The Triangular Dynamics

SANDEEP CHAVAN

Published by SANDEEP CHAVAN, 2024.

While every precaution has been taken in the preparation of this book, the publisher assumes no responsibility for errors or omissions, or for damages resulting from the use of the information contained herein.

THE TRIANGULAR DYNAMICS

First edition. November 24, 2024.

Copyright © 2024 SANDEEP CHAVAN.

ISBN: 979-8230261605

Written by SANDEEP CHAVAN.

Table of Contents

1: The Triangular Dynamics 1
2: Historical Roots of the Triangle 10
3: A Multipolar World and India's Role 29
4: The Great Neighbors: A Complicated Relationship 50
5: The Shadow of the Dragon 67
6: The Eagle's Embrace 85
7: Friendship with Conditions 102
8: When Titans Clash 116
9: The Technology Battlefield 131
10: The Power of Strategic Autonomy 147
11: Core Sectors for Resilience 162
12: Diversifying Global Dependencies 180
13: India's Vision for 2030 198
14: The Triangular Dynamics Redefined 214
References 227
Acknowledgments 230
About the Author 232

This book is dedicated to the visionary leaders who made courageous decisions and framed transformative policies, always keeping their nation's progress and prosperity at the forefront. Your wisdom and determination continue to inspire generations.

To the readers and experts across the globe, whose curiosity and commitment to understanding healthy geopolitics drive meaningful conversations and foster a more interconnected and harmonious world—this book is for you.

Disclaimer

The content of this book, *The Triangular Dynamics: India between China and USA*, is based on extensive research, personal insights, and the author's interpretations of global geopolitical, economic, and technological trends. While every effort has been made to ensure the accuracy and relevance of the information presented, the perspectives and conclusions drawn in this book reflect the author's views and are not intended to represent the positions of any government, institution, or organization.

This book is intended for educational and informational purposes only. It is not a substitute for professional advice in areas such as geopolitics, economics, or international relations. Readers are encouraged to consult experts or conduct their own research when making decisions based on the themes and ideas discussed in this work.

The scenarios, case studies, and analyses presented are based on publicly available data and historical trends at the time of writing. As global dynamics continue to evolve, some information may become outdated or subject to reinterpretation. The author and publisher assume no responsibility for any consequences arising from the use of the information contained in this book.

The references to specific countries, organizations, or individuals are used solely for the purpose of discussion and analysis and should not be construed as endorsements or criticisms. Any similarities to actual policies, events, or situations are coincidental and intended solely for illustrative purposes.

This book is the intellectual property of the author. Unauthorized reproduction, distribution, or use of its content is strictly prohibited without prior written consent.

By engaging with this book, readers acknowledge that they are interpreting its content with an understanding of the above disclaimers and accept full responsibility for how they choose to apply or act upon the information presented.

Sandeep Chavan

Preface

The world is witnessing a profound shift in its geopolitical and economic landscape, marked by the rising influence of China, the sustained power of the United States, and the aspirations of emerging nations like India. At the heart of this evolving dynamic lies the intricate triangular relationship between these three nations—a relationship that holds the key to shaping the future of the 21st century.

As an industrial engineer, educator, and counselor, I have spent over two decades analyzing the intersection of technology, economics, and global strategies. My experience working with diverse industries and mentoring students to think critically about the world has driven me to explore the forces that define our modern era. This book, *The Triangular Dynamics: India between China and USA*, is the culmination of years of reflection, research, and a deep desire to understand India's role in an increasingly multipolar world.

India, with its vast potential, strategic geographic location, and growing economic and technological capabilities, stands at a pivotal crossroads. The United States, a long-standing global superpower, and China, an assertive and rapidly rising power, each offer opportunities and challenges that India must navigate with wisdom and agility. This triangular dynamic is not merely about competition or alliances—it is about understanding how India can assert its sovereignty, balance its relationships, and leverage its unique strengths to shape its destiny.

This book delves into India's nuanced approach to diplomacy, its pursuit of strategic autonomy, and its efforts to balance partnerships while fostering self-reliance. It examines how India is leveraging its technological prowess, economic resilience, and cultural heritage to assert its influence on the global stage. From navigating trade challenges and technological dependencies to leading the global South in climate action and equitable development, India's role is evolving as both a bridge and a balancer in this complex geopolitical equation.

The Triangular Dynamics aims to provide readers with a comprehensive understanding of India's strategic choices and their broader implications. It seeks to inspire policymakers, academics, business leaders, and citizens to think critically about India's future and the collective responsibility of shaping a more inclusive and harmonious global order.

As I present this work to you, I am deeply grateful to all those who have contributed to my understanding of these issues—mentors, colleagues, students, and fellow thinkers. This book is not just an analysis of geopolitics; it is a vision for how India can thrive as a force for stability, equity, and innovation in a rapidly changing world.

I invite you to join me on this journey of exploration and reflection. Together, let us unravel the dynamics of this triangular relationship and envision a future where India, alongside the United States and China, plays a pivotal role in creating a more balanced and prosperous world.

Sincerely,

Sandeep Chavan

(Industrial Engineer, Educator, and Author)

Part I: Setting the Stage

1: The Triangular Dynamics

In a world shaped by shifting alliances and growing rivalries, the triangular relationship between **India, China, and the United States** stands as one of the most pivotal dynamics of the 21st century. These three nations, each with its unique strengths and aspirations, are not just competing for influence but also navigating a web of interdependence. At the heart of this triangle lies India, a rising power that balances the aspirations of global superpowers while charting its own path to sustainable growth. This chapter unpacks the historical roots, current complexities, and India's strategic position in this ever-evolving relationship, setting the stage for the nuanced interplay between competition and collaboration that defines this triangular dynamic.

Introduction to the India-China-U.S. Relationship

The global stage in the 21st century is witnessing a fascinating interplay of power, ambition, and strategy among three major players: **India, China, and the United States**. Each of these nations brings its distinct strengths and priorities to the table, influencing the global economic, political, and strategic order in profound ways. While the U.S. and China dominate the global narrative as the world's two largest economies and technological titans, **India stands apart as a key balancer**, uniquely poised to navigate this dynamic and carve out its own influential role.

At first glance, this triangular relationship may seem like a straightforward alignment of power: the U.S. and China as dominant forces, with India gradually rising to global prominence. However, the reality is far more nuanced and layered. This is not a static or uniform equation but rather a dynamic and evolving interplay of **competition, collaboration, and conflict**. Each nation is pursuing its national interests, but their trajectories are constantly shaped—and often redirected—by the strategies, policies, and ambitions of the others.

For India, this relationship is both an opportunity and a challenge. On the one hand, it offers a chance to leverage its growing economic and geopolitical clout. India's strategic location, vast consumer market, and technological potential make it an attractive partner and a critical player in shaping the global future. On the other hand, India faces the formidable task of maintaining **strategic autonomy**—balancing its ties with both the U.S. and China without becoming overly reliant on either, all while navigating their intensifying rivalry.

This triangular relationship also needs to be understood in the broader context of global shifts. The **rise of China** as a global economic powerhouse and an assertive geopolitical actor has dramatically altered the balance of power, challenging the long-standing dominance of the U.S. in several domains. Meanwhile, the U.S., though still a formidable force, is grappling with the reality of a **multipolar world**, where its unilateral dominance is increasingly contested. Against this backdrop, India's emergence as a pivotal player in Asia, with aspirations of global leadership, adds another layer of complexity to this dynamic.

India's interactions with China and the U.S. extend far beyond the realm of bilateral interests. They are deeply rooted in global trends and realities. The economic interdependence of nations, the rapid advancements in technology, and the shared challenges of climate change, pandemics, and security threats are threads that weave these relationships together. In this context, India is not just a participant but an influencer, whose actions and policies have the potential to reshape the contours of this triangular dynamic.

The stakes are high. For the U.S., India represents a critical partner in countering China's growing influence, especially in the Indo-Pacific region. For China, India is both a competitor in Asia and a potential partner in regional and global economic frameworks. And for India, the challenge lies in managing these relationships to secure its own growth, stability, and global standing.

This chapter serves as a gateway to understanding the complexities of this triangular relationship. By exploring its historical roots, current realities, and evolving dynamics, we aim to uncover the opportunities and challenges that lie ahead for India as it navigates the intertwined destinies of these two global superpowers. This is a story not just of power and politics but also of choices and vision—choices that India must make to chart its course in an increasingly interconnected yet divided world.

Historical Context of Power Struggles and Alliances

The triangular relationship between India, China, and the United States did not emerge in isolation. Its roots lie in the **post-World War II era**, a period marked by seismic shifts in global politics and the emergence of new power centers. Understanding the historical context is crucial to appreciating the current dynamics, as it reveals how alliances, rivalries, and ideological conflicts have shaped the interactions among these three nations over decades.

The U.S. and China During the Cold War

The Cold War era (1947–1991) was defined by ideological battles between capitalism and communism, with the United States and the Soviet Union leading opposing camps. The rise of **China as a communist state under Mao Zedong in 1949** added a third axis to this rivalry. Mao's victory in the Chinese Civil War not only unified China but also aligned it ideologically with the Soviet Union, creating an early adversary for the U.S.

However, the alliance between China and the Soviet Union proved short-lived, fracturing in the 1960s over ideological and territorial disputes. Sensing an opportunity, the United States shifted its strategy, seeking to exploit this Sino-Soviet split. The **Nixon-Kissinger diplomacy of the 1970s** marked a dramatic thaw in U.S.-China relations. Nixon's historic visit to Beijing in 1972 symbolized a strategic rapprochement, aimed at countering Soviet influence. This engagement set the stage for China's gradual opening to the world and its eventual rise as a global economic power.

India's Non-Alignment and Early Choices

India, newly independent in 1947, chose a different path. Guided by Prime Minister Jawaharlal Nehru, India adopted a policy of **non-alignment**, refusing to align itself with either the U.S.-led capitalist bloc or the Soviet-led communist bloc. This approach, while rooted in the ideal of maintaining sovereignty, was also pragmatic, as it allowed India to engage with both sides based on its developmental needs.

However, India's relationship with China took a significant turn in the early 1960s. Initially, the two nations shared a sense of solidarity as post-colonial states striving for independence and growth. But territorial disputes over the Himalayan border escalated into the **1962 Sino-Indian War**, a conflict that exposed India's strategic vulnerabilities and left a lasting impact on its foreign policy. The defeat pushed India closer to the Soviet Union, leading to a reliance on Soviet military and economic support during the 1970s and 1980s.

The Post-Cold War Recalibration

The end of the Cold War in 1991 marked a turning point in global geopolitics. The **collapse of the Soviet Union** left the United States as the sole superpower, while China capitalized on decades of economic reforms initiated under Deng Xiaoping to emerge as a **global manufacturing hub**. Meanwhile, India embarked on its own transformation, initiating **economic liberalization** under Prime Minister P.V. Narasimha Rao and Finance Minister Manmohan Singh.

This period saw India recalibrate its relationships with both the U.S. and China. On the one hand, India began **deepening ties with the U.S.**, particularly in technology, defense, and trade. The U.S., recognizing India's potential as a democratic counterweight to China, welcomed this partnership. On the other hand, India maintained a cautious but growing economic engagement with China, even as mutual distrust lingered over unresolved border issues.

China's rapid economic rise during this period reshaped global supply chains and tilted the balance of power in Asia. India, while benefiting from China's economic boom as a trading partner, also grew wary of Beijing's increasing assertiveness in the region.

21st Century Dynamics

The 21st century has been characterized by a dramatic escalation of U.S.-China rivalry and the concurrent rise of India as a pivotal player in the global order. The early 2000s witnessed the United States formally recognizing **India as** a strategic partner, evident in the signing of the **U.S.-India Civil Nuclear Agreement (2005)** and deepening defense ties. These moves were not just about strengthening bilateral relations but also part of a broader strategy to counterbalance China's influence in Asia.

Simultaneously, China's meteoric rise as the world's second-largest economy and its increasing regional assertiveness—manifested in initiatives like the **Belt and Road Initiative (BRI)** and military expansion in the South China Sea—heightened tensions with the U.S. India, with its strategic location in the Indo-Pacific and its growing economic clout, became a critical piece in this geopolitical puzzle.

India's rise has added complexity to the triangular dynamic. Its **economic growth**, **large consumer market**, and **technological advancements** make it a valuable partner for the U.S. in its efforts to counter China. At the same time, India's continued engagement with China in trade and regional multilateral forums reflects its need to maintain a degree of balance in its foreign policy.

In conclusion, the historical interactions among India, China, and the U.S. reveal a fascinating evolution of power struggles, alliances, and recalibrations. From Cold War rivalries and ideological divides to post-Cold War realignments and 21st-century strategic partnerships, this triangular relationship has been shaped by the shifting sands of global geopolitics. As India positions itself as a **key balancer between two superpowers**, the lessons of history will undoubtedly inform its strategies for navigating the challenges and opportunities of the future.

The Unique Positioning of India in this Dynamic

In the evolving triangle of global power that includes **India, China, and the United States**, India occupies a **distinct and pivotal position**. Unlike the other two, India is not a traditional superpower, yet its role as a balancer and influencer has made it indispensable in shaping the geopolitical and economic dynamics of the 21st century. This unique positioning is the result of a combination of its **geopolitical location, economic potential, strategic autonomy, and cultural influence**, each of which reinforces its importance in this global interplay.

Geopolitical Location: A Strategic Crossroads

India's **geopolitical position in South Asia** and its proximity to critical maritime routes in the **Indian Ocean Region (IOR)** make it a linchpin for regional and global stability. The IOR is a vital conduit for global trade, with nearly **80% of the world's maritime oil trade** passing through its waters. India's ability to influence this region places it at the center of power dynamics in Asia and beyond.

As a Stabilizing Force: India's geographic location allows it to act as a stabilizing force in a volatile neighborhood that includes Pakistan, Afghanistan, and Myanmar, while also countering China's expanding footprint in the region. Its presence in the IOR is a critical element of the U.S.'s **Indo-Pacific strategy**, which aims to counterbalance China's maritime ambitions.

Influence in Asia's Security and Politics: India's land borders with both China and Pakistan have made it an active participant in addressing regional security challenges. This positioning also gives India the ability to influence the **political, economic, and security landscape** of Asia, making it a critical ally for the U.S. and a competitor for China.

Economic Potential: A Rising Giant

India's **economic potential** is one of its greatest strengths, making it a key player in the triangular dynamic. With a population of over **1.4 billion people**, India represents one of the world's largest consumer markets. Its **rapid GDP growth** and diverse industrial sectors—ranging from **technology** and **pharmaceuticals** to **renewable energy**—make it a lucrative destination for global investments.

A Magnet for Investments: Global powers, including the U.S. and China, are drawn to India's economic opportunities. The U.S. views India as a strategic market for its technology and defense sectors, while China engages economically through trade and investments, despite geopolitical tensions.

Self-Reliance and Global Integration: India's government has launched initiatives like **Atmanirbhar Bharat (Self-Reliant India)** and **Make in India**, which aim to reduce import dependencies, especially on China, while attracting foreign direct investments (FDI) from the U.S. and other nations.

These programs also highlight India's ambition to emerge as a **global manufacturing hub**, providing an alternative to China in global supply chains.

Technological Leadership: India's thriving **IT sector**, growing **startup ecosystem**, and advancements in **renewable energy technologies** underscore its economic resilience and innovative capacity. These attributes not only strengthen India's economic position but also enhance its appeal as a partner for both superpowers.

Strategic Autonomy: Balancing Act with Precision

India has masterfully maintained **strategic autonomy**, navigating its relationships with the U.S. and China without becoming overly dependent on either. This balanced approach has allowed India to engage in **multi-alignment**, a foreign policy strategy that leverages partnerships while maintaining independence.

Participation in Diverse Alliances: India's involvement in the **Quad** (with the U.S., Japan, and Australia) positions it as a key player in countering China's influence in the Indo-Pacific. At the same time, India remains an active member of **BRICS** and the **Shanghai Cooperation Organisation (SCO)**, forums where China has a strong presence. This dual engagement allows India to hedge its bets and play a diplomatic balancing act.

Defense and Security Partnerships: While India has deepened its defense ties with the U.S. through arms deals, joint exercises, and technology transfers, it continues to maintain a cautious yet cooperative relationship with China in multilateral settings. This reflects India's commitment to preserving its sovereignty and avoiding entanglement in great power rivalries.

Cultural and Historical Influence: The Power of Soft Diplomacy

India's **soft power** is another unique asset that sets it apart in the global arena. Its democratic values, cultural richness, and historical connections make it a natural partner for the U.S. and a point of contrast with China's authoritarian model.

Democracy and Shared Values: India's democratic framework resonates with the U.S.'s emphasis on freedom and individual rights, creating a strong ideological alignment. This shared value system strengthens bilateral ties and distinguishes India from China in the eyes of the global community.

The Indian Diaspora: The vast **Indian diaspora**, particularly in the U.S., acts as a bridge between the two nations. This community not only contributes to the U.S. economy but also influences policymaking and fosters cultural ties.

Cultural Diplomacy: India's global outreach through initiatives like **International Yoga Day**, the popularity of Bollywood, and the appeal of Indian cuisine and traditions enhances its image as a culturally vibrant and inclusive nation. These efforts complement its hard power strategies, building goodwill and fostering engagement.

Thus, India's unique positioning in the India-China-U.S. triangle is a testament to its **geopolitical significance, economic potential, strategic autonomy, and cultural influence**. Unlike China and the U.S., whose interactions are often marked by rivalry, India operates as a **balancer and bridge**, engaging both powers on its own terms. This ability to navigate complexity while maintaining independence underscores India's growing role as a global power and a key player in shaping the future of international relations. As the world continues to evolve, India's unique attributes will remain critical to its success in managing this triangular dynamic.

Conclusion

The interplay between India, China, and the United States is not just a regional phenomenon; it is a defining element of the **global power structure** in the 21st century. This triangular relationship encapsulates the complexities of modern geopolitics, shaped by competing ambitions, shared interests, and a growing interdependence that transcends borders. India's ability to navigate this dynamic reflects its **resilience, strategic foresight, and adaptability** in an era where alliances are fluid and rivalries often define the narrative.

As the world transitions from a predominantly unipolar system, dominated by the United States, to a more **multipolar future**, India stands uniquely poised to play a pivotal role. It is not merely a passive participant in this dynamic; it is a nation actively shaping outcomes to **balance power, safeguard its sovereignty, and secure its economic and strategic objectives**. India's

THE TRIANGULAR DYNAMICS

geographic location, coupled with its rising economic influence and strategic autonomy, makes it an indispensable player in crafting the global order.

This triangular dynamic is characterized by its **dual nature**—competition and collaboration. India's economic interdependence with China coexists with geopolitical tensions along disputed borders. Meanwhile, its growing partnership with the United States is balanced by the need to avoid excessive reliance on any single power. This balancing act, while complex, showcases India's **maturity as a global player** capable of engaging with both giants on its own terms.

India's unique positioning offers a rare opportunity to **bridge divides** and influence global power structures. By leveraging its strengths—its vast consumer market, technological prowess, and commitment to democratic principles—India can create a **model of inclusive growth and strategic independence** that appeals to nations navigating similar challenges.

This chapter lays the groundwork for understanding how India's approach to the China-U.S. dynamic is rooted in both pragmatism and vision. The **strategic choices India makes today** will not only shape its relationships with these two superpowers but also determine its broader role in the evolving global landscape. As we delve deeper into subsequent chapters, the focus will shift to the **specific opportunities, challenges, and strategies** that define India's engagements with China and the United States. These explorations will illuminate the intricacies of this triangular relationship, revealing how India can continue to thrive as a central force in a world marked by complexity and change.

2: Historical Roots of the Triangle

Understanding the triangular relationship between **India, China, and the United States** requires a journey through the **historical roots** that have shaped these nations' interactions over the decades. Each has traversed unique paths since the mid-20th century, with distinct ambitions and challenges that have interwoven their destinies. From India's principled neutrality during the Cold War to the recalibration of alliances in the post-Cold War era, these historical milestones provide the foundation for the current dynamics of competition, collaboration, and power balance.

India's Non-Alignment Strategy during the Cold War

In the aftermath of **World War II**, the global stage was dominated by the ideological rivalry of two powerful blocs: the **capitalist West**, led by the United States, and the **communist East**, dominated by the Soviet Union. For newly independent nations, this bipolar world posed a dilemma—aligning with one bloc often meant alienating the other. Amid this polarization, **India emerged as a unique voice**, choosing a path of **non-alignment** under the visionary leadership of **Prime Minister Jawaharlal Nehru**. This strategy was not a passive neutrality but a deliberate and deeply philosophical approach aimed at preserving India's sovereignty and enabling it to focus on its internal development without external interference.

THE TRIANGULAR DYNAMICS

Rationale behind Non-Alignment

India's choice to adopt non-alignment as its guiding foreign policy stemmed from its historical experiences, geopolitical realities, and the visionary aspirations of its leaders. Emerging from the shadows of colonial subjugation, India sought to define an independent role in global politics, free from the constraints of Cold War alliances.

After centuries under colonial rule, India approached the global stage with a deep wariness of aligning with hegemonic powers that could compromise its hard-won independence. Jawaharlal Nehru, deeply inspired by the principles of freedom, equality, and justice, championed a policy that safeguarded India's sovereignty while enabling independent decision-making in its international engagements. Non-alignment became the cornerstone of this vision, ensuring that India remained the arbiter of its own destiny.

Nehru also envisioned India as a beacon for global peace in a world fractured by ideological hostilities. In an era marked by the rivalry between the United States and the Soviet Union, India aspired to serve as a bridge, advocating for peaceful coexistence and dialogue. This approach allowed India to mediate conflicts and foster cooperation rather than align with divisive blocs, carving out a unique space for itself in global diplomacy.

Non-alignment was not merely a moral stance but a pragmatic strategy. By steering clear of rigid alliances, India gained the flexibility to secure aid and resources from both superpowers. The United States supported India with agricultural advancements and industrial development, while the Soviet Union contributed to its burgeoning infrastructure and defense capabilities. This balanced approach allowed India to draw benefits from both sides without being ensnared in their ideological battles.

Underlying this policy was a profound moral responsibility. India's non-alignment reflected its commitment to decolonization, disarmament, and racial equality, positioning the country as a voice of justice and fairness in global forums like the United Nations. Through this approach, India not only preserved its autonomy but also became a symbol of hope for newly independent nations navigating the turbulent waters of post-colonial geopolitics.

Challenges of Non-Alignment

While non-alignment provided India with diplomatic flexibility and an independent voice on the global stage, it also exposed the country to significant challenges, particularly during periods of geopolitical tension and regional conflicts. The limitations of this policy became increasingly apparent in critical moments that tested India's strategic resilience.

One of the most glaring challenges emerged during the **Sino-Indian War of 1962**. India's commitment to non-alignment left it without strong allies during this pivotal conflict. While the United States offered limited support, its involvement was constrained by Cold War commitments and its broader strategic priorities. The Soviet Union, traditionally an ally of China, maintained neutrality, reflecting the inherent limitations of non-alignment when faced with an adversary backed by one of the global blocs. This diplomatic isolation during a moment of existential threat highlighted the vulnerabilities in India's strategy.

India's non-aligned stance also invited skepticism from both sides of the ideological divide. The **United States**, though supportive at times, often viewed India's policy as veiled pro-Soviet neutrality, especially as India began to rely heavily on Soviet military and economic aid in the 1970s. Conversely, the **Soviet Union**, despite its collaboration with India, remained cautious of India's outreach to the West, particularly its growing trade ties with Western democracies. This dual suspicion complicated India's efforts to build trust and leverage consistent support from either bloc.

Economically, non-alignment did not shield India from the hardships of being a developing nation. Balancing relations with both blocs often meant navigating a web of **aid dependencies**, **trade barriers**, and limited industrial capabilities. While India benefited from aid and investments, these were not always sufficient to address its ambitious growth targets or reduce its economic vulnerabilities. This reality underscored the limitations of relying on external partnerships without the strategic advantages of formal alliances.

Additionally, India's refusal to align with either bloc left it without the kind of robust **strategic partnerships** that could have bolstered its defense and infrastructure during moments of conflict. This was particularly evident in the wars with Pakistan in **1965** and **1971**, where non-alignment limited India's access to advanced military technologies and logistical support that aligned nations often received. While non-alignment granted India the freedom to chart its course, it also underscored the challenges of navigating a polarized world without the security of steadfast allies.

Despite its successes, non-alignment's challenges reveal the complexities of maintaining independence in a world dominated by competing powers. These difficulties became critical learning points, shaping India's evolving approach to strategic autonomy in the decades that followed.

The Enduring Legacy of Non-Alignment

Despite its inherent challenges, India's policy of non-alignment left an indelible mark on global politics, shaping its identity as a moral force and a champion of justice on the international stage. It was a bold and visionary approach that sought to redefine how nations could engage with a polarized world while retaining their sovereignty and ideals.

One of the most significant contributions of non-alignment was India's role as a **champion of decolonization**. In the aftermath of its own independence, India emerged as a leading voice supporting the liberation movements across **Asia**, **Africa**, and **Latin America**. Aligning itself with countries striving for independence from colonial rule, India became a symbol of global solidarity. This vision was institutionalized with the establishment of the **Non-Aligned Movement (NAM)** in 1961, of which India was a founding member. NAM provided a platform for newly independent nations to collectively assert their rights and aspirations in a world dominated by superpowers.

India's advocacy for **disarmament** further cemented its moral standing in global affairs. Amid the intensifying Cold War arms race, India's consistent calls for **nuclear disarmament** and **peaceful coexistence** resonated with nations worldwide. This commitment positioned India as a responsible actor in global security debates, emphasizing dialogue and diplomacy over aggression and conflict.

The principles of non-alignment also laid the **foundation for India's strategic autonomy**, a cornerstone of its modern foreign policy. While the policy evolved in response to changing global dynamics, its core tenets of maintaining balanced relationships and avoiding dependency on any single power remain central to India's international engagements. Today, India's ability to engage constructively with competing powers—whether through its partnerships with the **United States**, its economic ties with **China**, or its enduring relationship with **Russia**—can be traced back to the strategic flexibility that non-alignment fostered during the Cold War era.

Non-alignment also allowed India to establish itself as a **voice for peace and justice**, leveraging its moral authority to mediate conflicts and advocate for equitable global governance. Although the policy faced challenges, such as diplomatic isolation during the **Sino-Indian War**, it underscored India's resilience and its commitment to charting an independent course in world affairs.

The legacy of non-alignment continues to influence India's foreign policy, providing a framework for navigating the complexities of a multipolar world. As India engages with an evolving global order, the principles of independence, equity, and strategic balance remain deeply ingrained in its approach.

This enduring legacy will be explored further in the chapters ahead, as we examine how the foundations of non-alignment shaped India's engagements with both **China** and the **United States**, offering critical insights into the triangular dynamics that define contemporary geopolitics.

Key Milestones in India-China and India-U.S. Relations

The evolution of India's relationships with China and the United States has been defined by critical milestones that reflect shifting global dynamics and regional priorities. These milestones highlight the complexities of India's foreign policy and its efforts to balance competing interests in a rapidly changing world.

India-China Relations

India and China, as two ancient civilizations and emerging post-colonial states, have experienced a relationship marked by **early camaraderie, sharp conflicts, and cautious cooperation**.

Early Solidarity: From Brothers to Rivals

THE TRIANGULAR DYNAMICS

In the 1950s, India and China shared a rare sense of solidarity, born out of their shared struggles against colonial rule and their aspirations to shape a new world order. This was a period of optimism and camaraderie, marked by the belief that the two nations could lead the Global South into a new era of independence and cooperation.

The slogan **"Hindi-Chini Bhai-Bhai"** (India and China are brothers) encapsulated this spirit of unity. Leaders like **Jawaharlal Nehru** and **Zhou Enlai** championed the ideals of cooperation and non-alignment, positioning their nations as advocates for the developing world. Both saw themselves as torchbearers of a newly decolonized Asia, striving to create a future where Asian nations could assert their sovereignty and collective strength on the global stage.

India played a pivotal role in supporting China's international aspirations during this period. Nehru's government actively advocated for China's inclusion in global institutions, notably backing **Beijing's recognition in the United Nations** over Taiwan. This act underscored India's commitment to fostering Asian solidarity and its belief in China's rightful place in the global order.

The **Bandung Conference of 1955** marked a high point in this era of cooperation. As a significant milestone in the evolution of the **Non-Aligned Movement (NAM)**, the conference brought together leaders of newly independent nations to promote unity, non-alignment, and resistance to colonial and neo-colonial pressures. India and China stood shoulder to shoulder, signaling the potential for a powerful Asian bloc that could challenge Western dominance and shape a new geopolitical landscape.

Yet, beneath this surface of mutual respect and collaboration, cracks began to appear. **Territorial disputes** and **divergent strategic visions** started to strain the relationship. While both nations were united in their opposition to colonialism and imperialism, their aspirations for regional dominance often clashed, particularly as their geopolitical interests began to diverge.

The optimism of the **Hindi-Chini Bhai-Bhai** era, though sincere, was ultimately short-lived. These underlying tensions would later erupt, transforming the relationship from one of solidarity to rivalry. The seeds of future discord were sown even during this period of apparent unity, as the complexities of national interests and territorial ambitions started to overshadow the shared vision of Asian cooperation.

The 1962 Sino-Indian War: A Turning Point

The optimism and camaraderie of the 1950s gave way to **deep mistrust** and hostility with the outbreak of the **Sino-Indian War** in 1962. This conflict became a watershed moment in bilateral relations, fundamentally altering the trajectory of India-China interactions and leaving a legacy of unresolved tensions.

The war was rooted in **disputed borders**—a long-standing issue that had simmered beneath the surface of earlier cooperation. At the heart of the conflict were territorial disagreements over **Aksai Chin** in the western sector and **Arunachal Pradesh** in the eastern sector. China's unilateral construction of a strategic road through **Aksai Chin**, a region claimed by India, intensified the dispute. Combined with Beijing's territorial claims over large parts of Indian-administered Arunachal Pradesh, tensions escalated, leading to a breakdown in diplomatic efforts. In October 1962, these disputes culminated in a full-scale military offensive by China.

The war revealed **India's strategic vulnerabilities**. Ill-prepared for a conflict of this magnitude, India's military forces faced significant challenges against China's superior planning and execution. The defeat exposed gaps in India's defense infrastructure and strategic readiness, resulting in a national crisis that deeply impacted its political and public psyche. This humiliation left a lasting imprint on India's defense policies, spurring a renewed focus on military modernization in the years to follow.

The **aftermath of the war** reshaped India's foreign policy and alliances. India, having learned a harsh lesson about the perils of isolation, sought to strengthen its security through closer ties with the **Soviet Union**, securing military and economic assistance to rebuild its defenses. For China, the conflict reinforced its perception of India as a rival in the region, leading to an enduring mistrust that continues to influence bilateral relations.

The 1962 Sino-Indian War was not merely a border skirmish; it was a turning point that dismantled the spirit of **Hindi-Chini Bhai-Bhai** and replaced it with suspicion and hostility. This conflict entrenched a legacy of unresolved issues that persist in shaping the dynamics between the two nations, casting a long shadow over their efforts to rebuild trust and cooperation.

Post-War Relations: Distrust amid Growing Economic Ties

The aftermath of the 1962 war left a legacy of deep mistrust between India and China. However, the late 20th century saw a shift toward cautious engagement, driven by mutual economic interests and the broader imperatives of globalization. Despite this thaw, the relationship has remained fragile, marked by unresolved border disputes and strategic competition.

The **1980s and 1990s** witnessed a gradual normalization of ties as both nations turned their focus inward to address domestic economic challenges. With the advent of **economic liberalization**, India and China began to recognize the benefits of bilateral trade. By the 1990s, economic engagement became a cornerstone of their relationship, driven by China's rise as a manufacturing powerhouse and India's growing consumer market. China emerged as one of India's largest trading partners, with significant volumes of trade in sectors like **electronics**, **machinery**, and **pharmaceuticals**. This economic interdependence underscored the potential for collaboration even amid political differences.

Yet, the shadow of **strategic distrust** continued to loom over the relationship. Border disputes, particularly along the **Line of Actual Control (LAC)**, remained unresolved, and both nations frequently clashed over regional and geopolitical issues. The volatility of this dynamic was starkly illustrated during the **Galwan Valley clashes in 2020**, a violent confrontation that resulted in fatalities on both sides. This incident marked one of the most serious escalations since 1962, reigniting tensions and reinforcing mutual suspicion.

India's approach to China has evolved into a complex balancing act. On one hand, economic ties are essential for growth and development, with trade providing mutual benefits. On the other hand, strategic vigilance remains critical, as both nations compete for influence in the region and beyond. India's strategy reflects a dual commitment: fostering economic engagement where feasible while remaining prepared to counteract any threats to its sovereignty and regional interests.

This period of "distrust amid growing economic ties" captures the essence of the India-China relationship—a mix of pragmatic cooperation tempered by a cautious recognition of the enduring challenges posed by historical grievances and strategic rivalries.

India-U.S. Relations

India's relationship with the United States has evolved from **hesitation and mutual distrust during the Cold War** to **strategic alignment in the post-Cold War era**. Key milestones illustrate this transformation.

Early Hesitations: A Rocky Start

During the Cold War, India-U.S. relations were defined by a mix of misaligned priorities and deep-seated skepticism. While both nations shared democratic values, their geopolitical interests often clashed, leading to a relationship marked by mutual distrust and missed opportunities.

India's policy of **non-alignment** was a major point of contention. The United States, entrenched in its Cold War rivalry with the Soviet Union, perceived India's non-aligned stance as a veiled tilt toward Moscow. This perception intensified in the **1960s and 1970s**, as India deepened its ties with the Soviet Union through military and economic partnerships. For India, these ties were a pragmatic response to regional security threats and economic needs, but for the U.S., they symbolized a lack of alignment with the West.

Another source of strain was the U.S.'s **support for Pakistan**, India's adversary. This became particularly evident during the **1965 and 1971 wars**, when the U.S. provided military aid to Pakistan. For India, this support underscored a perceived bias in U.S. foreign policy, further widening the rift. The **1971 Bangladesh Liberation War** was a turning point, with India aligning more closely with the Soviet Union in response to U.S. support for Pakistan during the conflict.

Tensions were further exacerbated by **nuclear differences**. India's pursuit of nuclear capabilities, driven by regional security concerns and a desire for strategic autonomy, culminated in its first nuclear test in **1974** under the codename **Operation Smiling Buddha**. The U.S. strongly opposed this move, imposing sanctions and restricting technology transfers to India. This period saw the U.S. adopting a more punitive stance, which strained bilateral ties and limited cooperation in critical sectors like defense and technology.

These early years of India-U.S. relations highlight a complex dynamic shaped by divergent priorities and mutual misunderstandings. While the foundations for future collaboration were present, they were often overshadowed by geopolitical rivalries and conflicting strategic interests, setting the stage for a relationship that would evolve significantly in the post-Cold War era.

Strategic Shifts: The 1971 Bangladesh Liberation War

The **1971 Bangladesh Liberation War** was a defining moment in India-U.S. relations, exposing the deep-seated divergences in their strategic priorities and reshaping the geopolitical landscape of South Asia. This conflict not only highlighted India's regional ambitions but also underscored its willingness to align strategically when its national interests were at stake.

As tensions with Pakistan escalated over the independence movement in East Pakistan (now Bangladesh), India sought to strengthen its position through a **temporary alignment with the Soviet Union**. The **Indo-Soviet Treaty of Peace, Friendship, and Cooperation**, signed in August 1971, provided India with a critical security guarantee against potential Chinese or U.S. intervention. This marked a strategic pivot, allowing India to act decisively in the conflict while signaling its departure from strict non-alignment.

The United States, under **President Nixon** and **Secretary of State Henry Kissinger**, adopted a contrasting stance by supporting **Pakistan**, a key Cold War ally and a channel for U.S. rapprochement with China. The U.S. decision to side with Pakistan during the war was exemplified by the deployment of the **USS Enterprise**, a nuclear-powered aircraft carrier, to the **Bay of Bengal**. This move was widely perceived in India as an act of intimidation and a show of support for Pakistan, further straining India-U.S. relations.

Despite U.S. opposition, India's decisive victory in the war led to the creation of **Bangladesh**, a landmark achievement that solidified India's status as the **dominant power in South Asia**. The war showcased India's ability to shape regional dynamics independently, reinforcing its image as a nation capable of pursuing its strategic interests despite external pressures.

The 1971 war marked a turning point in India's foreign policy, demonstrating its willingness to forge temporary alliances and take bold actions to secure its national objectives. While it strained relations with the United States, it also underscored India's emergence as a regional power and set the stage for a more assertive role in South Asia in the decades to come.

Post-Cold War Recalibration: From Hesitation to Partnership

The collapse of the Soviet Union and the end of the Cold War marked a turning point in **India-U.S. relations**, providing an opportunity for both nations to reassess their strategic priorities. This recalibration, driven by shifting global dynamics, laid the groundwork for a partnership that has grown increasingly robust over time.

India's **economic liberalization** in 1991 played a pivotal role in transforming its relationship with the United States. By opening its markets to foreign investment, India created new opportunities for U.S. businesses across sectors like technology, pharmaceuticals, and infrastructure. This economic shift not only strengthened bilateral trade ties but also signaled India's willingness to engage with the global economy, aligning its aspirations with U.S. economic interests.

The **1998 nuclear tests** were another critical milestone, though initially fraught with tension. India's nuclear ambitions, aimed at bolstering its security and asserting its sovereignty, led to U.S. sanctions and diplomatic pushback. However, these tests also forced a deeper dialogue between the two nations, highlighting India's emergence as a more assertive global player. This period of strained relations ultimately culminated in the **2005 Civil Nuclear Agreement**, a landmark deal that recognized India as a responsible nuclear power and a key strategic partner. The agreement not only formalized India's status on the global stage but also paved the way for expanded cooperation in defense, energy, and technology.

As the 21st century unfolded, the United States began to view India as a critical partner in **counterbalancing China** in the Indo-Pacific region. The rise of China's economic and military influence prompted the U.S. to deepen its strategic alignment with India, resulting in initiatives like the **Quad alliance** with Japan and Australia. Increased defense collaborations, joint military exercises, and the signing of foundational defense agreements underscored this strategic shift, reflecting the shared goal of maintaining a free and open Indo-Pacific.

India's evolving relationship with the United States highlights a remarkable journey—from early hesitation to a deepening strategic partnership. This recalibration, driven by economic reforms, nuclear diplomacy, and shared concerns about regional stability, reflects India's growing prominence on the global stage.

These developments, along with India's complex interactions with China, underscore the fluid nature of global politics. With **China**, India has pursued economic engagement shadowed by strategic rivalry, while with the **United States**, it has fostered a partnership grounded in shared democratic values and mutual interests. These relationships, shaped by history and geopolitics, continue to define the triangular dynamics of the contemporary world.

As we delve deeper into this evolving triangle, the chapters ahead will explore how these historical trajectories shape India's present and future strategies, offering insights into its role as a key player in a multipolar global order.

How the Post-Cold War Order Shaped Current Dynamics

The collapse of the Soviet Union in **1991** marked a pivotal moment in global history, signaling the end of the Cold War and the advent of a **new world order**. The bipolar rivalry between the United States and the Soviet Union gave way to a more complex, multipolar landscape, defined by emerging powers, globalized markets, and shifting alliances. For **India, China, and the United States**, this period was transformative, presenting both opportunities for engagement and new challenges in the pursuit of national interests.

China's Economic Rise: From Reform to Dominance

The post-Cold War era witnessed **China's meteoric ascent** as an economic superpower, a transformation that reshaped the global economic landscape. Under the visionary leadership of **Deng Xiaoping**, China embraced market-oriented reforms in the late 1970s and 1980s, laying the groundwork for its unprecedented growth in the decades to follow. By the 1990s, these reforms had fully taken root, turning China into the **world's manufacturing hub** and a pivotal player in global trade.

Deng Xiaoping's policies, particularly the establishment of **Special Economic Zones (SEZs)**, marked a turning point for China's economy. These zones attracted foreign investment by offering tax incentives, streamlined regulations, and access to inexpensive labor. By opening its doors to global capital, China positioned itself as an attractive destination for Western businesses, particularly from the **United States**, which sought cost-effective production bases. This strategic integration into the global economy revolutionized supply chains, making China the **world's factory**, producing a vast range of goods from electronics to textiles and consumer products.

China's accession to the **World Trade Organization (WTO)** in 2001 further solidified its dominance in global trade. Membership in the WTO provided China with greater access to international markets, allowing it to expand its exports and deepen its economic ties with both developed and developing nations. This period marked the zenith of China's integration into the global economic order, as it leveraged its manufacturing capabilities to achieve extraordinary levels of growth.

For **India**, China's economic rise presented a mix of **opportunities and challenges**. On one hand, China's growth spurred **bilateral trade**, transforming it into one of India's largest trading partners by the early 2000s. The economic interdependence between the two countries created avenues for investment and market access, benefiting industries on both sides.

On the other hand, China's expanding **regional influence** raised significant strategic concerns for India. Initiatives like the **Belt and Road Initiative (BRI)** symbolized China's ambitions to establish economic and infrastructural dominance across Asia and beyond. Meanwhile, its increasing **military assertiveness**, particularly in contested regions like the South China Sea and along the **Line of Actual Control (LAC)** with India, heightened tensions and posed challenges to India's regional dominance and strategic security.

China's economic rise has been a defining feature of the modern global order. While its growth has created opportunities for collaboration, it has also underscored the need for India to strengthen its own economic and strategic position to navigate the complexities of this evolving dynamic.

India's Liberalization and U.S. Engagement

The early 1990s marked a transformative period for India as it embarked on a journey of **economic liberalization**, redefining its role in the global economic landscape. Faced with a severe **balance of payments crisis**, India introduced sweeping reforms under the leadership of **Prime Minister P.V. Narasimha Rao** and **Finance Minister Manmohan Singh**. These reforms not only stabilized the economy but also set the stage for closer ties with global powers, including the United States.

The **1991 economic reforms** dismantled restrictive trade policies, reduced state control over industries, and opened India's markets to **foreign investment**. By liberalizing key sectors, India aligned its economy with the global capitalist framework championed by the United States and other Western nations. This shift unleashed the potential of India's vast and skilled labor force, propelling sectors like **information technology (IT)**, **pharmaceuticals**, and **automobiles** into global prominence. Over time, India became a hub for **innovation**, **outsourcing**, and **highly skilled labor**, with companies like Infosys, Wipro, and Tata Motors symbolizing the country's economic ascent.

The economic transformation provided the foundation for a **new partnership with the United States**. By the late 1990s and early 2000s, the two nations began deepening ties in areas such as **technology**, **trade**, and **defense**. Shared democratic values and mutual interests in maintaining a stable global order further strengthened this alignment.

While the relationship was not without challenges, pivotal moments helped reshape India-U.S. engagement. The **1998 nuclear tests**, for instance, initially strained ties, with the U.S. imposing sanctions on India in response to its assertion of strategic autonomy. However, these sanctions ultimately highlighted India's growing geopolitical importance, prompting a reevaluation of its role in global security. By 2005, the two nations signed the landmark **U.S.-India Civil Nuclear Agreement**, a milestone that formalized India's status as a strategic partner. This agreement not only marked the normalization of ties but also opened avenues for collaboration in energy, technology, and defense.

India's liberalization and its engagement with the United States symbolized a pivotal shift in its foreign and economic policy. This era laid the groundwork for India's emergence as a global power, emphasizing the importance of adaptability, strategic partnerships, and economic integration in navigating a rapidly changing world.

Emergence of the Indo-Pacific Strategy

In the post-Cold War era, the **Indo-Pacific region** emerged as a strategic focal point for global powers, particularly as China's influence expanded across Asia. The United States, recognizing the growing importance of this region, began to recalibrate its foreign policy to counterbalance Beijing's rising dominance. This shift set the stage for India's pivotal role in shaping the Indo-Pacific framework.

The **U.S. Pivot to Asia**, announced during the Obama administration in the 2010s, underscored the Indo-Pacific's centrality in maintaining a **rules-based international order**. This strategy was a response to China's increasing assertiveness, marked by its militarization of the South China Sea and its aggressive economic initiatives through the **Belt and Road Initiative (BRI)**. By strengthening alliances and partnerships in the region, the United States aimed to curb China's influence while promoting stability and openness in one of the world's most critical geostrategic corridors.

Amid this realignment, India emerged as a **key partner** in the Indo-Pacific strategy. India's **geopolitical location**, straddling vital maritime routes in the Indian Ocean, positioned it as an indispensable player in ensuring regional security and connectivity. India's shared democratic values and its commitment to a rules-based order further aligned it with U.S. objectives in the region.

The formation of the **Quadrilateral Security Dialogue (Quad)**, comprising **India**, the **United States**, **Japan**, and **Australia**, solidified India's role in counterbalancing China's ambitions. The Quad, initially conceived as a security dialogue, has since expanded into a platform for collaboration on a wide range of issues, including **maritime security**, **critical infrastructure**, and **emerging technologies**. This partnership emphasizes collective efforts to uphold freedom of navigation, promote sustainable development, and ensure stability in the Indo-Pacific.

India's engagement in the Indo-Pacific framework reflects a nuanced strategy that balances its national interests with broader regional goals. By integrating defense collaborations, participating in joint naval exercises, and fostering partnerships in technology and infrastructure, India has reinforced its status as a critical stakeholder in the Indo-Pacific.

The rise of the Indo-Pacific strategy highlights the growing interdependence of geopolitics and economics in the 21st century. For India, it presents both challenges and opportunities: the challenge of navigating a complex regional landscape and the opportunity to assert itself as a stabilizing force in one of the most dynamic and contested regions in the world.

India's Dual Approach: Balancing Engagement and Vigilance

India's post-Cold War foreign policy exemplifies a **dual approach** of strengthening ties with the United States while maintaining a cautious yet pragmatic engagement with China. This strategy reflects India's commitment to **strategic autonomy**, navigating opportunities and threats from two global powers with nuanced diplomacy and calculated decisions.

Economic Cooperation with China

Despite a history of political and military tensions, India and China have developed significant **economic ties** over the past few decades. The 1990s and 2000s witnessed a surge in bilateral trade, fueled by **China's demand for raw materials** and **India's expanding consumer market**. By the 2010s, China emerged as one of India's largest trading partners, underscoring the interdependence between Asia's two largest economies.

However, this economic relationship is marked by **asymmetry**. India faces a substantial trade deficit with China, relying heavily on imports in critical sectors like **electronics**, **pharmaceutical ingredients**, and **machinery**. This imbalance exposes vulnerabilities in India's supply chains and highlights the need for enhanced domestic capabilities.

Strategic Distrust

While economic engagement has flourished, **strategic distrust** continues to define India-China relations. The unresolved **border disputes**, epitomized by the Doklam standoff in 2017 and the **Galwan Valley clashes** in 2020, serve as stark reminders of the deep-seated tensions. These incidents reinforced India's perception of China as a **strategic competitor** rather than a cooperative partner.

India's response to these challenges has been multifaceted:

- **Strengthening Border Infrastructure:** India has invested in building roads, bridges, and other infrastructure along its border areas to enhance connectivity and defense preparedness.
- **Boosting Defense Capabilities:** Modernizing the armed forces and acquiring advanced military technology, often through partnerships with countries like the U.S. and France, has been a critical component of India's strategy.
- **Diversifying Trade Relationships:** Efforts to reduce economic dependence on China include promoting domestic manufacturing under initiatives like **Atmanirbhar Bharat** and strengthening trade ties with alternative partners like ASEAN, Europe, and Japan.

Maintaining Strategic Autonomy

India's expanding partnership with the United States, particularly in areas like defense, technology, and the Indo-Pacific strategy, underscores its alignment with democratic values and shared security goals. However, India remains committed to **strategic autonomy**, ensuring its foreign policy is not overly reliant on any single power.

India's involvement in **multilateral platforms** like BRICS and the Shanghai Cooperation Organisation (SCO) demonstrates its willingness to engage with China and other global powers on equal terms. These forums provide opportunities for collaboration on shared challenges such as climate change, counterterrorism, and regional stability, even amid broader strategic rivalries.

India's dual approach reflects its ability to balance **economic engagement** with **geopolitical vigilance**, leveraging opportunities while safeguarding its sovereignty. As the dynamics of the post-Cold War world continue to evolve, India has emerged as a key player in the triangular interplay between itself, China, and the United States.

This nuanced strategy has positioned India as a **balancing force** in an increasingly multipolar world, laying the groundwork for its rise as a global power. In the chapters ahead, we will examine how these historical shifts and contemporary strategies influence India's role in shaping the future of international relations.

Conclusion

The historical journey of the India-China-U.S. triangle reveals a compelling narrative of **alliances, conflicts, and recalibrations**, reflecting the evolving nature of global power structures. This dynamic is not merely a product of contemporary geopolitics but a continuation of a complex interplay rooted in the past. India's strategy of **non-alignment during the Cold War** was a bold and pragmatic choice, laying the groundwork for its **independent foreign policy** in a world dominated by superpower rivalries. By refusing to align itself with either the capitalist West or the communist East, India positioned itself as a **sovereign actor** capable of pursuing its national interests without external coercion.

Key milestones in India's relationships with **China and the United States** have marked significant shifts in the global order. With China, India experienced a trajectory that began with post-colonial solidarity but soon devolved into strategic rivalry following the **1962 Sino-Indian War**. Despite periods of economic engagement, unresolved territorial disputes and border tensions have kept their relationship fraught with mistrust. Meanwhile, India's ties with the United States evolved from **Cold War skepticism** to **post-Cold War partnership**, underscored by increasing cooperation in technology, defense, and trade. These milestones not only highlight the **shifting dynamics** of **global power** but also underscore India's ability to **adapt and recalibrate** its foreign policy in response to changing circumstances.

The end of the Cold War in 1991 brought about **new challenges and opportunities** for India. The rise of China as a global manufacturing hub and the integration of its economy into the world stage reshaped trade, investment, and regional influence. For India, this economic transformation presented both an **opportunity for collaboration** and a **challenge to its regional aspirations**. Simultaneously, India's own liberalization reforms aligned its economy with global capitalism, creating a foundation for its deepening partnership with the United States. These shifts in the post-Cold War era have **positioned India as a rising power**, capable of engaging with two global superpowers on its own terms while safeguarding its strategic autonomy.

As the world transitions into a **multipolar system**, the lessons from India's historical experiences remain highly relevant. India's ability to **balance relationships with competing powers** while pursuing its own strategic goals highlights its potential as a **key player in global geopolitics**. The historical context not only offers insights into India's current strategies but also illuminates the paths it may take in navigating future challenges and opportunities. This balance of engagement, caution, and self-reliance is the hallmark of India's foreign policy, enabling it to thrive in an era of heightened competition and collaboration.

The complexities of the India-China-U.S. relationship will continue to shape the global order. The next chapters will delve deeper into these bilateral dynamics, exploring the **opportunities, challenges, and strategies** that define India's role within this triangular framework. By examining these relationships in detail, we aim to provide a clearer understanding of how India can maintain its unique positioning and advance its national interests in a rapidly evolving world.

3: A Multipolar World and India's Role

The world we live in today is no longer defined by the binary rivalries of the Cold War. Instead, it is characterized by a complex web of relationships among multiple centers of power, each vying for influence in an increasingly interconnected global landscape. This **multipolar world** has created opportunities for nations like India to assert themselves as key players, crafting their own narratives and shaping international policies. For India, this shift is both a challenge and a chance—a chance to rise as a global power while carefully navigating the competing interests of giants like the United States and China. Balancing these relationships, while safeguarding its sovereignty and pursuing its development goals, forms the cornerstone of India's approach in this new world order.

The Shift from Bipolar to Multipolar Geopolitics

The **collapse of the Soviet Union in 1991** marked a seismic shift in global politics, bringing an abrupt end to the **bipolar world order** that had dominated international relations since the end of World War II. During the Cold War, the United States and the Soviet Union stood as the two opposing poles, shaping a world divided along ideological lines of capitalism and communism. Most nations found themselves compelled to align with one bloc or the other, creating a starkly binary system. However, the Soviet Union's dissolution shattered this structure, heralding the dawn of a more **complex and fluid geopolitical landscape**.

From Bipolarity to Unipolarity

The end of the Cold War brought about a profound transformation in the global power structure. With the collapse of the Soviet Union in 1991, the world shifted from a bipolar order, dominated by the rivalry between the United States and the Soviet Union, to a period of **unipolarity**, where the United States stood as the sole superpower. This unprecedented position of dominance allowed the U.S. to wield unparalleled influence across military, economic, and technological spheres, shaping the trajectory of global politics for the decade that followed.

During this unipolar era, the United States became the central architect of international institutions and policies. Organizations like the **World Bank**, **International Monetary Fund (IMF)**, and **World Trade Organization (WTO)** reflected the ideological and economic priorities of the U.S., emphasizing free trade, market liberalization, and the promotion of democratic values. These institutions, guided by Washington's leadership, became vehicles for advancing the principles of **global capitalism** and integrating emerging economies into a U.S.-led global economic framework.

The United States also demonstrated overwhelming **military superiority**, which was evident in its swift and decisive role in the **Gulf War (1991)**. This conflict not only showcased America's unmatched military capabilities but also reinforced its position as the primary enforcer of global security. Its vast network of alliances, particularly through NATO, further cemented its dominance in international security affairs.

Technological innovation became another pillar of U.S. hegemony during this period. The rapid advancements in the **information technology sector**, driven by American companies, solidified its global leadership in shaping the digital age. The U.S. emerged as a hub of technological breakthroughs, from the proliferation of the internet to the rise of Silicon Valley as the epicenter of innovation.

However, the unipolar moment proved to be fleeting. As the world transitioned into the early 21st century, new power centers began to challenge the United States' dominance. The economic rise of **China**, the resurgence of **Russia**, and the growing aspirations of emerging economies like India signaled the gradual emergence of a **multipolar geopolitical order**. These developments marked the end of unipolarity and set the stage for a more complex and dynamic international landscape, where the United States would no longer dictate global affairs unilaterally.

This shift from unipolarity to multipolarity underscored the evolving nature of global power, laying the foundation for a world characterized by competition, collaboration, and the rise of regional powers.

China's Ascension

Among the emerging powers reshaping the global order, **China's rise** stands as the most transformative. Beginning in the late 20th century, China's integration into global trade and manufacturing elevated it from a developing nation to a global superpower, profoundly altering economic and geopolitical dynamics.

China's economic transformation began with the **market-oriented reforms** spearheaded by **Deng Xiaoping** in the late 1970s and 1980s. Policies like the establishment of **Special Economic Zones (SEZs)** and the liberalization of trade created an environment that attracted substantial foreign investment. Western nations, in particular, saw China as a cost-effective manufacturing hub, fueling its rapid industrial growth. By the 1990s, China had positioned itself as a central player in global trade, with its factories becoming the backbone of supply chains for industries ranging from **electronics** to **consumer goods**.

By the early 2000s, China's economic growth had accelerated to unprecedented levels. Its gross domestic product (GDP) surged, and by 2010, it had become the world's **second-largest economy**, a milestone that underscored its ascent on the global stage. This role as the **world's factory** not only reshaped supply chains but also rendered China indispensable to global economic stability.

China's economic rise was accompanied by a broader **strategic vision** aimed at increasing its geopolitical influence. The launch of the **Belt and Road Initiative (BRI)** in 2013 exemplified this ambition. Through massive investments in infrastructure and trade networks across Asia, Africa, and Europe, China sought to position itself as the hub of a new era of global connectivity. Simultaneously, its **military modernization**, exemplified by advancements in naval capabilities and assertive territorial claims in the **South China Sea**, signaled a willingness to challenge the status quo in regional and global power dynamics.

This dual pursuit of economic and strategic dominance placed China in direct competition with the **United States**, making it the most significant challenger to U.S. hegemony in the 21st century. The resulting rivalry between the two superpowers has become a defining feature of global politics, influencing trade, technology, and security frameworks worldwide.

China's ascension represents a profound shift in the balance of global power. As its influence continues to expand, it shapes a multipolar world where economic interdependence coexists with strategic competition, heralding a new chapter in international relations.

The Multipolar Era

By the early 21st century, the global order had shifted into a **multipolar framework**, where influence was no longer concentrated in a single superpower but dispersed among multiple nations. While the **United States** continues to wield considerable dominance, the rise of **China**, **India**, **Russia**, **Brazil**, **Japan**, and other regional powers has created a more interconnected and intricate geopolitical landscape.

The emergence of **regional powers** has been a defining feature of this multipolar era. Nations have asserted their influence, not only within their regions but also on the global stage:

> **Russia**, despite its economic vulnerabilities, has reasserted itself through military actions, such as in Ukraine and Syria, and energy diplomacy, leveraging its vast reserves of oil and natural gas.

> **India**, with its **demographic advantage**, rapid economic growth, and increasing global influence, has positioned itself as a pivotal player in global politics. Its leadership in technology, trade, and climate initiatives underscores its growing stature.

> **Brazil**, as the largest economy in Latin America, has emerged as a representative voice for the **Global South** in multilateral

institutions, advocating for equitable development and climate action.

The rise of alternative **global institutions** further underscores the multipolar nature of the current world order. Forums like **BRICS** and the **Shanghai Cooperation Organisation (SCO)** have gained prominence, providing platforms for emerging economies to collaborate and counterbalance the influence of Western-led institutions such as the **World Bank** and **IMF**. These organizations reflect a shift toward a more diverse and inclusive approach to global governance, emphasizing regional priorities and shared interests.

Unlike the Cold War, where rigid ideological divisions defined the global order, the **multipolar era** is marked by a paradoxical blend of **economic interdependence** and **technological competition**. Nations collaborate on shared challenges such as climate change, public health, and trade, while simultaneously competing in fields like artificial intelligence, defense, and space exploration. This duality has made international relations more dynamic, with shifting alliances and strategic partnerships reflecting the complexities of a multipolar world.

The multipolar era signifies a profound transformation in global politics. It is a world where no single power dictates the rules, and regional actors play critical roles in shaping the international agenda. This evolving framework, characterized by collaboration and competition, has created both opportunities and challenges for nations seeking to assert their influence and safeguard their sovereignty.

India's Opportunity in a Multipolar World

The shift to a multipolar world presents India with a unique combination of challenges and opportunities. The decline of dominance by any single superpower creates space for emerging nations like India to assert themselves on the global stage while carefully managing relationships with competing powers.

India's ability to navigate the **complex power dynamics** of a multipolar order is rooted in its position as a vibrant democracy with a commitment to **strategic autonomy**. This flexibility allows India to engage with diverse global actors without being tethered to a single bloc. Initiatives like the **Quad**—a partnership with the United States, Japan, and Australia—reflect India's alignment with democratic powers to uphold a rules-based international order, particularly in the Indo-Pacific. Simultaneously, India's active participation in platforms such as **BRICS** and the **Shanghai Cooperation Organisation (SCO)** highlights its willingness to collaborate with non-Western alliances, underscoring a balanced and pragmatic approach to foreign policy.

The multipolar era also offers India a **platform for leadership**, particularly as a voice for the **Global South**. By championing the interests of developing nations, India positions itself as a bridge between advanced economies and emerging markets. Its emphasis on **inclusive development**, climate action, and the equitable distribution of resources resonates with countries striving to overcome systemic inequalities. India's initiatives in renewable energy, such as its leadership in the **International Solar Alliance (ISA)**, and its advocacy for debt relief in global forums underscore its responsibility in shaping the global agenda.

In this evolving global landscape, India's adherence to the principle of **strategic autonomy** remains its cornerstone. This approach enables India to maintain independence in its decision-making while selectively pursuing partnerships that align with its national interests. For instance, while deepening defense and technological ties with the United States, India also continues to engage with Russia for energy and military supplies and with China for trade, despite underlying tensions. This balancing act demonstrates India's capacity to safeguard its sovereignty while leveraging global opportunities.

The multipolar world is a dynamic and complex environment, but it offers India an unprecedented opportunity to define its role as a key player in shaping global norms and policies. By maintaining its commitment to autonomy, fostering inclusive growth, and embracing strategic partnerships, India is poised to navigate the challenges of this new order while cementing its status as a pivotal force in the 21st century.

In conclusion, the shift from a bipolar to a multipolar world has redefined global politics, creating a more interconnected and competitive landscape. For India, this new order presents both opportunities to assert its influence and challenges in navigating the complexities of competing power dynamics. As one of the emerging powers in this multipolar era, India is uniquely positioned to shape the global agenda while balancing its relationships with dominant players like the United States and China. This balancing act, rooted in strategic autonomy and pragmatic diplomacy, will be central to India's role in the evolving world order.

India as an Emerging Global Power

India's emergence as a global power is one of the most significant geopolitical developments of the 21st century. Over the past three decades, it has transformed from a developing economy into a key player on the global stage. This transformation is driven by **rapid economic growth, strategic geographical positioning, and a youthful population**, which collectively give India a competitive edge in an increasingly multipolar world. Today, India is not just a regional leader but a nation with aspirations to influence global governance and international decision-making.

Economic Growth and Market Potential

India's economic ascent has been central to its emergence as a global power. Over the past three decades, it has consistently positioned itself among the fastest-growing economies, rising to become the fifth-largest in the world. With ambitious goals to secure the third spot in the coming decades, India's growth story is driven by robust policies, a massive consumer base, and thriving industrial sectors.

India's journey toward **robust GDP growth** began with the liberalization reforms of 1991, which dismantled restrictive trade policies and opened the economy to global markets. These reforms catalyzed investment, fostered entrepreneurship, and created a business-friendly environment. Despite global challenges such as the COVID-19 pandemic and economic slowdowns, India has demonstrated remarkable resilience, maintaining one of the highest growth rates among major economies.

At the heart of this growth lies **India's massive consumer base**, a population of over 1.4 billion people. This demographic advantage, coupled with rapid urbanization and a burgeoning middle class, drives demand across key sectors such as healthcare, retail, and technology. The scale and diversity of this market make India an unparalleled opportunity for businesses and investors worldwide.

India has also emerged as a leader in several **thriving industrial sectors**:

> **Information Technology (IT):** Home to global giants like TCS, Infosys, and Wipro, India's IT sector is a cornerstone of its economy, contributing significantly to exports and solidifying its reputation as a hub for innovation and technology services.

> **Pharmaceuticals:** Known as the "pharmacy of the world," India supplies affordable medicines and vaccines to global markets, playing a pivotal role in public health worldwide.

> **Renewable Energy and Green Technologies:** Initiatives such as large-scale solar power projects and electric vehicle (EV) production position India as a leader in the global transition to sustainable energy.

India's appeal as a **global investment hub** is further bolstered by initiatives like **Make in India** and **Atmanirbhar Bharat** (Self-Reliant India). These policies aim to attract foreign direct investment (FDI) while strengthening domestic manufacturing capabilities. Multinational corporations increasingly view India as a strategic destination, leveraging not only its vast market potential but also its skilled and cost-effective workforce.

India's economic growth, coupled with its market potential, reflects a trajectory of resilience and adaptability. Its ability to innovate, attract investment, and expand industrial capabilities ensures its continued rise as a critical player in the global economic landscape. This economic strength forms a solid foundation for India's broader aspirations as a global leader in trade, technology, and diplomacy.

Demographic Advantage

India's demographic profile stands as one of its most valuable assets, distinguishing it from major powers grappling with aging populations. With a median age of just over 28 years, India enjoys a youthful population poised to drive economic growth, innovation, and development well into the future. This

demographic dividend is a cornerstone of India's global competitiveness and a critical factor in shaping its ascent as a major power.

India's **youthful workforce** is a dynamic force in labor-intensive and technology-driven industries. The energy, adaptability, and productivity of this population ensure that India remains a vital player in global supply chains and cutting-edge fields. As industries worldwide shift toward digital transformation and sustainability, India's workforce is well-positioned to meet the evolving demands of the global market.

The nation's commitment to **STEM education (Science, Technology, Engineering, and Mathematics)** has created a robust pipeline of skilled professionals. Engineers, doctors, and scientists from India are not only fueling domestic growth but also contributing significantly to the economies of nations like the United States, the United Kingdom, and Australia. This global reputation for excellence highlights India's role as a **global skills hub**, providing critical expertise in IT, healthcare, and engineering.

India's youthful dynamism is also evident in its **thriving startup ecosystem**, one of the fastest-growing in the world. Cities like Bengaluru, Hyderabad, and Pune have emerged as global innovation hubs, fostering groundbreaking developments in technology, fintech, and e-commerce. Supported by initiatives like **Startup India**, Indian entrepreneurs are creating unicorns that redefine markets and disrupt traditional business models. This entrepreneurial spirit reflects the creativity and resilience of the nation's youth, driving India's reputation as a hub for innovation.

India's demographic advantage is not merely a statistic but a transformative force. By harnessing the potential of its young population through education, skill development, and entrepreneurial support, India is laying the groundwork for sustained economic growth and global influence. This youthful energy, combined with strategic policy initiatives, positions India as a leader in shaping the future of work, innovation, and global collaboration.

Strategic Location

India's geographic position is one of its most significant strategic assets, placing it at the heart of global trade, security, and regional diplomacy. Its location serves as a critical link between continents, making India a pivotal player in shaping the geopolitical and economic landscape of the 21st century.

Situated at the confluence of South Asia, the Middle East, and Southeast Asia, India's unique geographic position allows it to act as both a gateway to Asia and a bridge to the Middle East and Africa. These regions are vital for global energy supplies and trade flows, and India's ability to navigate these dynamics enhances its influence on international trade routes. The nation's economic policies and infrastructure initiatives aim to leverage this connectivity, making India an indispensable partner in regional integration and global supply chains.

India's strategic location along the Indian Ocean Region (IOR) gives it a commanding role in global maritime trade. Nearly 80% of the world's maritime oil trade passes through these waters, underscoring their economic and strategic importance. India's growing naval capabilities, coupled with strategic partnerships such as the Quad alliance (with the U.S., Japan, and Australia), reinforce its role as a stabilizing force in the region.

India's naval bases in the **Andaman and Nicobar Islands** provide a strategic vantage point, enabling it to monitor key maritime chokepoints such as the Strait of Malacca. This presence is crucial for countering China's expanding footprint in the Indo-Pacific and ensuring the security of critical sea lanes. As maritime tensions escalate in the region, India's ability to project power and maintain a free and open Indian Ocean is a cornerstone of its strategic relevance.

India's proximity to major geopolitical hotspots—China, Pakistan, and Southeast Asia—places it at the center of Asia's evolving power dynamics. Through initiatives like the **Act East Policy**, India is strengthening economic and security ties with ASEAN nations, bolstering regional cooperation and countering China's growing dominance. Its focus on building connectivity and fostering trade partnerships in Asia reflects its commitment to shaping the region's future.

India's geographic advantage is not just a matter of location but a platform for action. By leveraging its strategic position through enhanced infrastructure, naval modernization, and robust regional partnerships, India is asserting itself as a key player in global trade, security, and diplomacy. This geographical centrality, coupled with proactive policymaking, ensures India's continued relevance in an interconnected and competitive world.

Cultural and Diplomatic Soft Power

India's global influence extends well beyond its economic and strategic endeavors, driven by a profound cultural legacy, democratic ideals, and the significant impact of its diaspora. These elements collectively enhance India's soft power, enabling it to connect with nations and societies on a deeper, more human level.

India's democratic framework stands as a testament to its commitment to political pluralism and individual freedoms, offering a compelling counterpoint to authoritarian models of governance. As the world's largest democracy, India's institutions and values resonate with other democratic nations, fostering trust and mutual respect. This democratic credibility reinforces its partnerships with powers like the United States, the European Union, and other democracies, enabling India to champion values of human rights, justice, and equality on the global stage.

India's cultural heritage plays an equally pivotal role in its international standing. The global appeal of Indian cinema, especially Bollywood, has captivated audiences across continents, breaking cultural barriers and building a shared emotional connection. The universal adoption of yoga, formalized through initiatives like International Yoga Day, showcases India's ability to influence lifestyles and promote well-being worldwide. Indian cuisine, festivals like Diwali and Holi, and classical art forms further enrich this cultural narrative, making India a country that people across the globe feel a connection to, even without stepping onto its soil.

The Indian diaspora, with over 32 million members spread across the globe, acts as an extension of India's cultural and intellectual presence. This diaspora is not only a vibrant link to India's traditions but also a significant contributor to the economies and societies of their adopted countries. Leaders like Sundar Pichai (CEO of Alphabet), Kamala Harris (U.S. Vice President of Indian descent), and Rishi Sunak (Prime Minister of the U.K.) exemplify the impact and influence of Indians on the global stage. These individuals, alongside countless others in business, academia, and the arts, serve as ambassadors of

India's values, contributing to its soft power and strengthening its ties with host nations.

India's active leadership in global initiatives underscores its commitment to addressing shared challenges. The International Solar Alliance (ISA) is a prime example of how India has taken the lead in promoting sustainable energy solutions, uniting countries in the fight against climate change. During the COVID-19 pandemic, India's Vaccine Maitri initiative provided millions of vaccine doses to developing nations, cementing its role as a partner in global health.

Through its cultural richness, democratic values, and proactive diplomacy, India has cultivated a multifaceted soft power that complements its economic and strategic ambitions. This influence not only enhances its global image but also strengthens its ability to build bridges, foster collaboration, and lead on issues of shared human interest in an increasingly interconnected world.

In conclusion, India's rise as a global power is a testament to its **resilience, ambition, and adaptability**. Its robust economy, youthful population, strategic location, and cultural influence collectively position it as a nation capable of shaping the global agenda in the 21st century. As the world transitions into a multipolar era, India's ability to leverage these strengths will determine its success as a global leader. In this complex landscape, India is not just participating but actively shaping the rules of the game, asserting itself as a key player in both regional and international politics.

The Significance of Balancing Relations with the U.S. and China

As an emerging global power, India finds itself navigating a delicate balancing act between the **United States** and **China**, the two dominant forces shaping 21st-century geopolitics. Both nations are deeply intertwined with India's economic and strategic priorities, but their rivalry presents complex challenges that India must carefully manage. While the United States represents a critical partner in advancing India's security, economic, and technological ambitions, China poses both an opportunity for economic engagement and a challenge to India's regional dominance. Striking a balance between these two powers is essential for India's growth, stability, and long-term strategic autonomy.

THE TRIANGULAR DYNAMICS

Engaging with the United States

India's relationship with the United States has evolved from cautious interaction during the Cold War to a robust strategic partnership in the 21st century. This transformation is rooted in shared democratic values, mutual economic interests, and aligned security priorities. The collaboration now spans diverse domains, including trade, technology, defense, and regional stability, making the U.S. a critical ally in India's ascent as a global power.

The economic ties between India and the United States have reached unprecedented levels, with the U.S. emerging as one of India's largest trading partners. This economic partnership is bolstered by substantial U.S. investments in key Indian sectors like technology, pharmaceuticals, and infrastructure. American corporations such as Amazon, Google, and Apple have deepened their operations in India, tapping into its growing consumer base and contributing significantly to its digital economy. In return, Indian IT services, pharmaceutical exports, and engineering goods dominate trade with the U.S., ensuring a mutually beneficial economic relationship.

Technological collaboration has become a cornerstone of India-U.S. relations. Initiatives such as the U.S.-India Initiative on Critical and Emerging Technologies (iCET) reflect a shared commitment to advancing fields like artificial intelligence, quantum computing, and semiconductor manufacturing. The United States actively supports India's ambitions to emerge as a global innovation hub by fostering partnerships and providing expertise to its burgeoning startup ecosystem.

The Indo-Pacific region has emerged as a focal point of strategic cooperation between the two nations. India's inclusion in the Quad alliance (comprising the U.S., Japan, and Australia) underscores its critical role in promoting a free, open, and rules-based maritime order. This collaboration also addresses shared concerns about China's growing influence in the region, aligning India and the U.S. on regional security objectives.

Defense ties between India and the United States have deepened considerably, becoming a pillar of their strategic partnership. The procurement of advanced U.S. defense systems, such as Apache helicopters and P-8I maritime surveillance aircraft, has enhanced India's military capabilities, aligning with its modernization efforts. Regular military exercises, including

Malabar, strengthen interoperability between Indian and U.S. forces, ensuring readiness in critical theaters like the Indo-Pacific. Foundational agreements like LEMOA (Logistics Exchange Memorandum of Agreement) and COMCASA (Communications Compatibility and Security Agreement) have facilitated closer operational and technical cooperation, laying the groundwork for a long-term defense partnership.

The landmark 2005 U.S.-India Civil Nuclear Agreement marked a turning point in bilateral relations, granting India access to civilian nuclear technology and fuel. This agreement not only recognized India's status as a responsible nuclear power but also paved the way for deeper strategic and technological engagement.

India's partnership with the United States reflects its growing global influence and underscores the importance of collaborative efforts in addressing shared challenges. By fostering this relationship, India positions itself as a key player in shaping the geopolitical and economic dynamics of the 21st century.

Managing the China Challenge

India's relationship with China is a complex interplay of economic cooperation and strategic rivalry. While economic engagement with China has been mutually beneficial, growing geopolitical tensions and unresolved border disputes highlight the challenges of navigating this crucial bilateral relationship.

Economic engagement between the two nations has grown substantially, with China becoming one of India's largest trading partners. The trade relationship, however, is marked by significant imbalances. China supplies a substantial portion of India's imports, particularly in electronics, machinery, and chemicals. This dependence underscores vulnerabilities in India's supply chains and its reliance on Chinese goods for critical sectors like pharmaceuticals and consumer electronics. The resulting trade deficit remains a persistent concern, emphasizing the need for India to strengthen its domestic capabilities.

To address this dependency, India has launched initiatives like *Atmanirbhar Bharat* (Self-Reliant India), which aim to boost domestic manufacturing and encourage diversification of supply chains. Efforts to attract investments from partners like Japan, South Korea, and Europe further align with India's strategy to counterbalance its economic ties with China. These steps reflect India's determination to maintain its economic sovereignty while leveraging global partnerships to reduce vulnerabilities.

Border tensions have significantly strained India-China relations, adding a layer of strategic distrust to their economic interdependence. The 1962 Sino-Indian War left a lasting legacy of mistrust, with unresolved disputes in regions like Aksai Chin and Arunachal Pradesh frequently flaring into skirmishes and military standoffs. Incidents such as the Galwan Valley clash in 2020, which resulted in casualties on both sides, have deepened animosities and fueled anti-China sentiment within India.

China's growing influence in South Asia further complicates this relationship. Through its Belt and Road Initiative (BRI), China has invested heavily in India's neighboring countries, challenging India's traditional dominance in the region. Projects like the China-Pakistan Economic Corridor (CPEC), which runs through Pakistan-occupied Kashmir, are viewed by India as direct threats to its sovereignty. Similarly, China's infrastructure investments in Sri Lanka, Nepal, and Bangladesh have expanded its strategic footprint, posing a challenge to India's regional influence.

In response, India has pursued a multipronged strategy to counter China's assertiveness. Strengthening partnerships with like-minded nations, particularly in the Indo-Pacific, has become a cornerstone of India's foreign policy. Initiatives like the Quad alliance and enhanced maritime cooperation underscore India's commitment to a free and open Indo-Pacific. Domestically, India has bolstered its military presence along the border and accelerated infrastructure development in remote regions to improve connectivity and security.

India's approach to managing the China challenge reflects a delicate balance of engagement and vigilance. While economic ties remain crucial, India's strategic autonomy and regional security interests guide its broader strategy. By diversifying trade, building alliances, and reinforcing its defense capabilities, India is positioning itself to address the complexities of its relationship with its northern neighbor while safeguarding its long-term national interests.

Thus, balancing its relationships with the United States and China is one of India's most significant strategic challenges. With the U.S., India has developed a robust partnership that advances its economic and security goals, particularly in the face of China's growing assertiveness. However, India's economic interdependence with China, coupled with persistent border disputes, underscores the complexity of this relationship.

India's ability to navigate this balance will be crucial in defining its role as a global power in the 21st century. By deepening its partnerships with the United States while carefully managing its engagement with China, India can safeguard its sovereignty, advance its development goals, and strengthen its position in an increasingly multipolar world.

India's Balancing Act: Strategic Autonomy

India's foreign policy has long been anchored in the principle of **strategic autonomy**, reflecting its desire to maintain independence in decision-making while navigating the complexities of global power dynamics. This approach ensures that India avoids overdependence on any single power, allowing it to pursue its national interests in a multipolar world. Strategic autonomy has become particularly critical in managing India's relationships with the **United States** and **China**, two nations whose rivalry shapes much of today's geopolitics. By carefully balancing engagement with these global powers, India seeks to safeguard its sovereignty, enhance its economic resilience, and assert its leadership on the world stage.

Multi-Alignment Approach

India's foreign policy exemplifies a nuanced and pragmatic multi-alignment strategy, allowing it to engage with multiple global powers and platforms without compromising its independence. This approach reflects India's ability to navigate a multipolar world, leveraging diverse partnerships to advance its national interests while maintaining strategic autonomy.

India's participation in various multilateral platforms underscores its commitment to balancing global engagements. The Quad, comprising India, the U.S., Japan, and Australia, focuses on ensuring a free and open Indo-Pacific, countering maritime assertiveness, and fostering regional stability.

THE TRIANGULAR DYNAMICS

Simultaneously, India's involvement in BRICS highlights its willingness to collaborate with China and other emerging economies on shared goals of development and economic cooperation. Membership in the Shanghai Cooperation Organisation (SCO) further illustrates India's ability to engage constructively with powers like China and Russia on critical issues such as regional security and counterterrorism.

This strategic flexibility enables India to secure a voice in shaping regional and global policies. By engaging with forums that reflect diverse geopolitical priorities, India ensures it is not confined to the agenda of any single bloc, preserving its independence while maximizing its influence.

Beyond the dynamics of U.S.-China relations, India has also cultivated robust ties with other global players, broadening its network of partnerships. Its strategic relationships with European nations such as France, Germany, and the U.K. provide access to advanced technologies, defense cooperation, and trade opportunities. Europe's emphasis on sustainable development aligns with India's goals, fostering collaboration in renewable energy and climate action.

India's Act East Policy strengthens its economic and strategic engagements with ASEAN nations, creating opportunities for trade, connectivity, and regional security collaboration. This outreach counters China's growing dominance in Southeast Asia while building goodwill among its neighbors.

In Africa, India's investments in infrastructure, healthcare, and education underline its commitment to fostering development and strengthening bilateral ties. This engagement builds goodwill and enhances India's influence while creating new markets for Indian goods and services.

By embracing a multi-alignment approach, India reduces its dependence on any single global power while expanding its influence across regions. This strategy not only reflects India's aspirations for a greater role in global affairs but also ensures that it remains adaptable in an increasingly interconnected and competitive world.

Economic Resilience and Self-Reliance

Economic strength forms a cornerstone of India's strategic autonomy, enabling it to navigate complex global dynamics while reducing vulnerabilities in key sectors. Initiatives aimed at fostering self-reliance and diversification are integral to India's efforts to reduce economic dependencies, particularly on China, while promoting collaborations with global partners such as the United States, Europe, and Japan.

The Atmanirbhar Bharat (Self-Reliant India) initiative, launched in 2020, represents a bold vision to enhance domestic manufacturing, strengthen critical industries, and position India as a global production hub. This initiative has been pivotal in reducing import dependencies and creating new opportunities for technological and industrial growth. In electronics, for instance, India is scaling up domestic production of semiconductors, mobile phones, and IT hardware, addressing a significant reliance on Chinese imports. Similarly, in the defense sector, policies promoting indigenous production of military equipment aim to reduce dependence on foreign suppliers while fostering technological innovation and enhancing India's defense capabilities.

Diversifying trade and supply chains is another pillar of India's economic resilience. By expanding trade relationships with nations like Japan, South Korea, and Australia, India seeks to reduce overreliance on Chinese imports. Initiatives such as the Production Linked Incentive (PLI) scheme play a crucial role by encouraging global and domestic manufacturers to set up production units in India, driving job creation and bolstering exports. These measures are not only about reducing dependencies but also about integrating India more deeply into global value chains, ensuring long-term competitiveness in industries like electronics, pharmaceuticals, and renewable energy.

India's approach to economic resilience balances self-reliance with global collaboration. While strengthening domestic industries, India remains open to investments and partnerships with international players. For example, the United States continues to be a major investor in India's technology and defense sectors, facilitating collaborations in artificial intelligence, renewable energy, and healthcare. Similarly, partnerships with European nations and Japan bring advanced technologies and expertise, further enhancing India's economic capabilities.

This dual strategy of fostering self-reliance while engaging with global partners underscores India's commitment to maintaining strategic autonomy. By diversifying its economic relationships and investing in domestic capacities, India reduces its vulnerabilities while positioning itself as a critical player in the global economy.

India's economic strategy reflects its broader balancing act between the United States and China. Through initiatives like Atmanirbhar Bharat and its multi-alignment approach, India navigates the complexities of a multipolar world, ensuring that its sovereignty and economic resilience remain intact. As it continues to assert itself on the world stage, India's ability to balance relationships, foster innovation, and advance strategic autonomy will be pivotal in shaping its role as a global leader. This approach not only protects India's interests but also strengthens its capacity to address global challenges and collaborate on shared goals.

Conclusion

The transition to a multipolar world marks a transformative era for global politics, and for India, it presents a unique opportunity to assert itself as a key player on the world stage. Unlike the concentrated influence of the bipolar and unipolar periods, the multipolar order allows nations like India to shape international policies and alliances on their own terms. With its rapidly growing economy, youthful population, and strategic geographic position, India is poised to play a central role in this evolving landscape.

India's consistent economic growth and emergence as a global leader in industries such as information technology, pharmaceuticals, and renewable energy underscore its potential as a driver of global innovation and trade. Its democratic ethos and pluralistic values enhance its credibility and alignment with like-minded nations, particularly in the West, while its strategic location in the Indian Ocean Region underscores its importance in maintaining regional and global stability.

However, India's ascent is not without challenges. The ongoing rivalry between the United States and China remains a defining feature of contemporary geopolitics, requiring India to balance its relationships with these two powers. The United States, a critical economic and defense partner, offers opportunities for collaboration in advanced technologies, security, and trade. At the same time, China, despite being a strategic rival, remains deeply integrated into India's economy, necessitating a nuanced approach that addresses contentious issues such as border disputes and regional competition while maintaining avenues for economic engagement.

India's principle of strategic autonomy provides a vital framework for navigating these complexities. Through its multi-alignment approach, India engages with diverse partners across platforms such as the Quad, BRICS, and the Shanghai Cooperation Organisation (SCO), ensuring its voice is influential in global decision-making. Simultaneously, domestic initiatives like *Atmanirbhar Bharat* (Self-Reliant India) enhance India's resilience by reducing external dependencies and fostering growth in critical sectors such as manufacturing, technology, and defense.

To thrive in this multipolar world, India must continue to strengthen global partnerships, bolster its economic and military capabilities, and adapt to shifting international dynamics. Its ability to navigate these challenges will not only secure its national interests but also establish its role as a responsible and influential global leader. India's leadership will be essential in addressing global challenges such as climate change, international security, and sustainable development, reinforcing its reputation as a stabilizing force in an interconnected world.

The upcoming chapters will delve deeper into India's relationships with China and the United States, examining how these dynamics shape its strategies and influence its trajectory as a rising power. These relationships, though complex, are pivotal to India's emergence as a significant player in the 21st century and its journey toward becoming a leading voice in a multipolar world.

Part II: India-China Relationship: Competition and Collaboration

4: The Great Neighbors: A Complicated Relationship

The relationship between **India and China**, two of the world's largest and fastest-growing economies, is as complex as it is consequential. As neighbors with a shared border stretching over 3,400 kilometers, their interactions are shaped by a mix of **economic interdependence**, **geopolitical rivalries**, and a history marked by cooperation and conflict. While India and China collaborate on global platforms like **BRICS** and other multilateral forums, persistent challenges such as **trade imbalances** and **border disputes** underscore the fragility of their bilateral ties.

Trade Dependencies and Economic Imbalances

The economic relationship between **India and China** is a significant aspect of their bilateral ties, driven by the sheer scale and volume of trade between the two nations. Over the past few decades, this engagement has made them critical trading partners, with China emerging as one of India's largest sources of imports. However, the relationship is also marked by **asymmetries and vulnerabilities**, reflecting the challenges of managing economic interdependence in the context of geopolitical tensions.

The Growth of Bilateral Trade

The economic relationship between India and China has grown significantly over the years, reflecting the complex interplay of interdependence and rivalry. As China emerged as a global manufacturing powerhouse, its goods began to dominate markets worldwide, including in India, where the demand for high-value imports aligned with China's strengths in cost-effective production.

By 2022, bilateral trade between India and China had surpassed $125 billion, a testament to the scale and depth of their economic engagement. India's imports from China span a wide array of critical goods, including electronics, machinery, chemicals, and active pharmaceutical ingredients (APIs). These imports are indispensable for India's industrial sectors, from manufacturing and telecommunications to healthcare. For instance, in the pharmaceutical industry, over 70% of the APIs used in India are sourced from Chinese suppliers, underscoring a significant dependency on China's cost-efficient production capabilities. Similarly, Chinese inputs play a pivotal role in India's solar energy and automotive industries, with components such as solar panels and automotive parts powering these key sectors.

While imports from China are vital for India's industries, the trade relationship is marked by a pronounced imbalance. India's exports to China remain comparatively modest, largely comprising raw materials and commodities like iron ore, cotton, agricultural products, and seafood. These low-value exports highlight the asymmetry in the trade dynamic, as India supplies resources to fuel China's manufacturing base while importing finished products and technologically advanced goods.

Efforts to diversify India's export portfolio have encountered challenges, particularly in penetrating China's domestic markets. Sectors where India has significant strengths, such as IT services, pharmaceuticals, and processed foods, face limited access due to regulatory barriers and competition from domestic players in China. Despite this, India continues to explore avenues to reduce the trade deficit by enhancing competitiveness in these sectors and seeking greater market access.

The rapid growth in bilateral trade reflects both opportunity and vulnerability for India. While the relationship enables access to affordable, high-quality inputs that bolster India's industries, the heavy reliance on Chinese imports exposes critical sectors to supply chain disruptions and geopolitical risks. As India strives for greater self-reliance and diversification in trade, this relationship remains a focal point of its economic strategy, balancing immediate economic benefits with long-term resilience and strategic autonomy.

The Trade Deficit

A defining feature of the economic relationship between India and China is the persistent trade deficit, one of the largest India has with any trading partner. This deficit, exceeding $100 billion annually, highlights India's significant reliance on Chinese imports, particularly for essential goods and components that underpin key industries.

The magnitude of this deficit underscores structural challenges in India's trade dynamics. Sectors like electronics, chemicals, and advanced manufacturing remain heavily dependent on Chinese inputs due to the cost advantage and scale of Chinese manufacturers. For instance, India's dependence on China for electronics and machinery, coupled with its reliance on Chinese active pharmaceutical ingredients (APIs) for its pharmaceutical industry, reflects gaps in domestic production capabilities. This dependency leaves India vulnerable to supply chain disruptions and geopolitical uncertainties.

In response, India has initiated measures to address this imbalance by promoting domestic manufacturing and reducing import dependency. The Atmanirbhar Bharat (Self-Reliant India) campaign is a cornerstone of these efforts, focusing on boosting local production in critical sectors such as electronics, defense, and renewable energy. Programs like the Production Linked Incentive (PLI) scheme incentivize both domestic and foreign companies to establish manufacturing facilities in India. These efforts have already yielded results in sectors like smartphone production, where companies like Apple and Samsung have significantly expanded their manufacturing footprint in India. Similar strides are being made in renewable energy, with domestic solar panel and battery manufacturing gaining momentum.

However, reducing the trade deficit remains a challenging endeavor. The scale of India's reliance on Chinese goods, combined with the cost competitiveness and efficiency of Chinese manufacturers, makes it difficult to rapidly substitute imports with domestic production. Moreover, barriers to Indian exports, such as non-tariff measures and stringent regulatory frameworks in China, limit India's ability to capitalize on its strengths in sectors like IT services, pharmaceuticals, and agricultural products.

While progress is being made, bridging the trade deficit will require sustained efforts to strengthen India's industrial base, diversify its supply chains, and enhance the global competitiveness of its exports. Addressing these challenges is crucial not only for economic resilience but also for reducing strategic vulnerabilities in India's relationship with China.

Concerns of Economic Dependency

India's significant reliance on Chinese imports has long raised concerns about economic vulnerability, particularly in sectors deemed critical to national security and industrial growth. This dependency presents strategic risks that underscore the urgency of diversifying supply chains and bolstering domestic production capabilities.

The over-concentration of imports from China creates systemic challenges, especially in sectors like electronics and pharmaceuticals, where disruptions can have cascading effects. For instance, India's pharmaceutical industry, often referred to as the "pharmacy of the world," relies heavily on China for active pharmaceutical ingredients (APIs), making it susceptible to supply chain interruptions. Similarly, the electronics sector depends on Chinese components for manufacturing smartphones, telecom equipment, and other high-demand products.

The COVID-19 pandemic served as a stark reminder of these vulnerabilities. During the initial months of the pandemic, disruptions in Chinese manufacturing and logistics led to shortages of essential goods in India, including medical equipment and pharmaceutical ingredients. This experience not only highlighted the risks of over-dependence on a single source but also underscored the need for supply chain diversification and resilience.

In response, India has intensified efforts to mitigate these dependencies. Partnerships with nations like Japan, South Korea, Vietnam, and Taiwan are being explored to source electronics, machinery, and components, offering alternatives to Chinese suppliers. These collaborations are complemented by domestic initiatives aimed at strengthening India's industrial base.

Investments in research and development (R&D) and manufacturing capabilities are central to this strategy. The Atmanirbhar Bharat (Self-Reliant India) campaign and the Production Linked Incentive (PLI) schemes encourage the development of local production ecosystems in strategic industries. For instance, India is focusing on establishing domestic capacities for semiconductor manufacturing, renewable energy equipment, and defense production.

While these efforts represent a significant step toward reducing economic dependency, achieving self-reliance in critical sectors will require sustained investment, robust policy support, and international collaboration. By addressing its vulnerabilities, India not only enhances its economic resilience but also fortifies its strategic autonomy in an increasingly interconnected global economy.

The Vitality of Economic Engagement

Despite the complexities and challenges inherent in their relationship, economic engagement between India and China remains vital. Both nations acknowledge the significance of maintaining robust trade ties, even as geopolitical tensions ebb and flow. This interdependence, though asymmetrical, underscores the role of economic collaboration as a potential stabilizing factor in their often-contentious bilateral relationship.

For India, Chinese imports are integral to sustaining its manufacturing ecosystem. Critical sectors like electronics, automotive components, and telecommunications rely heavily on cost-efficient Chinese inputs to meet domestic and international demand. Simultaneously, India's exports of raw materials, including iron ore and agricultural products, contribute to China's industrial supply chain, reflecting the mutual benefits embedded in their trade relationship.

However, the inherent imbalance in this dynamic—characterized by India's significant trade deficit with China—necessitates a careful balancing act. India's strategy focuses on leveraging the economic opportunities presented by this engagement while addressing the risks of over-dependence. Key to this approach is strengthening domestic industries through initiatives like Atmanirbhar Bharat (Self-Reliant India), which promotes local manufacturing and technological innovation.

Additionally, India is actively diversifying its trade partnerships to reduce reliance on Chinese imports. Collaborations with nations such as Japan, South Korea, and Vietnam are creating alternative supply chains, while efforts to negotiate better market access for Indian goods in China aim to rectify the current trade imbalance.

The economic relationship between India and China is thus a complex interplay of dependence, opportunity, and strategic caution. While the scale of bilateral trade highlights the indispensability of their economic ties, it also presents challenges that demand sustained policy innovation and global collaboration.

As both nations navigate this intricate economic dynamic, the future of their trade relationship will be shaped not only by market forces but also by the broader geopolitical landscape. For India, maintaining a pragmatic balance between economic growth and strategic security will remain essential to fostering a stable and mutually beneficial relationship with its largest trading partner.

Border Conflicts and Their Impact on Bilateral Relations

The **unresolved border disputes** between India and China remain a persistent source of tension, casting a long shadow over their diplomatic and economic engagements. These disputes are rooted in **historical territorial claims** and have frequently flared into confrontations, affecting the broader trajectory of their bilateral relations. While the two nations have attempted to manage these tensions through dialogue, the **legacy of mistrust**, amplified by recent standoffs, continues to strain their relationship.

Historical Context

The territorial disputes between India and China have long been a source of tension, rooted in their unsettled border, which spans over 3,400 kilometers and is divided into three distinct sectors. These disputes trace their origins to colonial-era treaties and conflicting interpretations of historical maps, leaving both nations with competing claims and unresolved boundaries that have persisted for decades.

In the **Western Sector**, the focus of contention is Aksai Chin, a high-altitude region that China controls but India claims as part of its erstwhile

Jammu and Kashmir territory. Aksai Chin holds immense strategic value for China, serving as a vital link between Tibet and Xinjiang via the G219 Highway. This area became a flashpoint during the 1962 Sino-Indian War, during which China captured and consolidated its control over Aksai Chin, leaving a legacy of mistrust and resentment in India.

The **Middle Sector**, which includes parts of Himachal Pradesh and Uttarakhand, is less volatile than the western and eastern sectors. However, sporadic incursions and minor standoffs still occur, reflecting the unresolved nature of the boundary. While this sector sees fewer confrontations, it remains part of the broader border dispute that clouds bilateral relations.

In the **Eastern Sector**, China lays claim to the Indian state of Arunachal Pradesh, referring to it as "South Tibet." India, steadfast in its sovereignty, firmly rejects these claims. The presence of the Tawang Monastery, a culturally and religiously significant site tied to Tibetan Buddhism, further complicates the situation. China's assertions often cite historical and cultural links to Tibet, while India emphasizes its legitimate sovereignty over the region.

These unresolved disputes have deep historical roots but remain highly relevant today, shaping the contours of India-China relations. The enduring ambiguity and competing claims have resulted in periodic flare-ups along the border, reflecting the fragile and contentious nature of their bilateral dynamic. For both nations, resolving these issues is critical, yet the entrenched positions on either side make any resolution a complex and challenging endeavor.

Recent Standoffs

The long-standing border disputes between India and China have periodically flared into confrontations, but recent years have witnessed an escalation in both frequency and intensity, capturing global attention and further straining bilateral relations.

The **Galwan Valley Clash** in 2020 marked a turning point in the ongoing border tensions. This violent altercation, resulting in fatalities on both sides, was the first deadly clash along the Line of Actual Control (LAC) in over 45 years. The incident underscored the volatility of the LAC and exposed the deep mistrust that defines India-China relations. It not only hardened the positions of both nations but also led to heightened vigilance and a reevaluation of strategies along the border.

Another significant flashpoint has been **Pangong Tso**, where troops from both sides engaged in tense standoffs over strategic positions along the lake's north and south banks. The confrontations demonstrated the high stakes associated with control over critical terrain, with both nations unwilling to cede ground.

The **Tawang region** in Arunachal Pradesh has similarly remained a hotspot for tensions, with frequent skirmishes and incursions. This area holds strategic and symbolic significance for both nations, further complicating the already fraught dynamic.

In response to these confrontations, both India and China have significantly **militarized the LAC**, deploying additional troops, artillery, and advanced surveillance systems. The buildup reflects the persistent mistrust and the importance both nations place on securing their borders.

These recent standoffs underscore the fragile nature of peace along the LAC, where minor provocations can quickly escalate into significant confrontations. As both nations fortify their positions, the potential for de-escalation becomes increasingly complex, leaving the border disputes a critical and unresolved challenge in their bilateral relations.

Impact on Bilateral Relations

The recurring border conflicts between India and China have profoundly shaped the trajectory of their bilateral relationship, straining diplomatic ties and driving significant shifts in economic and strategic policies.

Erosion of Trust has been one of the most immediate and enduring consequences. The confrontations along the Line of Actual Control (LAC), particularly the violent clash in Galwan Valley, have deepened mistrust, making cooperative engagement increasingly difficult. In response, India has adopted a firm stance, imposing economic restrictions on Chinese entities. Measures such as banning popular apps like TikTok and WeChat, and increasing scrutiny of Chinese investments in critical sectors like telecommunications and technology, underscore India's strategy to reduce its reliance on Chinese goods and services. This economic decoupling reflects a broader geopolitical recalibration in light of the tensions.

Simultaneously, the border disputes have **strengthened India's strategic partnerships** with other nations, particularly those sharing concerns about China's regional ambitions. India's alliances with the United States, Japan, and Australia have grown more robust, with the Quad alliance emerging as a critical platform for collaboration in the Indo-Pacific. These partnerships are not just about military alignment but also extend to areas like technology, infrastructure, and supply chain resilience, offering India a counterbalance to China's influence.

Despite these shifts, the disputes have also led to a persistent **diplomatic stalemate.** Numerous rounds of military and diplomatic talks aimed at de-escalation have yielded limited progress. Both nations remain steadfast in their respective positions, with little indication of a comprehensive resolution to the territorial disagreements. This diplomatic impasse underscores the enduring complexity of the relationship and the challenges of fostering meaningful dialogue amidst heightened tensions.

The impact of these border conflicts on India-China relations is far-reaching, extending beyond immediate skirmishes to redefine economic ties, strategic alignments, and the broader geopolitical landscape in Asia.

Infrastructure and Security Measures

India has undertaken a comprehensive strategy to address vulnerabilities along its disputed border with China, emphasizing infrastructure development and military modernization. These measures aim to strengthen India's strategic position and improve its readiness in the face of potential conflicts.

Infrastructure Development Along the LAC has been a cornerstone of this strategy. India has accelerated the construction of roads, bridges, and airbases in border regions to enhance troop mobility and logistical efficiency. Projects like the Zojila Tunnel and initiatives by the Border Roads Organization (BRO) are pivotal in improving connectivity in remote areas, ensuring that resources and personnel can be deployed swiftly during crises. Such advancements not only bolster India's defensive posture but also provide critical infrastructure to local communities in otherwise inaccessible regions.

Equally significant is the **modernization of the military**, which has become a national priority. India has increased defense spending to acquire advanced technologies, including surveillance systems, drones, and long-range artillery. Collaborative defense agreements with key allies such as the U.S., Israel, and Russia have enabled India to access cutting-edge military equipment and technology, further enhancing its combat capabilities.

In parallel, India has deepened its **collaborations with allied nations** to counterbalance China's growing assertiveness. Joint military exercises with partners like the U.S., Japan, and Australia underline India's commitment to a free and open Indo-Pacific. These exercises not only enhance interoperability among forces but also send a clear signal of collective resolve in the region.

The enduring border disputes between India and China are more than just territorial disagreements—they are a defining feature of their complex bilateral relationship. Incidents like the Galwan Valley clash underscore the fragile and volatile nature of the Line of Actual Control (LAC), perpetuating a cycle of mistrust.

While India's initiatives to strengthen border infrastructure and military readiness represent significant progress, resolving the underlying disputes remains an uncertain and challenging endeavor. The broader impact of these tensions extends beyond the border, influencing India's recalibrated foreign policy, which now places greater emphasis on strategic partnerships and self-reliance.

As India continues to navigate its complicated relationship with China, the balancing act between addressing security concerns and maintaining necessary economic engagement will remain a central challenge in the years ahead.

Collaborations in BRICS and Other Multilateral Forums

Despite persistent bilateral tensions, **India and China** have found areas of collaboration within **multilateral platforms**, recognizing the importance of addressing shared global challenges. These platforms offer a space for dialogue and cooperation on critical issues such as **economic development, climate change, trade, and security**, even as bilateral disputes remain unresolved. By working together in these forums, both nations contribute to shaping the global agenda and advocating for the interests of developing countries.

BRICS: Strengthening Economic Cooperation

The BRICS coalition—comprising Brazil, Russia, India, China, and South Africa—has emerged as a crucial platform for fostering economic cooperation and reshaping global governance. For India, BRICS offers an avenue to engage with China on shared priorities, even amid bilateral challenges, while advocating for a more equitable international order.

The group's collective focus on promoting economic growth and financial stability reflects its members' ambition to reduce the dominance of traditional Western-led institutions such as the International Monetary Fund (IMF) and the World Bank. Both India and China, as leading voices within BRICS, have called for reforms to these institutions, seeking to enhance the representation and influence of emerging economies in global financial decision-making.

One of BRICS' most notable achievements is the establishment of the **New Development Bank (NDB)**, headquartered in Shanghai. This institution exemplifies the coalition's commitment to financial cooperation and sustainable development. The NDB provides funding for critical infrastructure projects across member states and other developing nations, offering an alternative to Western financial institutions. India has been a significant beneficiary of NDB resources, using these funds to advance its renewable energy goals and infrastructure development. This partnership underscores the pragmatic value of BRICS as a financial collaborator, even as geopolitical tensions persist among its members.

Another key initiative is the **Contingent Reserve Arrangement (CRA)**, a mechanism designed to provide liquidity support to BRICS nations during balance-of-payment crises. The CRA represents a shared resolve to enhance financial resilience, offering a safety net against global economic shocks. For India, this framework is particularly relevant in navigating periods of economic uncertainty without overreliance on Western financial systems.

Beyond financial initiatives, BRICS also serves as a platform for strategic dialogue on diverse global challenges. India and China, despite their bilateral tensions, actively participate in discussions on issues such as pandemic recovery, public health infrastructure, and digital economy policies. These dialogues highlight the coalition's potential to address pressing global concerns, fostering collaboration in areas of mutual interest.

While the dynamics within BRICS are often shaped by the broader geopolitical context, the group's ability to unite diverse voices around shared goals demonstrates its enduring relevance. For India, participation in BRICS reflects a pragmatic approach to engaging with China and other major economies, leveraging collective initiatives to advance its national priorities while contributing to a more balanced global order.

Shanghai Cooperation Organisation (SCO): Regional Stability and Security

The Shanghai Cooperation Organisation (SCO) serves as a vital multilateral forum for fostering dialogue and cooperation among its member states, including India and China. Despite their bilateral tensions, the SCO offers a platform for addressing shared challenges and advancing regional stability, economic integration, and cultural ties.

A cornerstone of the SCO's agenda is regional security, particularly in Central and South Asia. For both India and China, counterterrorism remains a critical area of convergence. The SCO provides a framework for intelligence sharing and collaborative efforts to combat extremism, recognizing that instability in the region poses threats to both nations. Through joint discussions and initiatives, the organization fosters a coordinated approach to addressing these complex security challenges.

Economic integration and connectivity are central to the SCO's mission. Discussions often center on infrastructure development and trade facilitation, key to enhancing regional economic cooperation. While China leverages the SCO to promote its Belt and Road Initiative (BRI), India has taken a more cautious approach, advocating for alternative connectivity projects. Initiatives like the Chabahar Port in Iran and the International North-South Transport Corridor (INSTC) reflect India's strategy to diversify regional trade routes. Despite differing priorities, the SCO facilitates dialogue on economic investments and trade opportunities, highlighting the potential for collaboration amidst competing visions.

Cultural and educational exchanges add a softer dimension to the SCO's objectives. Both India and China participate in initiatives aimed at fostering mutual understanding and regional cohesion. Programs promoting tourism, educational exchanges, and joint cultural events underscore the SCO's commitment to building bridges between diverse member states.

Through its broad scope of activities, the SCO enables India and China to engage constructively on issues of mutual interest, even as they navigate the complexities of their bilateral relationship. For India, the SCO represents an opportunity to assert its regional leadership while contributing to broader efforts for stability and development in the region.

Climate and Trade: Advocacy for Developing Countries

India and China, as two of the world's largest developing economies, share a mutual interest in advocating for equitable climate action and fair trade practices. Their collaboration in global forums underscores a collective commitment to representing the interests of the Global South while navigating the complexities of their bilateral relationship.

In the sphere of climate change, both nations play active roles within the United Nations Framework Convention on Climate Change (UNFCCC), emphasizing the principle of "common but differentiated responsibilities." This approach acknowledges the historical emissions of developed countries and the need for financial and technological support to assist developing nations in transitioning to sustainable, low-carbon economies. While their priorities differ—India focuses on renewable energy expansion, such as solar and wind power, whereas China emphasizes clean manufacturing and carbon-neutral technologies—their shared objective is to strike a balance between mitigating climate impacts and fostering equitable economic growth.

Trade protectionism is another area where India and China often align their positions, particularly in forums like the World Trade Organization (WTO). Both nations oppose protectionist policies from developed countries that could disproportionately impact developing economies. Their advocacy extends to preserving fair trade practices in areas such as agricultural subsidies, digital trade regulations, and tariff barriers. These efforts reflect a shared determination to safeguard the economic interests of the Global South against restrictive trade policies.

At the heart of their collaboration is a push for reforms in global economic governance. India and China jointly call for greater equity and inclusivity in institutions like the WTO, ensuring that developing nations have a stronger voice in shaping global trade policies. This shared agenda aims to create a more level playing field, enabling countries like India and China to compete effectively in the global market while advancing the developmental goals of emerging economies.

Despite their broader geopolitical and economic rivalries, India and China's cooperation on climate and trade highlights their capacity to converge on issues of global significance. This collaboration not only strengthens their individual standings in international diplomacy but also reinforces their roles as advocates for the developing world in shaping a fairer and more sustainable global order.

The Role of Multilateral Forums in Bilateral Relations

Multilateral forums like BRICS, the Shanghai Cooperation Organisation (SCO), and global climate platforms play a nuanced role in shaping India-China relations. While these platforms cannot resolve deep-seated bilateral tensions, they provide crucial avenues for dialogue, cooperation, and the exploration of common ground amidst rivalry.

Participation in such forums ensures open channels of communication between the two nations, even during periods of heightened bilateral tension. Regular diplomatic engagement in these settings allows India and China to address shared concerns, such as climate change, trade equity, and regional security, within a structured and neutral environment. These interactions, though indirect, create opportunities for constructive dialogue that might not be feasible in strictly bilateral settings.

Multilateral platforms also offer a unique framework for balancing the inherent rivalry in India-China relations with areas of potential collaboration. While the two nations compete for influence and leadership in Asia and beyond, these forums emphasize mutual benefits—whether through joint economic initiatives, shared security goals, or advocacy for the Global South.

This balancing act fosters a degree of stability, tempering the contentious aspects of their relationship with practical cooperation.

In essence, multilateral engagements serve as both a diplomatic buffer and a catalyst for constructive interactions. While they do not eliminate the challenges in India-China relations, these platforms underscore the importance of dialogue and collaboration, offering a blueprint for managing competition while pursuing shared goals on the global stage.

In conclusion, collaboration in multilateral forums like **BRICS**, the **SCO**, and global climate and trade platforms reflects the complex interplay of rivalry and cooperation between India and China. These platforms allow both nations to work together on shared global challenges while pursuing their respective national interests. While multilateral engagement does not eliminate bilateral tensions, it underscores the importance of maintaining open communication and fostering cooperation on global issues.

By leveraging these forums, India and China can contribute to a more inclusive and equitable global order, even as they navigate the complexities of their bilateral relationship. Such collaborations highlight the potential for diplomacy and shared leadership in addressing the pressing challenges of the 21st century.

Conclusion

The **India-China relationship** is a paradox of interconnectedness and rivalry. On one hand, the two nations are deeply intertwined economically, with trade playing a crucial role in their bilateral ties. On the other, **persistent border disputes and geopolitical tensions** have created an atmosphere of mistrust, influencing their diplomatic and security policies. This duality makes the relationship one of the most complex and consequential in global geopolitics today.

Economic Interdependence with Challenges

Trade has been the cornerstone of the India-China relationship, with both nations benefiting significantly from their economic engagement. However, this interdependence is marred by **imbalances** that disproportionately favor China. India's reliance on Chinese imports for critical sectors like **electronics,**

pharmaceuticals, and **machinery** highlights vulnerabilities that have prompted calls for greater **self-reliance** and diversification of trade partnerships. These economic dynamics underscore the paradox of a relationship where trade is both a bridge and a potential source of leverage in times of conflict.

Border Disputes and Strategic Rivalries

The unresolved **border disputes** along the Line of Actual Control (LAC) are a stark reminder of the historical and geopolitical complexities that define India-China relations. Incidents like the **Galwan Valley clash** and subsequent military standoffs have heightened tensions, pushing India to adopt a more assertive approach to its security and foreign policy. These disputes not only fuel mistrust but also drive India to strengthen its strategic alliances, particularly with countries like the **United States, Japan**, and **Australia** under the **Quad framework**. At the same time, both nations have fortified their military positions along the border, signaling the long-term challenges in achieving a resolution.

Collaborative Efforts in Multilateral Platforms

Despite these challenges, India and China have demonstrated the capacity for **constructive collaboration** in multilateral forums like **BRICS** and the **Shanghai Cooperation Organisation (SCO)**. These platforms provide avenues for dialogue on shared global challenges such as **climate change, trade reform**, and **regional stability**. Their ability to work together in these settings highlights the potential for **pragmatic engagement**, even amidst broader bilateral tensions. These forums serve as vital spaces where India and China can align on issues of mutual interest, reinforcing the importance of maintaining open channels of communication.

India's Strategic Path Forward

Navigating this complicated relationship requires India to maintain a delicate balance between **asserting its sovereignty** and leveraging opportunities for **economic and diplomatic collaboration**. To do so, India must:

Strengthen Domestic Capacities: Initiatives like **Atmanirbhar Bharat (Self-Reliant India)** are critical to reducing dependency on Chinese imports and building resilience in key sectors such as **manufacturing, defense**, and **technology**.

Diversify Trade Partnerships: Expanding trade and investment relationships with other nations, including **Japan, South Korea, ASEAN countries**, and **Europe**, will help mitigate risks associated with over-reliance on Chinese goods and supply chains.

Pursue Multilateral Diplomacy: Active participation in forums like **BRICS, SCO**, and the **United Nations** enables India to influence global decision-making while fostering constructive engagement with China on shared issues.

Enhance Strategic Alliances: Strengthening partnerships with like-minded nations, particularly in the **Indo-Pacific**, will bolster India's position as a counterbalance to China's assertiveness.

Looking Ahead

As India continues to assert itself as a key player in the region and the global order, managing its relationship with China will remain a critical challenge. This balancing act requires a blend of **pragmatism, resilience, and strategic foresight**, ensuring that India can advance its national interests while contributing to regional stability.

The next chapters will delve deeper into India's strategies for addressing these challenges, exploring its evolving relationships with other major powers, and analyzing how these dynamics shape India's aspirations as a rising global power in an increasingly multipolar world.

5: The Shadow of the Dragon

China's rapid ascent as a global superpower has been marked by ambitious initiatives, strategic investments, and increasing assertiveness, particularly in Asia. Among its most significant undertakings is the **Belt and Road Initiative (BRI)**, a vast infrastructure and connectivity project that seeks to reshape global trade routes and expand China's influence across continents. For India, the rise of China's influence presents significant challenges, necessitating counterstrategies like the **Act East Policy** and **domestic infrastructure development**. At the same time, the **competition for influence in South Asia** has added another layer of complexity to the India-China rivalry, shaping the region's geopolitical dynamics.

China's Belt and Road Initiative and Its Implications for India

China's **Belt and Road Initiative (BRI)**, launched in 2013, is one of the most ambitious global strategies of the 21st century. Designed to enhance connectivity and economic integration across continents, the BRI represents China's vision of becoming the central hub of global trade and infrastructure networks. While its proponents hail it as a transformative project for development and global commerce, the initiative has also raised concerns about **debt dependency**, **geopolitical dominance**, and **sovereignty violations**. For India, the BRI poses significant challenges, necessitating a nuanced response that balances strategic concerns with regional competition.

The Scope and Ambitions of the BRI

The Belt and Road Initiative (BRI) reflects China's sweeping ambition to reshape global trade networks and establish itself as a central player in international connectivity. This grand project operates through two primary components, each targeting distinct geographical and economic corridors while advancing Beijing's geopolitical and economic objectives.

The overland segment, known as the **Silk Road Economic Belt**, focuses on connecting China to Central Asia, Europe, and the Middle East through extensive infrastructure development. This includes constructing highways, railways, and energy pipelines that streamline the movement of goods, services, and resources. Major corridors such as the China-Central Asia-West Asia Economic Corridor and the New Eurasian Land Bridge link Chinese industrial hubs with European markets, revitalizing ancient trade routes in the process. These routes not only bolster China's trade capacities but also position it as a dominant economic force across continents.

Complementing the overland efforts is the **Maritime Silk Road**, which aims to establish a network of strategic sea routes and ports that stretch from Southeast Asia to South Asia, Africa, and Europe. Ports like Gwadar in Pakistan, Hambantota in Sri Lanka, and Djibouti in the Horn of Africa are integral to this maritime vision. These investments enhance China's foothold in critical maritime regions, allowing it to secure vital trade passages and assert its influence over global shipping lanes.

The BRI's reach extends to over 140 countries, with investments spanning diverse sectors such as transportation, energy, and trade facilitation. From railway networks crisscrossing Africa to modernized ports in Southeast Asia, the initiative underscores China's aspiration to weave a global web of trade with itself at the center. Beyond the economic scope, the BRI serves as a powerful tool for geopolitical strategy. It enables China to deepen its influence in developing regions, secure critical resource supply chains, and challenge the longstanding dominance of Western powers in shaping global governance.

By merging infrastructure development with strategic outreach, the BRI embodies China's vision of global integration under its leadership. While the initiative promises economic benefits for participating nations, its implications for sovereignty, debt dependency, and global power dynamics make it one of the most debated projects of the 21st century.

Implications for India

China's Belt and Road Initiative (BRI) poses significant challenges for India, transcending economic dimensions to touch on issues of sovereignty, strategic security, and regional influence. For India, the BRI symbolizes a geostrategic maneuver by China that could alter the balance of power in South Asia and beyond.

One of India's primary objections to the BRI is rooted in sovereignty concerns. The China-Pakistan Economic Corridor (CPEC), a marquee project under the BRI, passes through Pakistan-occupied Kashmir (PoK), a region that India claims as an integral part of its territory. By incorporating PoK into CPEC, China has implicitly recognized Pakistan's control over the disputed area, directly challenging India's sovereignty and territorial integrity. This contentious inclusion has led India to reject the BRI framework outright, positioning itself as a vocal critic of the initiative on global platforms. India's stance highlights its commitment to safeguarding its territorial claims, even as it navigates the diplomatic ramifications of opposing a globally influential project.

Beyond sovereignty, the BRI also raises alarms about strategic encirclement. China's investments in key South Asian ports and infrastructure projects are often perceived as part of its "string-of-pearls" strategy—establishing a network of strategic outposts to encircle India and project its influence in the Indian Ocean Region (IOR). The Gwadar Port in Pakistan, situated near the vital Strait of Hormuz, grants China a significant presence in the Arabian Sea, enabling it to monitor and potentially influence maritime activity in the region. Similarly, the Hambantota Port in Sri Lanka, leased to China for 99 years after Sri Lanka struggled to repay its debts, has sparked concerns about Beijing's use of "debt-trap diplomacy" to secure strategic assets. The Kyaukpyu Port in Myanmar further bolsters China's access to the Bay of Bengal, bypassing the vulnerable Malacca Strait and enhancing its connectivity to the Indian Ocean.

These developments directly challenge India's maritime security and its traditional dominance in the IOR. China's expanding presence in India's strategic backyard has compelled New Delhi to reassess its naval and regional security posture, intensify maritime collaborations with like-minded partners, and invest in its own strategic infrastructure.

Economically, the BRI enhances China's influence in South Asia, often at India's expense. Nations like Nepal, Sri Lanka, and Bangladesh have increasingly turned to Beijing for financial assistance and infrastructure development. China's ability to finance and execute large-scale projects quickly has made it an attractive partner for these countries. However, the economic allure often comes with strings attached, as seen in the rising debt burdens that align these nations more closely with Beijing. This growing economic dependence reduces India's leverage in the region, complicating its efforts to maintain its traditional sphere of influence.

India's response to the BRI reflects its broader strategic concerns about China's ambitions. By opposing the initiative and emphasizing alternative frameworks for regional connectivity and development, India seeks to counterbalance China's growing influence while safeguarding its own strategic interests. However, the BRI's expansive scope and reach continue to pose significant challenges, requiring India to adopt a multifaceted approach that blends diplomacy, economic resilience, and strategic partnerships.

Broader Geopolitical Implications

China's Belt and Road Initiative (BRI) presents significant challenges to India's regional and global strategies, reshaping power dynamics and influencing New Delhi's foreign policy priorities. By amplifying China's presence in South Asia and beyond, the BRI compels India to recalibrate its approach to regional leadership, economic partnerships, and security concerns.

The BRI has shifted regional power dynamics by bolstering China's influence in India's immediate neighborhood. Traditionally seen as the dominant power in South Asia, India now faces increasing competition from Beijing, which uses the BRI to deepen political and economic ties with countries like Sri Lanka, Bangladesh, Nepal, and Pakistan. This growing presence undermines India's leadership and forces New Delhi to navigate a more complex regional landscape. Competing for partnerships in such an environment is often challenging, particularly when smaller nations are drawn to China's generous infrastructure investments and swift project execution.

On the global stage, the BRI represents a significant challenge to the Western-led economic order, offering an alternative model of growth and financing to developing countries. This model appeals to nations seeking infrastructure development without the stringent conditions typically imposed by Western institutions. However, India's decision to abstain from the BRI framework limits its ability to influence this emerging order. In response, India has sought to strengthen alternative partnerships and frameworks, such as the Quad, while fostering deeper collaborations with nations that share its concerns about China's expanding influence.

Security concerns are another critical aspect of the BRI's broader implications. Many BRI projects, particularly ports, have a dual-use nature, serving both commercial and potential military purposes. This raises alarms about the militarization of critical infrastructure and the risks of regional instability. India views the BRI as a mechanism for China to project power far beyond its borders, threatening India's strategic and security interests. The development of ports like Gwadar in Pakistan and Hambantota in Sri Lanka underscores these concerns, as these facilities enhance China's ability to operate in the Indian Ocean, directly challenging India's maritime dominance.

The BRI has undeniably reshaped global trade and connectivity, but it also highlights risks such as sovereignty violations, debt dependencies, and intensified geopolitical competition. For India, the initiative serves as a reminder of the need for a comprehensive strategy to address these challenges. This includes safeguarding its sovereignty, countering China's influence in South Asia, and strengthening its presence in global governance platforms.

India's approach involves a multi-pronged response that balances addressing immediate threats with advancing long-term strategic goals. By leveraging initiatives like the Act East Policy, expanding infrastructure projects, and deepening ties with like-minded nations, India seeks to counterbalance China's growing influence. The next section will delve into these countermeasures, exploring how India is working to assert its leadership and secure its interests in the face of China's ambitious Belt and Road Initiative.

SANDEEP CHAVAN

India's Countermeasures: Act East Policy and Infrastructure Development

In response to China's expanding influence through its ambitious **Belt and Road Initiative (BRI)** and other strategic investments, India has devised a comprehensive strategy to **assert its regional leadership**, **enhance connectivity**, and **counterbalance China's dominance**. This multifaceted approach combines diplomatic outreach, domestic infrastructure development, and international partnerships to safeguard India's interests and promote sustainable regional development.

The Act East Policy

India's **Act East Policy**, launched in 2014 under Prime Minister Narendra Modi, represents a strategic evolution from the earlier Look East Policy of the 1990s. It underscores India's ambition to deepen its engagement with Southeast Asia and expand its influence across the Indo-Pacific region. By emphasizing trade, connectivity, and security, the Act East Policy reflects India's intent to position itself as a vital partner in a rapidly transforming Asia.

At its core, the policy prioritizes strengthening ties with the Association of Southeast Asian Nations (ASEAN), a bloc that includes ten Southeast Asian nations. ASEAN serves as a crucial platform for India's economic and strategic outreach, providing opportunities for collaboration in trade, investment, and cultural exchange. Through free trade agreements and active participation in forums like the East Asia Summit and the ASEAN Regional Forum, India has bolstered its presence in the region. Trade volumes between India and ASEAN have grown significantly, with Indian markets becoming a key destination for Southeast Asian goods and services.

Connectivity is a cornerstone of the Act East Policy, aiming to integrate India more closely with Southeast Asia and beyond. Major infrastructure projects such as the **India-Myanmar-Thailand Trilateral Highway** and the **Kaladan Multi-Modal Transit Transport Project** exemplify this focus. The Trilateral Highway is designed to connect India with Southeast Asian markets, enhancing cross-border trade and transportation. The Kaladan project links India's eastern seaboard to Myanmar's Sittwe Port, providing a strategic gateway to Southeast Asia while improving access to India's Northeast region. These initiatives not only facilitate trade but also drive economic development in regions historically underserved, bridging local economies with broader regional opportunities.

Security and maritime cooperation are equally critical components of the Act East Policy, reflecting India's strategic interests in the Indo-Pacific. Partnerships with nations like Vietnam, Indonesia, and the Philippines have intensified, focusing on countering growing assertiveness in the South China Sea. Joint naval exercises, defense agreements, and port access arrangements have enhanced India's maritime capabilities, ensuring freedom of navigation and contributing to regional stability. India's active participation in the Quad alliance, alongside the U.S., Japan, and Australia, complements these efforts by reinforcing a rules-based order in the Indo-Pacific.

The Act East Policy symbolizes India's proactive approach to leveraging its strategic location, economic potential, and democratic values to foster deeper regional integration. As India continues to build partnerships and infrastructure that connect it with Southeast Asia and the Indo-Pacific, the policy not only strengthens its position in Asia but also aligns with its broader vision of being a key player in shaping global and regional stability.

Domestic Infrastructure Development

India's domestic infrastructure development is a cornerstone of its strategy to enhance regional influence and counterbalance China's growing presence in Asia. Recognizing that robust infrastructure is pivotal for both economic growth and national security, India has prioritized transformative projects that improve connectivity, fortify border areas, and position the country as a key player in the Indian Ocean Region.

In border regions, infrastructure projects have gained momentum, addressing both logistical challenges and defense imperatives. The **Chardham Project**, for example, is designed to improve connectivity to pilgrimage sites in Uttarakhand, but its strategic significance lies in bolstering logistical support to areas near the China border. Similarly, the **Zojila Tunnel** in Ladakh ensures all-weather connectivity to India's northernmost regions, enabling swift troop movement and supply transport during crises. These initiatives reflect India's focus on strengthening its preparedness and sovereignty in sensitive border areas.

The **Northeast region** holds strategic importance due to its proximity to China and Southeast Asia. Investments in railways, highways, and airports aim to integrate this region with the rest of India while fostering economic development and social stability. The **Bogibeel Bridge**, India's longest rail-cum-road bridge, is a prime example of these efforts, enhancing connectivity in a region that has historically been underserved. These projects not only improve domestic integration but also position the Northeast as a gateway to Southeast Asia, aligning with India's Act East Policy.

On the maritime front, the **Sagarmala Project** plays a pivotal role in modernizing India's coastal infrastructure and strengthening its presence in the Indian Ocean Region (IOR). By developing ports and enhancing maritime connectivity, India counters China's expanding influence in the region while boosting its own global trade competitiveness. This initiative also focuses on reducing logistics costs and creating coastal economic zones, fostering economic growth and improving India's standing in global supply chains.

These infrastructure efforts reflect India's recognition that regional and global influence begins with a strong domestic foundation. By enhancing connectivity, improving logistical capabilities, and addressing strategic vulnerabilities, India is not only safeguarding its borders but also positioning itself as a resilient and influential power in a rapidly evolving geopolitical landscape.

Strategic Partnerships

India's strategy to counter China's influence is built on fostering strategic partnerships with like-minded nations. These collaborations aim to provide sustainable and inclusive alternatives to China's Belt and Road Initiative (BRI), promoting development models that prioritize transparency, local ownership, and long-term economic viability.

Japan has emerged as a key partner in India's infrastructure and development initiatives. Their collaboration reflects shared values of sustainability and mutual respect for regional sovereignty. A prominent example is the **Asia-Africa Growth Corridor (AAGC)**, a joint initiative by

THE TRIANGULAR DYNAMICS

India and Japan. This project focuses on infrastructure development in Africa and Asia but adopts a markedly different approach compared to the BRI. The AAGC emphasizes local ownership, transparency, and debt sustainability, ensuring that participating nations are not burdened by unsustainable financial commitments. This partnership highlights a commitment to empowering local communities and fostering equitable growth.

In the Indo-Pacific, India's partnerships with the **United States** and **Australia** play a significant role in countering China's regional dominance. These collaborations often focus on co-developing infrastructure and improving connectivity in strategically critical areas. Unlike the top-down approach associated with the BRI, these partnerships prioritize capacity-building and long-term sustainability. For smaller nations in the region, these initiatives offer an alternative that avoids the economic and political risks associated with debt-trap diplomacy.

India's engagement with **ASEAN nations** further strengthens its strategy. By working closely with Southeast Asian countries, India has focused on capacity-building projects designed to empower local communities and create equitable economic opportunities. This people-centric approach stands in contrast to China's model, which often prioritizes state-to-state agreements and large-scale infrastructure projects. Through its emphasis on inclusive development, India is carving a distinct identity as a reliable and responsible partner in the region.

These strategic partnerships reflect India's commitment to building a more balanced and sustainable regional order. By offering development models that prioritize fairness and shared growth, India not only counters China's influence but also strengthens its position as a trusted and cooperative leader in the global arena.

In summary, India's response to China's growing influence, particularly through the BRI, reflects a **comprehensive strategy** rooted in diplomacy, infrastructure development, and international partnerships. The **Act East Policy** underscores India's commitment to deepening its engagement with Southeast Asia and the Indo-Pacific, while domestic infrastructure initiatives bolster its strategic positioning and economic integration.

By strengthening its regional presence, building resilient infrastructure, and collaborating with global partners, India seeks to assert itself as a leader in the region while providing sustainable alternatives to China's model of development. These efforts are not merely reactive but represent a forward-looking approach to ensuring India's influence and sovereignty in an increasingly competitive geopolitical landscape. The next section will examine **South Asia's power dynamics**, where India and China vie for influence in their shared neighborhood, further shaping the trajectory of this rivalry.

South Asia's Power Dynamics: Competing for Influence

The competition between **India and China** for influence in **South Asia** is a defining aspect of their geopolitical rivalry. Both nations seek to secure strategic footholds in a region critical for their economic and security interests. However, their contrasting approaches—China's focus on large-scale infrastructure investments and India's emphasis on development partnerships and cultural ties—highlight their differing goals and strategies. This competition has not only redefined the region's **geopolitical landscape** but has also impacted the policies and trajectories of smaller South Asian nations.

China's Growing Influence

China's expanding presence in South Asia, fueled by its Belt and Road Initiative (BRI) and targeted bilateral agreements, has reshaped the region's geopolitical landscape. With strategic investments in infrastructure, trade, and diplomacy, China has positioned itself as a formidable competitor to India's traditional influence in the area. This assertive push challenges India's historical leadership in South Asia, compelling it to adapt its strategies to maintain its regional standing amidst growing Chinese influence.

Pakistan: A Cornerstone of China's Strategy

Pakistan plays a pivotal role in China's South Asia strategy, often described as its "all-weather ally." Central to this partnership is the China-Pakistan Economic Corridor (CPEC), a $62 billion flagship initiative under the Belt and Road Initiative (BRI). CPEC connects China's Xinjiang region to

Pakistan's Gwadar Port, offering China direct access to the Arabian Sea and bypassing the vulnerable Malacca Strait, thereby bolstering its energy security.

Gwadar Port, operated by China, serves as more than just an economic hub. It functions as a strategic outpost, enabling Beijing to project its influence in the Indian Ocean Region (IOR) and closely monitor maritime activities. This deepened collaboration extends beyond infrastructure, as Pakistan's growing economic reliance on Chinese loans and investments has strengthened their strategic alignment. For India, this partnership poses a significant challenge, intensifying security concerns and reshaping the regional power dynamics.

Sri Lanka: A Strategic Foothold in the Indian Ocean

Sri Lanka has become a strategic foothold for China in the Indian Ocean, with investments like the Hambantota Port exemplifying Beijing's ambitions to expand its maritime presence. The leasing of Hambantota Port to China for 99 years, after Sri Lanka struggled to repay Chinese loans, has sparked widespread concerns about debt-trap diplomacy. Positioned near critical shipping lanes, the port significantly enhances China's naval and commercial influence in the region, allowing it to monitor and potentially control maritime traffic.

While Sri Lanka maintains a historically strong relationship with India, its growing reliance on Chinese funding for infrastructure projects highlights a shifting dynamic. This dependence underscores the strategic challenges India faces in countering China's influence in a region critical to its own security and economic interests.

Nepal and Bangladesh: Strategic Diversification

Nepal and Bangladesh have pursued strategic diversification in their foreign engagements, increasingly turning to China for infrastructure funding and economic partnerships, challenging India's traditional dominance in the region.

In Nepal, agreements under China's Belt and Road Initiative (BRI) have led to investments in critical sectors like roads, railways, and energy. These projects aim to enhance Nepal's connectivity and trade, reducing its reliance on India as its primary economic partner. This shift underscores Nepal's efforts to balance its ties with both neighbors while seeking greater autonomy in its development agenda.

Bangladesh, too, has embraced Chinese investments in major infrastructure and energy projects, such as the Padma Bridge, which enhances internal connectivity and economic prospects. While maintaining a strong relationship with India, especially in areas like security and cultural ties, Bangladesh's pragmatic economic approach highlights its intent to leverage Chinese resources for growth. This dual engagement reflects a calculated strategy by both nations to diversify partnerships while navigating the complex regional dynamics shaped by India and China.

India's Regional Strategy

India has adopted a multifaceted approach to counter China's expanding influence in South Asia. By focusing on development assistance, cultural diplomacy, and military cooperation, India aims to strengthen its leadership while addressing the aspirations of its neighbors.

India's approach to development assistance is rooted in partnerships rather than dependency. Financial and technical aid is structured to foster sustainable growth, avoiding the pitfalls of debt often associated with Chinese loans. For example, India has played a pivotal role in Bhutan's energy sector by helping construct hydropower plants, enabling Bhutan to become a key exporter of clean energy to India. Similarly, in Bangladesh and Nepal, India's investments in hospitals, schools, and training programs underscore its commitment to enhancing healthcare and education. Infrastructure projects like the development of Chabahar Port in Iran and rail links in Nepal aim to improve regional connectivity while respecting sovereignty and ensuring mutual benefit.

Cultural diplomacy remains one of India's strongest assets in South Asia, leveraging shared languages, religions, and cultural traditions. India's rich cultural heritage creates a natural soft power advantage that China cannot replicate. Initiatives such as scholarships, educational exchanges, and the global popularity of Bollywood films deepen cultural ties and goodwill. Historical and religious connections, such as Buddhism's shared heritage with Sri Lanka and Nepal, further enhance India's cultural appeal.

THE TRIANGULAR DYNAMICS

Military cooperation is another critical pillar of India's regional strategy. India has deepened defense ties with key neighbors to counterbalance China's growing military presence. Regular joint military exercises with Nepal, Bangladesh, and the Maldives focus on areas like counterterrorism and maritime security. India also provides defense training and supplies equipment to nations such as Bhutan and Bangladesh, strengthening their security capacities and fostering trust.

Through these efforts, India seeks to reinforce its role as a trusted partner and regional leader. By prioritizing sustainable development, leveraging cultural connections, and enhancing military collaboration, India is working to build resilient relationships that reduce its neighbors' dependency on Chinese support while promoting stability and prosperity in South Asia.

Maritime Rivalry

The Indian Ocean Region (IOR) has emerged as a focal point of strategic competition between India and China, reflecting their broader contest for influence in Asia and beyond. This maritime rivalry underscores the critical importance of the IOR as a theater for both economic and military ambitions.

China's maritime expansion through its *string-of-pearls* strategy highlights its intent to establish a dominant presence in the IOR. By developing a network of ports and bases, such as Gwadar in Pakistan, Hambantota in Sri Lanka, and Kyaukpyu in Myanmar, China secures its trade and energy supply routes while enhancing its ability to project power in the region. These ports, while officially designated for commercial purposes, have dual-use potential, raising concerns about militarization and regional stability.

In response, India has positioned itself as a net security provider in the Indian Ocean, emphasizing regional stability, freedom of navigation, and equitable development. India's strategic efforts in the IOR include conducting joint maritime exercises with allies such as the United States, Japan, and Australia under the Quad framework. These exercises strengthen interoperability among navies and send a clear message of commitment to a rules-based maritime order.

India has also deepened its relationships with smaller littoral states like Seychelles, Mauritius, and the Maldives through port development, coastal security programs, and military aid. These collaborations not only enhance regional security but also counterbalance China's growing influence among these strategically located nations.

Strategic port development forms a cornerstone of India's maritime strategy. Investments in projects like Chabahar Port in Iran provide India with critical trade routes to Afghanistan and Central Asia, bypassing Pakistan and reducing dependence on Chinese-controlled corridors. Domestically, initiatives such as the Sagarmala Project aim to modernize Indian ports, enhance logistical efficiency, and strengthen India's maritime economy, bolstering its competitive edge in the region.

By expanding its naval capabilities and leveraging strategic partnerships, India continues to reinforce its position as a dominant maritime power in the IOR. This approach not only counters China's ambitions but also underscores India's broader commitment to ensuring peace, stability, and equitable development in the Indian Ocean. Through a combination of strategic investments, military readiness, and regional alliances, India seeks to maintain its leadership in this critical geopolitical arena.

In conclusion, the competition for influence in South Asia underscores the **geopolitical rivalry** between India and China. While China's **BRI investments** and strategic footholds have reshaped the region's dynamics, India's **development partnerships**, **cultural ties**, and **military collaborations** reflect a sustainable and inclusive approach to regional leadership.

As South Asian nations navigate this evolving power dynamic, their choices will significantly impact the region's future. For India, the challenge lies in balancing its **security and economic priorities** while strengthening its traditional role as the dominant power in South Asia. By leveraging its historical connections and forging partnerships rooted in trust and mutual benefit, India can counter China's influence and maintain its strategic edge in the region.

Conclusion

The rise of China as a global economic and strategic powerhouse, driven by initiatives like the Belt and Road Initiative (BRI), has significantly reshaped the geopolitical dynamics of South Asia. Through heavy investments in infrastructure, trade networks, and bilateral partnerships, China has extended its influence across the region, challenging India's traditional leadership and altering the balance of power.

China's assertiveness in South Asia presents a dual reality: it offers opportunities for economic growth to nations like Pakistan, Sri Lanka, Nepal, and Bangladesh while raising concerns about debt sustainability and sovereignty. For India, this evolving landscape represents a critical challenge to its regional influence and underscores the need for a recalibrated strategy.

India's Response: A Strategic Realignment

India has adopted a multifaceted approach to counter China's growing footprint while strengthening its leadership in South Asia. This strategy combines regional outreach, infrastructure development, and enhanced diplomatic and military engagement.

The **Act East Policy** has been pivotal in extending India's influence beyond South Asia to the broader Indo-Pacific region. By deepening ties with ASEAN nations and fostering maritime collaborations with partners like Vietnam and Indonesia, India is fortifying its role in regions where Chinese influence is expanding. Connectivity projects, such as the India-Myanmar-Thailand Trilateral Highway, enhance trade and cultural ties while reinforcing India's strategic presence.

Domestically, India's emphasis on infrastructure development in sensitive regions like the Northeast and border areas reflects its dual focus on national security and economic integration. Projects such as the Sagarmala initiative, which modernizes ports and coastal infrastructure, ensure India's competitive edge in regional trade and logistics, further bolstering its influence.

India has also prioritized equitable regional development through its partnerships with South Asian nations. By emphasizing trust, mutual benefit, and cultural diplomacy, India distinguishes itself from China's often-criticized debt-heavy investments. This approach not only preserves India's leadership but also strengthens its image as a reliable partner.

Broader Implications for Global Geopolitics

The India-China competition extends beyond South Asia, influencing the broader Indo-Pacific and global geopolitical landscape. China's assertiveness in the Indian Ocean Region (IOR) and strategic investments in South Asia are part of its larger ambitions in the Indo-Pacific. In response, India's participation in the Quad alliance and collaborations with the United States, Japan, and Australia highlight its commitment to maintaining a free and rules-based order in the region.

Globally, the rivalry between India and China is shaping their roles in multilateral institutions like the United Nations, WTO, and climate forums. While China's approach emphasizes economic dominance and infrastructure-driven influence, India's strategy focuses on inclusive development, democratic values, and shared prosperity.

Balancing Engagement and Assertiveness

India's challenge lies in balancing economic collaboration with China on shared global issues while maintaining its strategic autonomy and addressing security concerns. Achieving this balance requires proactive engagement with South Asian nations to ensure trust and reduce dependence on Chinese aid, while simultaneously strengthening domestic industries to minimize vulnerabilities.

Strategic partnerships with like-minded countries also play a vital role in providing alternatives to China's BRI and enhancing stability in the Indo-Pacific. These collaborations reinforce India's ability to project power while upholding its principles of inclusivity and mutual respect.

Looking Ahead

The India-China rivalry in South Asia reflects broader shifts in global power dynamics. As both nations vie for influence, their strategies will profoundly shape the region's political, economic, and security environment in the coming decades.

India's success in navigating this competition will depend on its ability to leverage its strengths—its democratic values, economic potential, and cultural ties—while addressing strategic vulnerabilities. By doing so, India has the opportunity not only to counterbalance China's growing presence but also to assert itself as a leading global power, capable of driving stability and progress in an increasingly multipolar world.

Part III: India-U.S. Relationship: Strategic Partnerships

6: The Eagle's Embrace

The relationship between **India and the United States** has evolved into a dynamic partnership characterized by mutual strategic, economic, and technological interests. As two of the largest democracies in the world, their collaboration has become increasingly critical in the face of shifting global power dynamics. From **defense collaborations** to **technology partnerships**, and from **U.S. investments** in India's burgeoning industries to their shared vision in the **Indo-Pacific region**, the India-U.S. partnership has become a cornerstone of India's global strategy.

Defense Collaborations and Technology Partnerships

The defense partnership between **India and the United States** has undergone a transformative shift in recent years, evolving from a **transactional arrangement** to a **strategic alliance**. This deepening collaboration reflects their shared commitment to addressing global security challenges and underscores India's growing importance as a key player in the international security architecture. The partnership encompasses **defense agreements, joint military exercises, technology transfers**, and a focus on **maritime security**, positioning India as a pivotal actor in the Indo-Pacific and beyond.

Strengthening Defense Ties

The India-U.S. defense relationship has evolved into a critical pillar of their strategic partnership, marked by foundational agreements and regular joint military exercises that enhance interoperability and mutual trust. These collaborations underscore a shared commitment to regional and global security.

Foundational Agreements

In recent years, key defense agreements have laid the groundwork for closer military cooperation between the two nations.

The **Logistics Exchange Memorandum of Agreement (LEMOA)**, signed in 2016, allows India and the United States to access each other's military bases for logistical support, including refueling and maintenance. This agreement not only enhances operational flexibility but also enables swift responses during joint missions or crises.

The **Communications Compatibility and Security Agreement (COMCASA)**, finalized in 2018, grants India access to advanced secure communication systems used by U.S. forces. This facilitates seamless coordination during joint operations and ensures compatibility with cutting-edge U.S. military platforms.

In 2020, the **Basic Exchange and Cooperation Agreement (BECA)** was signed, providing India access to geospatial intelligence from U.S. satellites. This data enhances the precision of India's missile systems, drones, and targeting capabilities, particularly in critical border and maritime zones.

Joint Military Exercises

Regular joint exercises between Indian and U.S. armed forces have become a cornerstone of their defense relationship, fostering a deeper understanding of each other's operational strategies.

Yudh Abhyas, an annual exercise between the armies of both nations, focuses on counter-terrorism and disaster response. This collaboration strengthens their ability to work together in complex, high-stakes scenarios.

The **Tiger Triumph** exercise, involving all three military services—army, navy, and air force—highlights their capacity to operate cohesively in multi-dimensional missions, from humanitarian assistance to combat operations.

The **Malabar Naval Exercise**, conducted with Japan and Australia, underscores the strategic alignment of the Quad nations in promoting maritime security. This exercise emphasizes the shared objective of ensuring a free and open Indo-Pacific region, countering challenges such as piracy and territorial assertiveness.

These defense initiatives reflect a deepening alignment between India and the United States in addressing global security challenges. By enhancing operational coordination, technological integration, and mutual trust, the India-U.S. defense partnership continues to play a vital role in shaping the regional balance of power, particularly in the Indo-Pacific.

Strengthening Defense Technology Collaboration

The defense partnership between India and the United States has become a cornerstone of India's modernization efforts, aligning closely with the *Make in India* initiative to bolster indigenous defense production. By facilitating technology transfers and supplying advanced military equipment, the U.S. has positioned itself as a key partner in enhancing India's defense capabilities and strategic autonomy.

Advanced Defense Equipment

The United States has provided India with cutting-edge military platforms that significantly enhance its operational readiness and strategic deterrence.

The **Apache AH-64E attack helicopters**, equipped with sophisticated avionics and precision-guided weaponry, have bolstered India's air combat capabilities. These helicopters are invaluable in counter-insurgency operations and battlefield support.

The **C-17 Globemaster transport aircraft** offers India unmatched airlift capacity, enabling the rapid deployment of troops, equipment, and humanitarian aid across challenging terrains.

The **P-8I maritime surveillance aircraft**, vital for monitoring the Indian Ocean Region (IOR), enhances India's maritime domain awareness. These aircraft are critical for tracking potential threats, ensuring maritime security, and safeguarding vital sea lanes.

Collaborative Defense Initiatives

The **Defense Technology and Trade Initiative (DTTI)** has emerged as a key framework for co-developing and co-producing defense technologies. This collaboration fosters innovation and strengthens India's defense industrial base.

Under DTTI, projects such as unmanned aerial systems, advanced sensor technologies, and lightweight materials have been explored, reflecting a shared commitment to technological innovation.

Private sector partnerships have further amplified this collaboration. Joint ventures between Indian and U.S. defense manufacturers facilitate technology transfers and local production, contributing to the development of India's defense ecosystem.

Synergy with *Make in India*

India's pursuit of self-reliance in defense is strongly supported by U.S. collaboration. The partnership enables the integration of advanced technologies and global best practices into Indian manufacturing processes.

Collaborative production of aircraft components, weapons systems, and cyber defense solutions underscores the synergy between the two nations. These initiatives not only reduce India's reliance on imports but also position it as a competitive player in the global defense market.

Through its technology transfers, defense production collaborations, and supply of state-of-the-art military equipment, the U.S. has become an essential partner in India's efforts to modernize its armed forces. This partnership strengthens India's strategic capabilities, fosters innovation, and aligns with its vision of becoming a self-reliant defense power.

Strengthening India's Maritime Security

India's strategic position in the Indian Ocean Region (IOR) underscores its critical role in maintaining regional stability and addressing emerging security challenges. With the increasing assertiveness of China and the broader complexities of the Indo-Pacific, India's maritime capabilities are central to its defense strategy. The partnership with the United States has been instrumental in bolstering these capabilities, fostering both modernization and strategic alignment.

Enhancing Maritime Capabilities

The United States has played a pivotal role in advancing India's naval strength, supplying advanced systems for surveillance, reconnaissance, and anti-submarine warfare. These contributions have enhanced India's ability to monitor and respond to threats across the vast expanse of the IOR.

Collaborative naval exercises further deepen this partnership. Joint operations and port visits not only improve interoperability between the Indian and U.S. navies but also strengthen coordinated responses to transnational challenges like piracy, terrorism, and illegal fishing. These exercises underscore a shared commitment to upholding security in one of the world's most vital maritime corridors.

Commitment to Freedom of Navigation

A shared vision of a free and open Indo-Pacific forms the cornerstone of India-U.S. maritime collaboration. This commitment is particularly significant against the backdrop of China's growing assertiveness in the South China Sea and its expanding naval presence in the Indian Ocean.

India's emphasis on freedom of navigation aligns with U.S. efforts to ensure a rules-based international order, where all nations can access critical sea lanes without coercion. This alignment not only strengthens bilateral ties but also reinforces a collective stance against unilateral actions that threaten regional stability.

Advancing Maritime Domain Awareness

Improving maritime domain awareness has become a key focus of India-U.S. cooperation. Platforms like the Information Fusion Centre for the Indian Ocean Region (IFC-IOR) enable both nations to share real-time intelligence on maritime activity. This proactive approach allows for timely responses to emerging threats and enhances regional security coordination.

A Strong Foundation for Regional Stability

The evolving defense partnership between India and the United States reflects their shared commitment to addressing both immediate and long-term security challenges. Foundational agreements like LEMOA, COMCASA, and BECA provide the structural framework for closer military cooperation, while joint initiatives in maritime security exemplify the depth of their collaboration.

As India continues to modernize its naval forces and expand its strategic reach, U.S. support remains a critical enabler. By focusing on advanced technology integration, interoperability, and a shared vision for the Indo-Pacific, the India-U.S. partnership contributes to a more secure and stable maritime environment.

This collaboration not only addresses pressing challenges in the IOR but also sets the stage for a robust, future-ready alliance capable of navigating the complexities of a dynamic and interconnected world.

U.S. Investments in India's Tech, Pharma, and Startup Ecosystems

The **India-U.S. economic partnership** is a cornerstone of their bilateral relationship, underpinned by robust collaboration across **technology, pharmaceuticals, and startups**. The United States has been instrumental in fostering innovation, driving growth, and creating jobs in India, leveraging the country's **vast talent pool and consumer base**. These investments not only benefit both economies but also strengthen their strategic alignment in addressing global challenges.

Technology Partnerships

The technology partnership between India and the United States stands as a cornerstone of their bilateral relationship, fostering innovation and positioning both nations at the forefront of digital transformation. This collaboration leverages India's thriving IT ecosystem and its vast talent pool, alongside the technological expertise and investment capabilities of leading American companies.

American Tech Giants in India

Major U.S. technology companies have deeply integrated into India's economic and technological landscape, capitalizing on its burgeoning digital economy and skilled workforce. Companies like Google, Microsoft, Amazon, and Apple have made substantial investments, not only in India's market but also in its infrastructure and innovation ecosystem.

Amazon Web Services (AWS), for instance, has established multiple data centers across India, powering cloud infrastructure that supports industries ranging from healthcare to retail. Similarly, Microsoft's Azure platform is pivotal in driving innovation, particularly in education and healthcare, where digital solutions are bridging gaps in accessibility and efficiency. Google's contributions in digital payments and artificial intelligence (AI) are helping address critical challenges, such as financial inclusion and language barriers.

Apple's expansion of manufacturing operations in India further underscores the growing synergy between the two nations. By increasing production facilities for devices like iPhones, Apple not only diversifies its supply chain but also reinforces India's status as a global manufacturing hub.

India's IT Services Sector

India's IT services industry, led by companies like Tata Consultancy Services (TCS), Infosys, and Wipro, plays a central role in the technology collaboration between the two countries. These firms are globally recognized for their expertise in software development, cybersecurity, and digital transformation, offering services that underpin the operations of U.S. businesses.

Collaborations between Indian and American tech companies focus on cutting-edge fields such as cloud computing, AI, and blockchain. This partnership is instrumental in delivering innovative solutions to global clients, addressing challenges in industries as diverse as banking, healthcare, and e-commerce.

India's IT workforce, renowned for its technical acumen, is a vital component of this collaboration. From driving advancements in machine learning to developing scalable software systems, Indian professionals contribute significantly to the technological leadership of U.S. firms.

Joint Research and Development

Research and development initiatives are a key facet of the India-U.S. technology partnership, reflecting a shared commitment to innovation. Collaborative programs, such as the U.S.-India Artificial Intelligence (AI) Partnership, focus on areas like robotics, quantum computing, and sustainable technology.

These efforts go beyond economic benefits, addressing global challenges like climate change, healthcare accessibility, and cybersecurity. For example, AI-driven solutions are being developed to enhance disaster response, optimize renewable energy usage, and improve early disease detection.

A Synergy for Global Impact

The technology partnership between India and the United States exemplifies the power of collaboration in an increasingly interconnected world. By combining India's IT expertise and resource-rich ecosystem with American technological innovation and investment, the two nations are not only advancing their own economies but also driving solutions to pressing global issues.

This dynamic relationship reflects a mutual vision for a future shaped by innovation, inclusivity, and shared prosperity, setting a benchmark for how technology can unite diverse economies for the greater good.

Pharmaceuticals and Healthcare

The pharmaceutical and healthcare sectors epitomize the synergy between India and the United States, showcasing how mutual strengths can enhance global healthcare outcomes. This partnership leverages India's expertise in affordable generic drug production and vaccine manufacturing alongside U.S. advancements in healthcare innovation and investment capabilities. Together, they address critical health challenges while driving research and development.

India's Role as a Global Supplier

Indian pharmaceutical companies have cemented their role as indispensable players in the global healthcare supply chain. With 40% of the generic drugs consumed in the U.S. originating from India, the country plays a vital role in making essential medicines more affordable and accessible.

Prominent companies like Sun Pharma, Dr. Reddy's Laboratories, and Cipla have successfully penetrated the U.S. market by adhering to stringent regulatory standards and maintaining high manufacturing quality. Their contributions not only reduce healthcare costs for American consumers but also underscore India's capacity to meet global demands efficiently.

COVID-19 Collaboration

The COVID-19 pandemic brought India's pharmaceutical capabilities into sharp focus. As one of the world's largest vaccine producers, India supplied vaccines like Covishield and Covaxin to over 100 countries, reaffirming its position as the "pharmacy of the world."

Collaboration between India and the United States during this crisis exemplified the importance of global partnerships. Initiatives under the Quad

Vaccine Partnership saw both nations working together to enhance vaccine production and distribution, addressing supply shortages and expanding access to life-saving doses.

Partnerships between Indian manufacturers and U.S. companies, including Pfizer and Johnson & Johnson, highlighted the seamless integration of expertise across borders, enabling rapid innovation and distribution during a global emergency.

R&D and Healthcare Innovation

The United States has played a pivotal role in supporting India's biopharmaceutical research, particularly in high-impact areas such as oncology, biologics, and clinical trials. These collaborations have accelerated the development of breakthrough treatments and improved healthcare outcomes globally.

Additionally, American investments in telemedicine and healthcare startups have expanded access to quality healthcare in India's rural and underserved regions. Digital platforms supported by U.S. technology companies are bridging gaps in healthcare delivery, enabling remote consultations, diagnostics, and treatment management.

A Model for Global Health Collaboration

The partnership between India and the United States in pharmaceuticals and healthcare underscores the transformative potential of cross-border collaboration. By combining India's manufacturing expertise with U.S. technological innovation and investment, both nations contribute significantly to advancing global health equity.

As the world continues to face evolving health challenges, the India-U.S. partnership serves as a model for leveraging complementary strengths to improve healthcare access, affordability, and innovation on a global scale.

The Startup Ecosystem

India's thriving startup ecosystem, now the third-largest in the world, has become a focal point for U.S. venture capital and corporate investments. This vibrant sector is driving innovation across industries such as e-commerce, fintech, education, clean energy, and biotechnology, reshaping India's economy and addressing its unique challenges.

U.S. Venture Capital and Corporate Influence

Prominent U.S. venture capital firms like Sequoia Capital, Accel, and Tiger Global have been instrumental in fueling the growth of Indian startups. Their investments have nurtured numerous unicorns, including Flipkart, Zomato, and BYJU'S, empowering these companies to scale globally while solving critical challenges in areas such as education access, digital payments, and financial inclusion.

The success of these startups is a testament to the synergy between India's entrepreneurial spirit and the financial backing provided by U.S. investors. By fostering innovation and creating jobs, these ventures are playing a vital role in driving India's economic growth.

Transforming E-Commerce and Digital Access

The entry of U.S. corporate giants like Amazon and Walmart (via Flipkart) has revolutionized India's e-commerce landscape. Their investments in logistics, digital payments, and supply chain networks have not only expanded market access for small businesses but also provided consumers with unprecedented convenience and affordability.

These collaborations have accelerated India's digital transformation, enabling millions of people to participate in the digital economy and boosting economic inclusivity.

Clean Energy and Electric Vehicles

Collaboration between India and the United States is also evident in emerging sectors like clean energy and electric vehicles (EVs). Companies such as Tesla and SunPower are exploring opportunities to contribute to India's ambitious goals for renewable energy and its target to achieve net-zero emissions by 2070.

These partnerships are driving advancements in solar energy, wind power, and EV infrastructure, positioning India as a leader in sustainable development and green technologies.

Innovations in Biotechnology and Life Sciences

U.S. investments in biotechnology startups in India are paving the way for advancements in agriculture, healthcare, and environmental sustainability. Innovations in precision farming, gene therapy, and renewable energy solutions are helping India address pressing challenges related to food security, health, and climate change.

These collaborations are not only transforming industries but also creating pathways for India to achieve sustainable and inclusive growth.

A Resilient and Innovation-Driven Partnership

The partnership between India and the United States has been pivotal in shaping India's technology, pharmaceutical, and startup ecosystems. From fostering innovation to addressing global challenges, this collaboration exemplifies the power of economic cooperation.

As India's economy continues to grow and diversify, the partnership is set to deepen further, particularly in cutting-edge areas such as artificial intelligence, clean energy, and biotechnology. By leveraging their complementary strengths, India and the U.S. are not only transforming industries but also building a robust, forward-looking relationship that benefits both nations and contributes to global progress.

The Quad and India's Role in the Indo-Pacific Strategy

The **Indo-Pacific region** has become the epicenter of global geopolitics, shaped by the contest between rising Chinese assertiveness and the efforts of regional and global powers to ensure a **rules-based international order**. For India, the **Quadrilateral Security Dialogue (Quad)** has emerged as a critical platform for advancing its strategic goals in the region. The Quad, comprising **India, the United States, Japan, and Australia,** focuses on fostering **maritime security, connectivity, and regional stability** while promoting shared democratic values.

India's Strategic Role in the Indo-Pacific

India's pivotal geographic position, straddling the Indian Ocean Region (IOR) and key maritime chokepoints, underscores its critical role in shaping the security and stability of the Indo-Pacific. With expanding naval capabilities and a steadfast commitment to a free, open, and inclusive Indo-Pacific, India is emerging as a central player in this strategically significant region.

Geostrategic Importance

India's location at the crossroads of vital sea lanes, such as the Strait of Malacca, underscores its importance in global trade and energy flows. This chokepoint connects the Indian and Pacific Oceans, facilitating a significant portion of international commerce.

China's growing presence in the Indian Ocean, evidenced by port acquisitions, naval deployments, and initiatives under the Belt and Road Initiative (BRI), has heightened the need for India's maritime vigilance. India's ability to maintain a robust presence in these waters is vital for ensuring regional balance and safeguarding its strategic interests.

Leadership in the Quad

India's role in the Quadrilateral Security Dialogue (Quad) demonstrates its proactive engagement in regional security and cooperation. The Quad, comprising India, the United States, Japan, and Australia, serves as a platform to address shared challenges in the Indo-Pacific, including maritime security, economic connectivity, and technological collaboration.

Through the Quad, India asserts its leadership in counterbalancing China's growing influence, promoting a rules-based international order, and advancing inclusive regional development. This partnership also aligns with India's principle of strategic autonomy, enabling it to collaborate with like-minded democracies while maintaining its independent foreign policy.

A Vision for a Stable Indo-Pacific

India's commitment to the Indo-Pacific extends beyond strategic counterbalancing. Its vision encompasses fostering sustainable development, ensuring freedom of navigation, and enhancing regional connectivity. Collaborative initiatives with partners like ASEAN nations further solidify India's position as a key player in advancing economic integration and shared prosperity across the region.

As the Indo-Pacific becomes an increasingly contested space, India's role is both vital and multifaceted. By leveraging its geographic advantages, strengthening its naval capabilities, and fostering regional partnerships, India is not only addressing immediate security challenges but also shaping the future of this dynamic region.

Quad's Pillars of Cooperation

The Quad's framework of cooperation reflects a shared commitment to regional stability, sustainable development, and technological progress, aligning closely with India's strategic and economic goals. Its multifaceted agenda strengthens collective capabilities while addressing challenges across the Indo-Pacific.

Maritime Security as a Cornerstone

Maritime security remains central to the Quad's mission, tackling issues like freedom of navigation, piracy, and illegal fishing. Joint naval exercises, such as the Malabar Exercise, exemplify this focus by enhancing interoperability among member nations. These coordinated efforts enable the Quad to respond collectively to security threats and maintain order in contested waters, such as the South China Sea.

India's robust naval presence, coupled with the advanced technologies and resources of the United States, Japan, and Australia, creates a formidable deterrent against unilateral actions that threaten the region's stability. This collaboration underscores the Quad's role in safeguarding maritime trade routes and upholding international norms.

Promoting Sustainable Infrastructure

The Quad places significant emphasis on developing sustainable infrastructure as an alternative to China's Belt and Road Initiative (BRI). Member-funded projects prioritize transparency, accountability, and local ownership, steering clear of the debt dependency often associated with BRI investments.

India's own initiatives, such as the India-Myanmar-Thailand Trilateral Highway, align seamlessly with the Quad's vision of fostering regional integration and economic growth. By enhancing connectivity and empowering local communities, these efforts contribute to building a more inclusive and resilient Indo-Pacific.

Climate Action and Technological Advancement

Addressing climate change is a critical pillar of Quad cooperation. The focus on clean energy technologies—such as solar power, hydrogen, and energy storage solutions—complements India's ambitious renewable energy goals, including its target of achieving 500 GW of non-fossil fuel capacity by 2030.

Beyond climate action, the Quad drives collaboration in cutting-edge technologies, including artificial intelligence (AI), cybersecurity, and space exploration. These initiatives not only promote innovation but also bolster resilience against emerging challenges, ensuring the region remains adaptive and competitive in a rapidly changing global landscape.

A Collaborative Vision

The Quad's pillars of cooperation resonate deeply with India's broader strategic priorities, enhancing its capacity to lead and influence in the Indo-Pacific. Through a focus on maritime security, sustainable development, and technological progress, the Quad fosters a balanced and inclusive approach to regional challenges, solidifying its role as a stabilizing force in the Indo-Pacific.

Countering China's Influence

Countering China's growing influence in the Indo-Pacific is a central focus of the Quad, which addresses concerns over military assertiveness, economic coercion, and challenges to the established regional order. This strategic collaboration aligns with India's own priorities and strengthens its position as a key player in the region.

Challenging Unilateral Actions

China's activities in the South China Sea, such as constructing artificial islands, deploying military assets, and exerting control over critical waterways, have undermined international norms and raised significant concerns among regional and global powers. The Quad's united stance on a rules-based order reinforces principles like freedom of navigation and territorial sovereignty, serving as a counterbalance to China's unilateral actions.

For India, this commitment resonates deeply with its vision of an inclusive and stable Indo-Pacific. The Quad provides India with a platform to collaborate with like-minded nations, ensuring that regional dynamics are not dictated by a single power.

Promoting Democratic Values

The Quad's emphasis on democratic governance, transparency, and inclusive development offers a compelling alternative to China's state-led economic and political practices. This focus underscores the importance of fair and participatory growth models in addressing the region's challenges.

India's active involvement reflects its alignment with these values while highlighting its ability to navigate partnerships with global powers without compromising its strategic autonomy. As the world's largest democracy, India's role in promoting these principles further solidifies its leadership in the Indo-Pacific.

Balancing Strategic Autonomy

While India engages deeply with Quad partners to address shared concerns, it also maintains its strategic autonomy. India continues to collaborate with China on multilateral platforms like BRICS and the Shanghai Cooperation Organisation (SCO), fostering dialogue and cooperation on global issues.

This dual approach allows India to leverage its partnerships with the Quad while ensuring that its regional and global interests remain independent and pragmatic. This balance reinforces India's position as a stabilizing force in the Indo-Pacific and beyond.

Shaping the Regional Order

India's geostrategic location, expanding naval capabilities, and leadership within the Quad position it as a pivotal player in shaping the Indo-Pacific's future. By addressing maritime security, promoting sustainable development, and countering unilateral actions, India and its Quad partners are working to redefine the regional order. Their shared commitment to democracy, inclusivity, and shared prosperity underscores a vision for a secure and equitable Indo-Pacific.

As China continues to assert its influence, the Quad represents a vital mechanism for maintaining a balance of power. For India, this partnership not only strengthens its strategic footprint but also reinforces its role as a leader in ensuring that the Indo-Pacific remains a region of opportunity and stability for all.

Conclusion

The evolving India-U.S. partnership has become a cornerstone of India's aspirations in a multipolar world, marked by a dynamic collaboration across defense, economics, and regional stability. This relationship is rooted in shared democratic values, complementary strengths, and a mutual commitment to addressing global challenges, transitioning beyond transactional arrangements to a more strategic alignment.

The India-U.S. defense relationship has bolstered India's position as a regional security provider. Foundational agreements such as LEMOA, COMCASA, and BECA have enhanced military interoperability, while the supply of advanced equipment and technology has strengthened India's defense capabilities.

Joint military exercises and a strategic focus on maritime security underscore the critical importance of this partnership in ensuring stability in the Indo-Pacific region, countering threats, and upholding a rules-based international order.

U.S. investments in technology, pharmaceuticals, and startups have accelerated India's economic transformation. These collaborations have fostered innovation, created jobs, and advanced sectors like artificial intelligence, renewable energy, and biotechnology, enhancing India's global competitiveness.

The synergy between India's talent pool and U.S. technological expertise exemplifies how the partnership drives growth while addressing critical challenges such as climate change and digital transformation.

The Indo-Pacific strategy, anchored by the Quad, highlights the convergence of India and the U.S. in promoting stability, freedom of navigation, and countering unilateral actions in the region.

India's active role in the Quad reflects its commitment to regional security while asserting its position as a key player shaping the Indo-Pacific's future.

Balancing Strategic Autonomy with Collaboration

While the U.S. partnership offers India access to advanced technology, defense capabilities, and economic opportunities, India remains committed to its principle of strategic autonomy. This balanced approach ensures that India leverages the benefits of diverse partnerships without becoming overly reliant on any single power.

India continues to engage with other global powers, including China and Russia, through multilateral platforms like BRICS and the Shanghai Cooperation Organisation (SCO). This flexibility enables India to pursue its national interests while maintaining an independent foreign policy.

India's leadership in South Asia and the broader Indo-Pacific depends on its ability to address economic and security challenges equitably and sustainably. By fostering partnerships based on mutual trust and shared benefits, India solidifies its role as a trusted regional power and a voice for developing nations.

The Eagle's Embrace and the Path Ahead

The India-U.S. partnership provides India with a strategic advantage in navigating the complexities of a rapidly evolving geopolitical landscape. Defense collaborations, economic ties, and shared regional goals offer India the tools to assert its global position while addressing critical challenges.

However, India's success lies in maintaining its strategic autonomy, regional leadership, and focus on inclusive growth. The "Eagle's embrace" symbolizes India's ability to leverage its partnership with the U.S. while safeguarding its sovereignty and advancing its long-term ambitions.

7: Friendship with Conditions

While the **India-U.S. relationship** has strengthened over the past two decades, it is not without challenges. The partnership, though rooted in shared democratic values and strategic interests, often faces friction in areas such as **trade policies**, **visa regulations**, and **strategic autonomy**. Additionally, the evolving **U.S.-China rivalry** presents both challenges and opportunities for India. This chapter explores the complexities of this friendship, highlighting areas of contention and how India navigates its path amid global power dynamics.

Challenges in Trade Relations and Visa Policies

While economic collaboration is a central pillar of the **India-U.S. relationship**, persistent challenges in **trade policies, market access**, and **immigration regulations** occasionally strain their otherwise robust partnership. These issues highlight the complexity of balancing national priorities with the mutual benefits of bilateral cooperation.

Trade Disputes

Trade relations between India and the United States, while robust and mutually beneficial in many areas, have also been shaped by recurring disputes and negotiations. These challenges stem from differences in economic priorities, trade policies, and regulatory frameworks, reflecting the complexities of engagement between two of the world's largest economies.

One of the primary points of contention has been tariff barriers and market access. The United States has frequently criticized India for its high tariffs on products such as automobiles, agricultural goods, and medical devices. These tariffs are seen by American exporters as significant obstacles to entering the Indian market. India, however, defends its tariff structure as essential for protecting domestic industries and supporting the livelihoods of its farmers. As a developing country, India emphasizes the need to shield vulnerable sectors from excessive foreign competition, pointing to its domestic economic realities. At the same time, India has highlighted U.S. agricultural subsidies as unfair trade practices that distort global markets, reflecting a broader clash over trade fairness.

Another area of friction lies in the protectionist measures enacted by the United States. India has raised concerns over policies such as restrictions on pharmaceutical exports, tariffs on steel and aluminum, and broader measures perceived as targeting foreign imports to safeguard American jobs. For example, U.S. tariffs on Indian steel and aluminum products, imposed under Section 232 of the Trade Expansion Act, have created challenges for Indian manufacturers and exporters, particularly in metals and industrial goods. These measures have added strain to bilateral trade, particularly in sectors where both nations have significant stakes.

Intellectual property rights (IPR) have also been a source of recurring disagreements. The United States advocates for stricter IPR enforcement, arguing that strong protections are vital to fostering innovation and safeguarding its industries, particularly pharmaceuticals and technology. India, on the other hand, stresses the importance of balancing IPR enforcement with the need to ensure affordable access to medicines and technology, especially for developing nations. As a global leader in the production of generic drugs, India has often found itself at odds with U.S. pharmaceutical companies that seek tighter patent protections, highlighting a fundamental divergence in priorities.

The revocation of India's preferential trade status under the Generalized System of Preferences (GSP) in 2019 further underscored the complexities of the trade relationship. The United States cited insufficient market access for American goods as the reason for this decision, impacting Indian exports worth approximately $6 billion across sectors such as textiles, jewelry, auto parts, and agriculture. While India has sought to address these issues and negotiate the reinstatement of GSP benefits, the episode highlighted the fragility of trade ties and the need for sustained dialogue to address underlying differences.

Despite these disputes, both nations recognize the importance of their economic relationship and continue to engage in discussions to resolve trade tensions. The enduring strength of India-U.S. trade lies in their ability to navigate these challenges through negotiation, compromise, and a shared commitment to fostering deeper economic ties.

Visa and Immigration Policies

Visa and immigration policies have long been a point of contention in the India-U.S. relationship, particularly due to their significant impact on the movement of skilled professionals. This dynamic, central to the bilateral partnership, has often been challenged by restrictive policies that create hurdles for Indian workers and companies.

The H-1B visa program, a cornerstone for skilled migration, has faced increasing restrictions, creating challenges for Indian professionals who form a substantial part of the U.S. tech workforce. Caps on H-1B visa allocations, higher fees, and stricter eligibility requirements have made it more difficult for Indian IT firms such as Infosys, Wipro, and TCS to deploy their employees to U.S.-based operations. These restrictions not only hinder the operations of Indian companies but also risk disrupting the talent pipeline that has been instrumental in driving U.S. technological innovation. India views such policies as counterproductive, given the mutual economic benefits of skilled migration.

The impact of these restrictions extends beyond companies to the broader technology sector, where Indian professionals play a critical role. Workers from India have been central to the success of leading U.S. companies like Google, Microsoft, and Amazon, contributing to advancements in software development, research and development, and innovation. Any disruption to this flow of talent threatens to undermine the competitiveness of U.S. industries that rely on global expertise.

Changing immigration policies under successive U.S. administrations have introduced additional uncertainty for Indian professionals and their employers. Measures targeting spousal work permits (H-4 visas) and increasing compliance costs for employers have added complexity to an already challenging system. These policy shifts often create a sense of instability for

Indian workers, many of whom are key contributors to critical sectors like healthcare, technology, and engineering.

Despite these challenges, Indian professionals have demonstrated remarkable resilience and continue to make substantial contributions to the U.S. economy. From driving innovation in Silicon Valley to advancing medical research and strengthening the operations of multinational corporations, the impact of India's talent pool is profound. Indian-origin leaders such as Satya Nadella (Microsoft) and Sundar Pichai (Google) exemplify this transformative influence, highlighting the potential benefits of more open and collaborative immigration policies.

In conclusion, while visa restrictions and immigration policies present significant challenges, they also underscore the need for ongoing dialogue and negotiation. Addressing these issues in a constructive manner could unlock new opportunities for economic growth, technological innovation, and shared prosperity. By finding common ground on immigration and skilled migration, India and the U.S. can further strengthen their partnership, ensuring that it remains a driving force for global progress in the years to come.

Balancing Autonomy with Strategic Alignment

India's foreign policy has long been guided by the principle of **strategic autonomy**, which allows it to engage with global powers without compromising its independence. This approach reflects India's determination to navigate a complex and competitive geopolitical landscape while prioritizing its **national interests**. The **India-U.S. partnership**, though robust and multifaceted, is a prime example of this balancing act, requiring India to align strategically with the U.S. while maintaining relationships with other influential powers, such as Russia and China.

Maintaining Autonomy

India's emphasis on maintaining strategic autonomy is deeply rooted in its historical non-alignment policy, which has evolved to navigate the complexities of modern global relationships. This approach allows India to assert its independence while fostering diverse partnerships tailored to its national interests.

A clear demonstration of India's independent stance is its measured response to contentious global issues such as the Russia-Ukraine conflict. Despite significant pressure from the United States and other Western nations to condemn Russia and curtail energy imports, India has prioritized its strategic and economic interests. Robust ties with Moscow, particularly in defense and energy sectors, remain vital for India. Russia is a key supplier of defense equipment and plays a crucial role in bolstering India's energy security through the supply of oil and natural gas. This balanced engagement underscores India's commitment to charting its foreign policy course without undue external influence.

India's active participation in multilateral organizations further illustrates its nuanced approach to diplomacy. Platforms such as BRICS and the Shanghai Cooperation Organisation (SCO), where Russia and China are prominent members, provide India with avenues to engage constructively with diverse global powers. These forums enable India to advocate for shared goals, including economic development, climate action, and counterterrorism, while simultaneously reinforcing its strategic independence.

The delicate balance between engagement and vigilance is especially evident in India's relationship with China. While regional rivalries persist, India engages with China through platforms like the Asia Infrastructure Investment Bank (AIIB) and collaborative initiatives under BRICS. These economic partnerships reflect a pragmatic approach to harness opportunities for mutual benefit. At the same time, India remains strategically cautious, particularly in addressing border tensions and competing regional ambitions.

India's approach to strategic autonomy is not about isolation but about ensuring that its foreign policy serves its long-term interests. By maintaining this balance, India continues to assert its sovereignty on the global stage while fostering partnerships that align with its vision for inclusive development and regional stability. This nuanced strategy highlights India's capacity to navigate the intricate dynamics of a multipolar world.

Strategic Alignment with the U.S.

India's alignment with the United States highlights a strategic convergence of interests in areas such as security, technology, and regional stability, particularly within the Indo-Pacific. This partnership, while deepening, remains carefully calibrated to safeguard India's sovereignty and uphold its principle of strategic autonomy.

A cornerstone of this relationship is security and counterterrorism cooperation. India and the U.S. have significantly enhanced intelligence sharing and collaborative efforts to combat transnational threats. Joint military exercises, including *Yudh Abhyas* and the *Malabar Naval Exercise*, underscore their shared commitment to regional and global security. These exercises enhance interoperability and preparedness, particularly in addressing emerging challenges in the Indo-Pacific.

India's role in the Quad alliance with the U.S., Japan, and Australia further emphasizes its strategic collaboration with like-minded democracies. The Quad serves as a platform to promote a free, open, and inclusive Indo-Pacific while countering unilateral actions that threaten regional stability. Key priorities include ensuring freedom of navigation, enhancing maritime domain awareness, and addressing the assertiveness of powers like China. India's active participation reflects its commitment to fostering a balanced and rules-based maritime order.

On the technological and economic fronts, the U.S. is a vital partner in advancing India's innovation ecosystem. Collaborations in fields such as artificial intelligence (AI), clean energy, and cybersecurity contribute to India's technological modernization. Initiatives like the U.S.-India Strategic Energy Partnership (SEP) drive joint efforts to expand renewable energy capacities, addressing both India's developmental aspirations and global climate challenges.

This strategic alignment with the U.S. exemplifies India's ability to foster robust partnerships while maintaining its independent foreign policy. By leveraging shared goals and complementary strengths, India enhances its role as a key player in regional stability and global innovation, ensuring its national interests remain at the forefront of this collaboration.

Navigating the Balance

India's strategic approach to balancing its alignment with the United States while maintaining autonomy highlights its nuanced and pragmatic foreign policy. As it strengthens ties with the U.S. to address shared strategic and economic priorities, India carefully navigates relationships with other global powers, particularly China and Russia, to safeguard its sovereignty and broader interests.

India's growing partnership with the U.S., particularly its active role in the Quad and collaborations in the Indo-Pacific, often draws sharp responses from China. These engagements are perceived by Beijing as counterbalancing efforts, adding tension to an already complicated relationship. Despite these frictions, India avoids overt hostility, choosing diplomacy as the primary tool to address disputes. Simultaneously, it bolsters its military readiness and economic resilience to counter potential threats and assert its regional influence.

Even as India deepens its partnership with the U.S., it remains committed to its long-standing relationship with Russia. Moscow continues to be a critical defense partner, providing advanced military equipment and technology. Additionally, Russia serves as a geopolitical counterweight to China in Asia. India's ability to sustain this partnership, even amid global polarization and Western pressure, reflects its diplomatic agility and steadfast commitment to maintaining strategic autonomy.

India's foreign policy extends beyond its relationships with the U.S., China, and Russia. By cultivating ties with European nations, ASEAN members, and Middle Eastern states, India creates a diversified network of partnerships. These relationships enhance its global standing and reduce dependency on any single power or bloc. For instance, collaborations with Europe in technology, climate action, and defense complement India's economic ties with ASEAN and energy partnerships in the Middle East.

India's ability to navigate this intricate web of relationships underscores its role as a key player in a multipolar world. By balancing competing interests and fostering diverse alliances, India secures its autonomy while advancing its strategic and economic goals on the global stage.

In summary, India's engagement with the United States is a masterclass in balancing **strategic alignment with autonomy**. While leveraging its partnership with the U.S. to advance goals in security, technology, and regional stability, India remains steadfast in preserving its independence in foreign policy decisions. This delicate balance is critical to India's vision of becoming a **leading global power** in a multipolar world.

THE TRIANGULAR DYNAMICS

By maintaining constructive relationships with Russia, engaging diplomatically with China, and fostering partnerships with other nations, India demonstrates its ability to navigate complex global dynamics. This approach not only enhances India's strategic flexibility but also reinforces its position as a key player in shaping the future of global geopolitics.

How India Benefits from the U.S.-China Rivalry

The escalating rivalry between the **United States and China** has transformed global geopolitics, creating significant opportunities for **India** to enhance its **economic, strategic**, and **diplomatic influence**. By positioning itself as a **trusted partner** to the U.S. while maintaining pragmatic engagement with China, India has adeptly leveraged this competition to advance its national interests and bolster its global standing.

Economic Opportunities

India's growing prominence as a global economic hub has been amplified by the ongoing U.S.-China decoupling in trade and technology. This shift presents India with unparalleled opportunities to position itself as a reliable alternative for manufacturing, supply chains, and foreign investments.

India's rise as a preferred destination for global manufacturing is underpinned by initiatives like *Make in India* and the Production-Linked Incentive (PLI) schemes, which have attracted significant interest from U.S. companies seeking to diversify their operations away from China. In particular, sectors such as electronics, pharmaceuticals, and automobiles have gained momentum. For instance, Apple has significantly expanded its production in India, moving key manufacturing processes from China to Indian facilities. These developments not only boost India's industrial base but also enhance its integration into global value chains.

India's vast and rapidly growing consumer market, bolstered by its large middle class, makes it an attractive destination for U.S. investments in sectors such as technology, retail, and e-commerce. Companies like Amazon, Walmart (via Flipkart), and Google have made substantial investments in India, capitalizing on the country's digital economy and evolving consumer preferences. These investments not only drive innovation but also create employment opportunities, fueling India's economic growth.

The pharmaceutical and healthcare sectors exemplify the symbiotic relationship between India and the U.S. India's leadership in the production of affordable generic drugs plays a pivotal role in global health, attracting U.S. investments that enhance research, development, and distribution capabilities. Collaborations in clean energy and electric vehicles (EVs) also highlight India's alignment with global sustainability goals. Partnerships with U.S. firms in renewable energy projects and EV production are pivotal in supporting India's transition to a low-carbon economy.

As the U.S.-China decoupling reshapes global trade and investment patterns, India stands poised to seize the opportunities presented by this shift. By strengthening its industrial capabilities, fostering innovation, and leveraging its demographic advantages, India cements its role as a key player in the emerging global economic order.

Strategic Importance

India's strategic importance in the evolving global order is underscored by its geostrategic location, defense modernization, and active participation in alliances like the Quad. These factors position India as a pivotal partner for the United States in addressing security challenges posed by China's assertive actions in the Indo-Pacific and beyond.

At the heart of key maritime routes, India's presence in the Indo-Pacific is vital for maintaining freedom of navigation and countering China's growing militarization in the region. Collaborating with the U.S., Japan, and Australia through the Quad, India addresses shared security concerns, including Chinese aggression in the South China Sea and its expanding influence in the Indian Ocean Region (IOR). India's leadership in ensuring a rules-based international order reinforces its critical role in regional stability.

The U.S. has been instrumental in supporting India's military modernization, providing advanced technologies and equipment that bolster India's ability to address security challenges. Platforms such as Apache helicopters, C-17 Globemaster transport aircraft, and sophisticated maritime surveillance systems enhance India's readiness along its Himalayan borders and its strategic oversight in the IOR. Joint military exercises like *Malabar* and *Yudh Abhyas* demonstrate the growing interoperability between the armed forces of both nations, enabling coordinated responses to emerging threats.

India's leadership in South Asia has received U.S. backing as part of a broader strategy to counterbalance China's expanding footprint in the region. Collaborative efforts focus on providing South Asian nations with sustainable alternatives to China's Belt and Road Initiative (BRI). Initiatives in infrastructure development, economic aid, and regional connectivity aim to strengthen ties with countries like Sri Lanka, Nepal, and Bangladesh, offering solutions that prioritize sovereignty and long-term stability.

India's strategic partnership with the U.S. not only enhances its defense capabilities but also reinforces its position as a key player in shaping the security architecture of the Indo-Pacific. By addressing shared concerns and countering unilateral actions, this collaboration ensures a stable and inclusive regional order, reflecting a shared vision for global peace and security.

Diplomatic Leverage

India's growing diplomatic leverage in the context of the U.S.-China rivalry underscores its rising prominence on the global stage. As both nations vie for influence, India has adeptly positioned itself as a strategic partner to both, while maintaining its autonomy and advancing its national interests.

The geopolitical tensions between the U.S. and China have enhanced India's stature as a pivotal player in shaping the global order. India's active role in multilateral forums such as the United Nations, G20, and BRICS highlights its ability to influence global policies and advocate for the interests of the developing world. As a democratic and rapidly emerging economic power, India's alignment with U.S.-led efforts to uphold a rules-based international order complements its position as a leader among like-minded nations.

Despite challenges along the Line of Actual Control (LAC), India has maintained a pragmatic approach to its relationship with China. Recognizing the importance of economic interdependence and regional stability, China remains invested in sustaining a functional relationship with India. India's leadership in forums like BRICS and the Shanghai Cooperation Organisation (SCO) allows it to engage constructively with China while preserving its strategic independence. This dual approach enables India to leverage its partnerships with both the U.S. and China to its advantage.

India has skillfully used its growing diplomatic clout to secure benefits that advance its economic and developmental goals. Its partnership with the U.S. has facilitated access to advanced technologies, foreign direct investments (FDI), and collaboration on critical projects in sectors like renewable energy, defense, and infrastructure. These strategic gains not only strengthen India's domestic capabilities but also enhance its ability to navigate an increasingly multipolar world.

India's ability to balance its relationships with competing powers while asserting its strategic autonomy reflects its diplomatic agility. By leveraging its partnerships and leadership in multilateral platforms, India is poised to shape the evolving global order in alignment with its values and aspirations. This dynamic positioning underscores India's emergence as a significant global influencer in the face of shifting power dynamics.

In summary, the intensifying rivalry between the **United States and China** has opened doors for India to strengthen its **economic foundations**, enhance its **strategic capabilities**, and assert its leadership on the global stage. By presenting itself as a **trusted partner** to the U.S. while maintaining a **pragmatic relationship with China**, India has skillfully navigated this geopolitical competition to its advantage.

As global supply chains shift, India is emerging as a hub for **manufacturing and innovation**, driven by policies that align with U.S. interests and global trends. Strategically, its **geopolitical location and growing defense capabilities** have made it indispensable in maintaining stability in the **Indo-Pacific**. Diplomatically, India's ability to balance relationships with the U.S. and China has enhanced its global influence, enabling it to address both regional and global challenges.

By leveraging these opportunities effectively, India is not only securing its national interests but also positioning itself as a key player in shaping the future of global geopolitics.

Conclusion

The India-U.S. partnership is a reflection of modern geopolitics, characterized by shared values, mutual benefits, and strategic alignment, yet not without its challenges. Trade disputes, visa policies, and differing positions on global issues occasionally create friction. However, the depth of shared interests ensures the partnership remains resilient and relevant.

India's approach to managing this relationship is rooted in its principle of strategic autonomy, which has long guided its foreign policy. This independence allows India to align with the U.S. on critical areas like counterterrorism, technological advancement, and Indo-Pacific security, while simultaneously maintaining productive relationships with other major powers such as Russia and China. By doing so, India secures its national interests without being drawn into exclusive alliances or compromising its broader global aspirations.

Opportunities amid U.S.-China Rivalry

The escalating competition between the U.S. and China has amplified India's role on the global stage, offering avenues to advance its economic, strategic, and diplomatic goals.

Economic Leverage

India is increasingly seen as a viable alternative for global manufacturing and investments as the U.S. seeks to reduce its dependence on China. Programs like *Make in India* and the Production-Linked Incentive (PLI) schemes have attracted significant U.S. investments in electronics, pharmaceuticals, and renewable energy. These initiatives position India as a key player in global supply chains, driving economic growth and innovation.

Strategic Importance

India's location in the Indo-Pacific and its expanding defense capabilities make it a critical partner for the U.S. in addressing security challenges posed by China. Collaboration within the Quad alliance underscores India's pivotal role in maintaining regional stability, safeguarding maritime routes, and countering assertive actions in contested areas like the South China Sea.

Diplomatic Clout

The dynamics of U.S.-China rivalry have elevated India's diplomatic influence. India has skillfully leveraged this to secure favorable trade agreements, attract foreign investments, and assert leadership in multilateral forums like the G20 and BRICS. By positioning itself as a neutral and constructive player, India strengthens its global standing.

The Path Forward

India's ability to navigate the complexities of this geopolitical environment will determine its success as a rising global power. Key priorities include:

Enhancing Domestic Resilience

Strengthening domestic industries, fostering innovation, and diversifying supply chains are crucial for reducing vulnerabilities. Investments in technology, infrastructure, and education will ensure that India remains competitive in a rapidly evolving global economy.

Fostering Regional Leadership

By deepening its engagement with South Asian neighbors and Indo-Pacific nations, India can reinforce its role as a stabilizing force and counterbalance to China's influence. Initiatives that promote regional connectivity, equitable development, and mutual trust will be critical.

Maintaining Strategic Balance

India must continue to collaborate with the U.S. while engaging constructively with other global powers. This balanced approach will preserve its autonomy, ensuring flexibility in addressing complex challenges and capitalizing on opportunities.

Looking Ahead

The India-U.S. relationship, while complex, holds immense potential for driving mutual growth and global impact. As India asserts its place as a global power, its ability to balance partnerships and navigate the intricacies of an interconnected world will define its future role in shaping the global order.

The following chapter will explore how India leverages relationships not only with the U.S. but also with other global actors to realize its ambitions as a rising power. By examining its strategies and navigating its challenges, we will uncover the roadmap for India's evolving influence in the international arena.

Part IV: The U.S.-China Rivalry and Its Impact on India

8: When Titans Clash

The intensifying economic rivalry between the **United States and China**, often epitomized by **trade wars**, has far-reaching implications for the global economy. The clash between these two economic giants disrupts **supply chains**, creates **opportunities for emerging economies**, and introduces significant **risks for nations like India** that must navigate the shifting dynamics of global trade. This chapter explores the ripple effects of U.S.-China trade wars, the opportunities they create for India, and the challenges India faces in avoiding the economic crossfire.

Trade Wars and Their Effects on Global Supply Chains

The **U.S.-China trade war**, initiated in 2018, marked a significant turning point in global trade relations. Characterized by **tariff escalations, protectionist measures**, and retaliatory policies, it was aimed at curbing China's economic dominance and addressing long-standing trade imbalances. These actions, however, sent shockwaves through the global economy, disrupting **supply chains**, altering trade patterns, and forcing businesses to rethink their operational strategies.

Disruption of Global Trade Flows

The imposition of tariffs on hundreds of billions of dollars' worth of goods between the U.S. and China sent ripples through global trade, forcing industries to reevaluate their heavy reliance on China-centric supply chains. Sectors such as electronics, textiles, automotive, and technology components were among the hardest hit, as production costs surged and goods became less competitive in global markets. The technology sector, for instance, faced delays and higher costs as critical components like semiconductors and batteries—often sourced from China—were subjected to steep tariffs. Similarly, the textiles and apparel industry, reliant on both the U.S. and China for raw material supply and manufacturing, encountered significant disruptions, affecting product timelines and inflating costs.

In response to these challenges, businesses began to realign their supply chains, seeking alternative manufacturing bases to avoid tariffs and ensure continuity. This shift was not merely about cost-saving but a strategic necessity to enhance supply chain resilience. Countries like Vietnam, India, and Mexico emerged as viable alternatives, offering companies opportunities to diversify their operations and reduce dependency on a single supplier or region. The reconfiguration of supply chains highlighted the vulnerabilities of centralized production models, emphasizing the importance of adaptability and resilience amid escalating geopolitical tensions.

Ultimately, the trade disputes between the U.S. and China revealed the fragility of global supply networks, compelling industries to adopt more balanced and sustainable strategies to navigate the uncertainties of a rapidly changing economic landscape.

Rethinking Supply Chain Strategies

The trade war between the U.S. and China triggered a reevaluation of global supply chain management, compelling businesses to diversify their manufacturing and sourcing strategies to minimize risks and ensure continuity. Countries like Vietnam, Thailand, Mexico, and India quickly emerged as attractive alternatives, offering competitive labor costs, improving infrastructure, and preferential trade agreements with major economies. Vietnam, for example, saw a significant influx of foreign investments as companies like Samsung, Nike, and Apple suppliers shifted parts of their operations to the region, taking advantage of its favorable business environment and proximity to key markets.

This disruption also highlighted the vulnerabilities inherent in highly globalized supply chains, prompting a shift toward regionalization and localization. Businesses began favoring regional supply chains that prioritized stability and nearshoring to reduce dependency on any single country. Regional trade agreements, such as the Comprehensive and Progressive Agreement for Trans-Pacific Partnership (CPTPP), gained importance by providing stable frameworks for trade and fostering closer economic ties among participating nations.

In parallel, companies turned to technology and automation to enhance supply chain efficiency and mitigate risks. Smart technologies like blockchain for transparency and AI for predictive analytics became integral tools for improving visibility, agility, and responsiveness in supply chain operations. Investments in digitization not only reduced reliance on low-cost labor but also allowed businesses to adapt swiftly to changing market dynamics.

The combined effect of these strategies marked a significant transformation in global supply chain management, as businesses prioritized resilience and adaptability in the face of ongoing geopolitical and economic uncertainties. This rethinking of supply chains represents a paradigm shift, ensuring that operations remain robust and agile in an increasingly interconnected yet volatile world.

Impact on Global Markets

The U.S.-China trade war sent shockwaves through global markets, affecting economies worldwide and creating significant challenges for both developed and emerging nations. The uncertainty generated by escalating tariffs and retaliatory measures led to a slowdown in global economic growth, particularly in export-driven economies deeply connected to China-centric supply chains. Countries like South Korea and Japan experienced reduced trade volumes as businesses adjusted to the new trade realities. The World Bank estimated that global growth slowed by approximately 0.3% annually during the height of the trade war, as companies postponed investments and undertook costly restructuring of their operations.

Inflationary pressures further compounded these challenges. Tariffs on goods such as electronics, consumer products, and automotive parts drove up costs for both businesses and consumers, disrupting spending patterns and deepening economic uncertainty. Higher prices for essential goods strained household budgets and placed additional pressure on industries already grappling with supply chain disruptions.

Emerging economies were particularly vulnerable to the fallout. Currency volatility and fluctuations in commodity prices, often tied to the broader trade war, created instability in countries dependent on raw material exports. For instance, nations like Brazil and South Africa faced unpredictable demand and price swings for their commodities, affecting their economic performance. While some emerging markets, such as Vietnam and India, benefited from the diversification of supply chains and attracted new investments, others struggled to adapt to the intensified competition for resources and market share.

The trade war underscored the interconnected nature of the global economy, revealing both the vulnerabilities and opportunities that arise when major economic powers reshape trade dynamics. It highlighted the need for resilience and adaptability in global markets, as businesses and governments alike navigated the complex and shifting landscape of international commerce.

In conclusion, the U.S.-China trade war reshaped the global trade landscape, revealing the fragility of **interdependent supply chains** and prompting businesses to rethink their strategies. The disruptions, while challenging, also created opportunities for nations like **India, Vietnam**, and **Mexico** to position themselves as viable alternatives in global markets.

For India, the trade war underscored the need to strengthen its **manufacturing capabilities, infrastructure**, and **trade policies** to capitalize on these shifts effectively. As global supply chains become more regionalized and less dependent on China, the trade war serves as a catalyst for structural changes in global trade, presenting both challenges and opportunities for economies worldwide.

Opportunities for India to Fill Gaps Left by China in Global Markets

The disruption of **China-centric supply chains**, accelerated by the U.S.-China trade war and growing geopolitical tensions, presents India with a strategic opportunity to assert itself as a **reliable and competitive alternative** in global markets. Armed with a **skilled workforce, government-backed initiatives**, and a growing infrastructure, India is well-positioned to step into roles previously dominated by China across key industries. This chapter explores India's potential to expand its manufacturing base, enhance its export profile, and leverage strategic partnerships to reshape global trade dynamics.

Expanding Manufacturing Capabilities

India's strategic focus on expanding its manufacturing capabilities is supported by targeted policies and incentives aimed at transforming the nation into a global manufacturing hub. Through initiatives like **Make in India** and the **Production-Linked Incentive (PLI) schemes**, the government has provided a strong foundation for industrial growth, attracting significant foreign investment while fostering domestic production. These programs simplify regulatory frameworks, encourage technology transfer, and offer financial incentives to businesses, creating a favorable environment for industrial expansion.

The **PLI scheme**, in particular, has yielded notable success, drawing investments across sectors such as electronics, pharmaceuticals, automotive components, and renewable energy. By aligning incentives with production targets, the initiative has boosted India's competitiveness in global markets and established it as a reliable manufacturing destination.

India's electronics industry has seen transformative growth, with global giants like Apple, Samsung, and Xiaomi significantly expanding their manufacturing footprints in the country. Apple's decision to assemble flagship products such as the iPhone in India exemplifies the growing confidence in India's production capabilities. The pharmaceutical sector, already a global leader in generic drug production, is poised for even greater prominence. The COVID-19 pandemic exposed vulnerabilities in Chinese pharmaceutical supply chains, underscoring India's potential to serve as a trusted supplier of active pharmaceutical ingredients (APIs) and finished pharmaceutical products.

The textiles sector, one of India's traditional strengths, has witnessed modernization efforts that position the country as a viable alternative for global brands looking to diversify away from China. Export-oriented clusters in Gujarat, Tamil Nadu, and Punjab are experiencing renewed interest from international buyers, leveraging India's rich heritage in textiles and its ability to scale production efficiently.

The burgeoning electric vehicle (EV) market is another area of rapid growth, supported by government incentives and collaborations with global automakers. India's focus on sustainable mobility solutions is creating opportunities for local manufacturing of EVs and related components, establishing the nation as a significant player in the future of automotive innovation.

India's emphasis on expanding its manufacturing capabilities reflects its ambition to not only become a reliable global supplier but also to foster self-reliance and resilience in critical industries. By capitalizing on its policies, infrastructure, and workforce, India is well-positioned to seize opportunities in a shifting global economic landscape.

Becoming a Global Export Hub

India's transformation into a global export hub is driven by its vast consumer market, improving trade connectivity, and robust infrastructure development. These factors have positioned the country as a magnet for foreign direct investment (FDI) and a critical player in the evolving dynamics of global trade.

India's infrastructure advancements, including industrial corridors, smart cities, and expansive logistics networks, are attracting significant international investment. Key sectors like semiconductors, renewable energy, and automotive manufacturing are witnessing strong FDI inflows. Investments in solar energy projects and battery manufacturing, for example, align with India's sustainability ambitions while addressing global demand for clean energy solutions.

Trade agreements with strategic partners such as ASEAN, Japan, and Australia have further bolstered India's role as a regional trade hub. Initiatives like the **India-Australia Economic Cooperation and Trade Agreement (ECTA)** and the **India-Japan Comprehensive Economic Partnership Agreement (CEPA)** are enhancing market access and promoting collaboration across critical sectors. India's active participation in supply chain resilience initiatives, including the **Indo-Pacific Economic Framework (IPEF)** and

Quad collaborations, underscores its commitment to ensuring stable and diversified supply chains in a rapidly shifting global economy.

Export-led growth in strategic sectors is central to India's ambitions. In renewable energy, India's leadership in solar technology and its plans to become a global hub for green hydrogen production highlight its alignment with global sustainability goals. These initiatives not only meet domestic needs but also position India as a key exporter of renewable technologies to the world.

In semiconductors, India's push to develop a domestic ecosystem, bolstered by investments from U.S. and Japanese firms, is addressing the global chip shortage and enhancing its role in high-tech manufacturing. Similarly, India's focus on defense exports, including drones, artillery, and armored vehicles, reflects its evolving capabilities in high-value manufacturing and its ambition to become a significant player in global defense markets.

India's journey toward becoming a global export hub is a testament to its strategic vision, leveraging its infrastructure, trade partnerships, and industrial strengths. By aligning with global trends and addressing critical gaps in supply chains, India is poised to play a pivotal role in shaping the future of international trade.

Leveraging Strategic Partnerships

India's strategic partnerships with global powers in technology, defense, and infrastructure development have significantly enhanced its capacity to address gaps in global trade left by China's shifting role. These collaborations position India as a key player in fostering innovation, building resilient supply chains, and driving economic transformation.

Partnerships with the United States, Japan, and Europe have been instrumental in bringing cutting-edge technologies, financial investments, and best practices to India. Joint ventures with U.S. companies in aerospace, information technology, and clean energy are fueling innovation and bolstering India's capabilities in critical industries. Japanese investments in transformative infrastructure projects, such as high-speed rail and industrial corridors, are reshaping India's logistical and connectivity framework, making it an attractive destination for global businesses.

THE TRIANGULAR DYNAMICS

The Quad's **Supply Chain Resilience Initiative** highlights India's central role in global efforts to diversify and strengthen supply chains, reducing dependence on China. This initiative focuses on sectors such as rare earth minerals, pharmaceuticals, and advanced technology components, where India's growing manufacturing and R&D capabilities offer sustainable alternatives. India's active participation underscores its strategic importance in creating a stable and diversified global trade environment.

India's involvement in platforms like **BRICS** and the **G20** complements its bilateral partnerships, allowing it to influence global trade policies and advocate for equitable growth. Through these multilateral engagements, India promotes collaboration on critical issues, from sustainable development to digital trade, ensuring its voice is integral to shaping the future of international commerce.

Collaborations on digital trade and cybersecurity with partners in Europe and the U.S. further underscore India's potential to lead in emerging technologies. These partnerships not only enhance India's technological capabilities but also strengthen its position as a global hub for innovation and secure digital infrastructure.

By leveraging its strategic partnerships, India is not only addressing immediate trade realignment needs but also positioning itself as a cornerstone of the future global economy. These collaborations reflect India's ability to align its national interests with global priorities, ensuring sustainable growth and shared prosperity.

In conclusion, the disruption of China-centric supply chains offers India a rare opportunity to redefine its role in the global economy. By expanding its manufacturing capabilities, strengthening its position as an export hub, and leveraging strategic partnerships, India can fill critical gaps in global markets left by China's diminishing dominance.

To fully capitalize on these opportunities, India must continue investing in **infrastructure, skill development**, and **technological innovation**. Additionally, fostering an environment of **policy stability and ease of doing business** will be crucial in attracting long-term foreign investments and ensuring sustainable growth.

As global supply chains evolve, India's ability to align its domestic priorities with international demands will determine its success in becoming a trusted and indispensable player in global trade. This strategic positioning not only enhances India's economic resilience but also strengthens its influence in shaping the future of global markets.

Risks of Being Caught in the Crossfire of Economic Policies

While the ongoing **U.S.-China trade war** and geopolitical rivalry present India with unique opportunities, they also introduce significant **economic, diplomatic, and strategic risks**. India's position as an emerging global power and a key player in the **Indo-Pacific** makes it vulnerable to the fallout of competing interests between the two superpowers. Navigating these challenges requires **careful economic planning, diplomatic agility,** and **strategic foresight**.

Economic Uncertainty

Economic uncertainty driven by U.S.-China tensions poses significant challenges for India, potentially disrupting trade, investment flows, and overall economic stability. These tensions create ripple effects across global markets, impacting key sectors and commodities critical to India's economy.

Global trade disruptions stemming from the trade war could dampen demand for Indian exports in industries like textiles, information technology, and agriculture. At the same time, interruptions in Chinese supply chains might lead to increased costs for essential imports such as electronics components, solar panels, and active pharmaceutical ingredients (APIs), which are integral to India's manufacturing and healthcare sectors.

Volatility in commodity prices, particularly for oil and metals, adds another layer of economic strain. As a major importer of crude oil, India is acutely vulnerable to price spikes, which can inflate production costs, strain energy-intensive industries, and widen the trade deficit. Rising oil prices also exert inflationary pressures on the economy, potentially impacting consumer spending and fiscal health.

Currency fluctuations further complicate the landscape. Trade tensions often trigger exchange rate volatility, making imports more expensive and adding financial uncertainty for industries reliant on foreign goods and raw materials. Such instability can disrupt planning and budgeting, particularly in sectors with high import dependency.

Navigating this economic uncertainty requires India to adopt measures that enhance domestic production capabilities, diversify trade partnerships, and bolster energy security. These efforts are crucial to mitigating vulnerabilities and maintaining resilience amid the shifting dynamics of global trade.

Pressure to Align with One Side

India faces mounting pressure to navigate the delicate balance of aligning with either the United States or China, as both nations vie to strengthen their coalitions in the ongoing global power struggle. This geopolitical tug-of-war presents India with competing expectations that require careful diplomacy to safeguard its strategic autonomy.

The United States, as a vital strategic and economic partner, encourages India to take a more assertive role in supporting its Indo-Pacific strategy. This includes collaboration in security, technology, and trade, particularly through platforms like the Quad. In contrast, China, as a major regional power and India's largest trading partner, expects India to adopt a less confrontational stance. Beijing is especially sensitive to India's participation in the Quad and its firm positions on regional border disputes, seeking to temper hostilities for the sake of trade and regional stability.

The risks of overdependence on either side are significant. A closer alignment with the U.S. could provoke retaliatory actions from China, including disruptions in essential supply chains or heightened tensions along the border. On the other hand, leaning too heavily toward China risks alienating the U.S., potentially jeopardizing crucial investments in defense, technology, and infrastructure that are pivotal to India's economic and strategic growth.

India's ability to navigate this complex dynamic lies in its commitment to strategic autonomy, ensuring that its partnerships serve its national interests without becoming entangled in the binary rivalries of global superpowers. By maintaining a balanced and independent approach, India can leverage its relationships with both nations to secure its long-term growth and regional influence.

Dependence on Chinese Imports

India's heavy reliance on Chinese imports in critical sectors underscores a significant vulnerability, particularly in the context of escalating U.S.-China tensions. Despite ongoing efforts to diversify supply chains and bolster domestic production, this dependency remains a key challenge to India's economic resilience and strategic ambitions.

Electronics is one of the most affected sectors, with India sourcing a substantial portion of its components, including semiconductors and displays, from China. This reliance hampers India's goal of becoming a global electronics manufacturing hub. Similarly, the solar energy sector, where India has emerged as a global leader in adoption, is overwhelmingly dependent on Chinese imports, with over 80% of solar panels sourced from Chinese manufacturers. This creates a critical vulnerability in India's renewable energy drive, which is central to its sustainability goals.

The pharmaceutical industry also illustrates this reliance. Indian companies, renowned for their dominance in global generic drug markets, depend on Chinese manufacturers for the majority of active pharmaceutical ingredients (APIs). Any disruption in this supply chain, whether from geopolitical tensions or trade restrictions, poses a direct threat to the availability of essential medicines and the stability of India's healthcare sector.

Escalations in U.S.-China tensions exacerbate these risks, potentially leading to further delays and cost increases for critical imports. Such disruptions could ripple through India's economy, impacting production timelines in key industries and slowing domestic growth. The consequences are particularly dire for sectors integral to India's energy security, healthcare infrastructure, and electronics manufacturing ambitions.

Addressing this dependency is imperative for India. Strengthening domestic manufacturing capabilities, fostering technological innovation, and diversifying import sources will be crucial to reducing vulnerabilities and ensuring long-term economic stability in an increasingly uncertain global landscape.

THE TRIANGULAR DYNAMICS

Geopolitical Ramifications

India's engagement in strategic partnerships, particularly with the Quad and its deepening ties with the U.S., carries significant geopolitical implications, potentially straining its already fragile relationship with China and complicating its role in maintaining regional stability.

China perceives India's alignment with the U.S. and its active role in the Quad as a direct challenge to its regional and global ambitions. This perception risks intensifying tensions along the Line of Actual Control (LAC), where past incidents, such as the 2020 Galwan Valley clash, highlight the volatile and sensitive nature of their border dynamics. Any escalation in these disputes not only threatens peace along the border but also disrupts the broader strategic balance in South Asia.

Beyond the border, China's growing assertiveness in South Asia further complicates India's geopolitical environment. Beijing's deepening ties with Pakistan, exemplified by the China-Pakistan Economic Corridor (CPEC), and its strategic investments in countries like Sri Lanka and Nepal challenge India's traditional influence in its neighborhood. These developments risk marginalizing India's leadership in South Asia, especially as China strengthens its economic foothold through projects that align these nations closer to Beijing's sphere of influence.

India's counterbalancing efforts, including its leadership role in the Quad, may inadvertently polarize the region, making multilateral cooperation on shared challenges such as climate change, trade, and counterterrorism more difficult. Smaller South Asian nations, many of which are economically dependent on China, could find themselves navigating conflicting pressures from both powers. This dynamic poses a significant challenge for India as it seeks to assert its regional leadership while managing complex relationships with its neighbors.

Balancing these competing interests requires India to exercise diplomatic finesse. Strengthening regional partnerships based on mutual benefit, fostering economic resilience, and maintaining open communication channels with China will be crucial to mitigating tensions and safeguarding stability in South Asia. At the same time, India's engagement with global strategic alliances must be calibrated to enhance its influence without escalating regional polarization.

In conclusion, the intensifying rivalry between the U.S. and China presents a **double-edged sword** for India. While it opens opportunities to fill gaps in global markets and assert its strategic importance, it also introduces significant **economic, diplomatic,** and **geopolitical risks**. India's ability to navigate these challenges hinges on maintaining a delicate balance between its partnerships with both nations while safeguarding its **strategic autonomy**.

To mitigate these risks, India must:

Strengthen **domestic manufacturing** and reduce dependency on Chinese imports, especially in critical sectors like **electronics** and **pharmaceuticals**.

Diversify its trade partnerships to reduce overreliance on any single nation and build resilience against global economic disruptions.

Pursue **diplomatic engagement** with both the U.S. and China to ensure open channels of communication and avoid being drawn into their escalating rivalry.

India's long-term success in managing the risks of the U.S.-China conflict will depend on its ability to remain **strategically agile** and **economically resilient**, ensuring that its growth trajectory is not derailed by external pressures.

Conclusion

The U.S.-China trade war has marked a turning point in global trade dynamics, offering both significant challenges and unique opportunities for India. As global supply chains face disruption and geopolitical rivalries intensify, India finds itself at a crossroads. The upheaval exposes vulnerabilities in existing systems while creating avenues for emerging economies like India to fill critical gaps and assert their influence.

On one side, India faces economic risks, including market volatility, rising commodity prices, and the delicate task of managing relationships with two global superpowers. On the other, the shifting global landscape presents India with opportunities to position itself as a global manufacturing hub, attract foreign direct investment (FDI), and expand its presence in international markets. This dual reality highlights the need for India to exercise strategic foresight, bolster domestic resilience, and demonstrate diplomatic agility.

THE TRIANGULAR DYNAMICS

To capitalize on these opportunities and mitigate risks, India must focus on three interconnected priorities. First, strengthening domestic manufacturing and infrastructure is imperative. Initiatives like *Make in India* and the Production-Linked Incentive (PLI) schemes must be accelerated to expand manufacturing capacities in critical sectors such as electronics, pharmaceuticals, and renewable energy. Enhanced infrastructure—spanning logistics, industrial zones, and energy supply—will attract multinational corporations while ensuring the seamless operation of global trade networks.

Second, diversifying supply chains is essential to reducing reliance on Chinese imports in key areas like technology components, solar panels, and pharmaceutical ingredients. India should deepen regional trade networks and strengthen ties with partners such as Vietnam, Japan, and Australia. These partnerships not only enhance supply chain resilience but also position India as a central player in the evolving Indo-Pacific economic framework.

Finally, India must maintain a nuanced approach in its engagements with both the U.S. and China. Aligning with the U.S. on Indo-Pacific security and technology collaboration offers strategic advantages, but simultaneously engaging China on trade and regional stability will preserve India's autonomy and balance. Diplomatic agility is critical to navigating the complexities of this rivalry without being drawn into direct confrontation, safeguarding India's broader economic and geopolitical interests.

Looking forward, India's ability to navigate these global challenges will determine its trajectory as a rising power. Success will hinge on its capacity to leverage global shifts, enhance domestic resilience, and assert diplomatic leadership. By positioning itself as a reliable alternative in global supply chains, India can attract investments and partnerships that fuel industrial and technological growth. Building resilience in critical sectors will insulate India from external shocks, while its active participation in multilateral forums will allow it to shape global trade norms and advocate for equitable growth.

The U.S.-China trade war is not merely an economic conflict but a significant reordering of global power structures. For India, this is an opportunity to assert a more prominent role on the world stage. By balancing risks and opportunities, India can strengthen its position as a pivotal player in global trade and geopolitics. The journey ahead will test India's adaptability and vision as it navigates the intricacies of an interconnected and competitive world.

9: The Technology Battlefield

The **U.S.-China technological rivalry** has emerged as one of the defining features of modern geopolitics. This contest for dominance in **semiconductors, artificial intelligence (AI), green technology**, and **digital infrastructure** not only shapes the strategies of these two superpowers but also offers a unique opportunity for nations like **India** to assert their position in the global technology landscape. For India, navigating this "technology battlefield" involves balancing its role as a potential partner in global tech alliances, advancing its self-reliance in critical sectors, and leveraging tech disruptions to accelerate its **economic growth**.

The U.S.-China Tech Race and India's Role as a Potential Partner

The intensifying **technological rivalry** between the United States and China reflects a battle for dominance in the **21st-century economy**, with both nations vying to lead in critical fields such as **5G, artificial intelligence (AI), semiconductors, quantum computing,** and **green energy technologies**. As these two superpowers increasingly **decouple their tech ecosystems**, it creates significant opportunities and challenges for other nations. India, with its **large consumer market, skilled talent pool,** and **emerging tech ecosystem**, is uniquely positioned to play a pivotal role in reshaping the global technology landscape.

The U.S.-China Decoupling

The U.S.-China decoupling in technology reflects a deepening rift between the two economic giants, driven by their competing aspirations for global dominance in emerging industries. This division has fragmented the global tech landscape, compelling nations and corporations to adapt to a polarized environment shaped by export controls, sanctions, and strategic investments.

The United States has taken decisive steps to limit China's access to advanced technologies, implementing stringent export controls and sanctions targeting companies like Huawei and ZTE. These measures aim to protect U.S. intellectual property, secure supply chains, and curtail China's influence in transformative technologies such as 5G and semiconductors. Restrictions extend to critical resources, including semiconductor manufacturing equipment, sophisticated software, and advanced chip designs, creating significant barriers for China's technological progress. The goal is to safeguard U.S. leadership in the tech sector while diminishing China's ability to challenge it on a global scale.

In response, China has accelerated its drive for technological self-reliance. Massive government investments in sectors like semiconductors, artificial intelligence, and quantum computing underscore its determination to reduce dependence on Western technologies. Flagship programs such as *Made in China 2025* illustrate China's ambitions to achieve dominance in high-tech industries by nurturing indigenous innovation and building resilient domestic supply chains. Simultaneously, China has fortified its leadership in areas like solar energy and electric vehicles, leveraging its manufacturing expertise to remain competitive amid increasing restrictions.

This decoupling is not just an economic phenomenon but a strategic battle for technological supremacy, with global implications. Countries and companies must navigate this shifting terrain, balancing alliances and dependencies as they adapt to a tech landscape increasingly defined by division and competition. The ripple effects of this decoupling will shape the future of innovation, trade, and global power dynamics, forcing stakeholders to recalibrate their strategies in an era of heightened technological rivalry.

THE TRIANGULAR DYNAMICS

India's Strategic Position

India's strategic position amidst the technological decoupling between the U.S. and China places it at the heart of global power dynamics. Its geopolitical significance, burgeoning digital economy, and government-backed initiatives in technology make India an indispensable player and a sought-after partner for both superpowers.

India's alignment with the U.S. in the Indo-Pacific region solidifies its role as a trusted ally in countering China's technological and strategic ambitions. Collaborations with American technology giants like Google, Microsoft, Apple, and Amazon have enhanced India's reputation as a hub for research and development, software engineering, and cloud computing. Furthermore, India's active engagement in emerging technologies such as semiconductors, artificial intelligence, and quantum computing aligns with U.S. objectives to diversify supply chains and reduce reliance on China. This collaboration reflects India's growing stature as a critical partner in reshaping global technology ecosystems.

Simultaneously, India's pragmatic engagement with China highlights its ability to balance competition with economic interdependence. Despite geopolitical tensions, India remains a significant importer of Chinese electronics components and hardware, which are vital for its thriving smartphone and electronics manufacturing industries. However, through initiatives like *Make in India*, India is progressively localizing production to reduce dependency while fostering domestic innovation and capacity building.

India's dual role in the global technology ecosystem is underscored by its vast consumer market and unparalleled talent pool. As one of the world's fastest-growing markets, India attracts global technology investments, while its skilled workforce excels in areas like software engineering, data analytics, and AI. These strengths position India as both a lucrative market and a global hub for technological innovation.

By maintaining strong partnerships with the U.S. and managing its economic engagement with China, India deftly navigates a complex geopolitical landscape. This balanced approach not only safeguards India's strategic autonomy but also advances its national interests, allowing it to emerge as a pivotal player in the evolving global tech order.

India as a Bridge Between Tech Ecosystems

India's unique ability to engage with both the U.S. and China positions it as a bridge between competing global tech ecosystems. This role reflects its capacity to foster collaboration, promote domestic innovation, and align with global standards while safeguarding its strategic autonomy.

India's involvement in regional alliances underscores its significance in shaping alternative technology supply chains. Participation in frameworks like the Quad's supply chain resilience initiative strengthens its role in the Indo-Pacific, where collaborative efforts with nations like Japan, South Korea, and Australia provide access to critical resources and expertise. These partnerships not only enhance India's technological capabilities but also position it as a vital player in regional stability and innovation.

On the domestic front, India's focus on digital sovereignty highlights its proactive approach to securing its digital economy. Initiatives such as the Data Protection Bill and regulations on big tech companies reflect a commitment to creating a competitive, secure, and fair digital landscape. These measures ensure that India's growing digital economy aligns with its national interests while maintaining robust global engagement.

India's balanced strategy in the U.S.-China tech rivalry exemplifies pragmatism and foresight. By fostering domestic manufacturing under programs like *Make in India* and leveraging international partnerships, India mitigates vulnerabilities and reduces overdependence on any single global power. This dual approach enables India to seize opportunities for economic and technological advancement while ensuring it retains the flexibility to chart its own path.

As a bridge between two competing tech ecosystems, India's ability to maintain this balance reinforces its role as a pivotal player in global technology and geopolitics. By aligning its interests with both regional and global priorities, India is well-positioned to lead in innovation, foster sustainable growth, and influence the future of technology on the world stage.

In summary, the **U.S.-China tech race** has created a polarized global technology landscape, but it has also opened doors for India to assert its role as a critical player in shaping the future of innovation. By strategically aligning with the U.S. while maintaining pragmatic ties with China, India has positioned itself as a **trusted partner** and a **rising leader** in the global tech ecosystem.

India's ability to navigate this rivalry hinges on its commitment to **self-reliance, international collaboration,** and **domestic innovation**. As the global demand for advanced technologies grows, India's role as both a consumer and a producer will play a decisive role in reshaping the global technology order. This dual engagement strategy, combined with its strong fundamentals, ensures that India remains at the forefront of the evolving **technology battlefield**.

India's Push for Self-Reliance in Semiconductors, AI, and Green Tech

India's ambition to become a **self-reliant technology leader** is central to its strategy in navigating the global tech battlefield. The government, along with private sector participation, is undertaking significant initiatives to **reduce dependence on imports**, **foster innovation**, and position India as a global hub for **emerging technologies**. The focus on **semiconductors**, **artificial intelligence (AI)**, and **green technology** reflects India's commitment to advancing its economic growth and securing strategic autonomy.

Semiconductors

The semiconductor industry, the foundation of modern electronics, is indispensable for sectors ranging from consumer technology to defense. Recognizing its strategic importance, India has embarked on a transformative journey to establish a robust domestic semiconductor ecosystem, aiming to reduce dependency on imports and position itself as a global player in this critical industry.

India Semiconductor Mission (ISM): A Strategic Vision

The India Semiconductor Mission (ISM), backed by substantial government incentives, represents a comprehensive strategy to attract global semiconductor manufacturers. Its objectives are clear: foster domestic manufacturing capabilities, create a self-reliant semiconductor supply chain, and elevate India's status in the global technology landscape. Through the ISM, the government aims to entice leading companies such as Intel, Taiwan Semiconductor Manufacturing Company (TSMC), and Samsung to set up fabrication units (fabs) in India. The initiative includes substantial capital expenditure subsidies, tax incentives, and infrastructure support to ensure the viability and competitiveness of investments.

Global Collaborations for Expertise and Technology

India is actively collaborating with international partners to leverage their expertise and accelerate the establishment of a semiconductor ecosystem.

> **Japan**: India's partnership with Japan focuses on technology transfer and joint ventures, particularly in semiconductor equipment and processes. These collaborations are aimed at establishing knowledge-sharing frameworks and fostering innovation.

> **Taiwan**: Leveraging Taiwan's dominance in semiconductor fabrication, India is engaging Taiwanese companies to set up wafer fabrication plants and chip testing facilities. These efforts include technology transfer agreements that will enable India to build advanced manufacturing capacities.

> **United States**: Cooperation with the U.S. centers on joint research and development initiatives, with a particular focus on advanced technologies and supply chain resilience. These partnerships seek to strengthen India's foothold in the semiconductor value chain.

Strategic Importance and National Imperatives

The development of a domestic semiconductor industry holds immense strategic and economic significance for India. From a national security perspective, a reliable and secure supply of semiconductors is critical for defense systems, communications, and surveillance equipment. This independence minimizes vulnerabilities associated with global supply chain disruptions. Economically, the establishment of semiconductor manufacturing aligns seamlessly with the *Make in India* initiative. It catalyzes growth in electronics production, creates high-skilled jobs, and drives innovation in areas like artificial intelligence, renewable energy, and automotive technologies.

India's foray into semiconductor manufacturing is not merely an industrial initiative but a strategic imperative that promises to reshape its technological and economic trajectory. By fostering global partnerships and creating a conducive environment for investments, India is laying the foundation for a self-reliant and globally competitive semiconductor ecosystem.

Artificial Intelligence (AI)

Artificial Intelligence (AI) is revolutionizing industries across the globe, and India is strategically positioning itself to harness its transformative potential in key sectors like agriculture, healthcare, education, and infrastructure. With a blend of government-led initiatives, private sector investments, and a thriving startup ecosystem, India aims to emerge as a global leader in AI innovation and deployment.

The National AI Strategy, spearheaded by NITI Aayog, serves as the cornerstone of India's efforts to integrate AI into its socio-economic fabric. This initiative focuses on leveraging AI for critical domains such as smart cities, precision farming, and efficient healthcare systems. The policy emphasizes fostering research, innovation, and ethical AI practices, ensuring that India's AI journey is inclusive and sustainable.

India's "AI for All" program is a testament to the government's commitment to making AI accessible to every citizen. This initiative prioritizes education and skill development, offering training programs tailored for students, professionals, and policymakers. By equipping individuals with AI expertise, the program aims to democratize access to technology and empower a workforce capable of addressing local and global challenges.

The program also encourages innovation at the grassroots level. Through grants, incubators, and accelerators, small businesses and startups are supported in developing AI-driven solutions that tackle pressing issues in areas like healthcare accessibility, disaster management, and agricultural productivity.

India's leading IT firms, including Infosys, Tata Consultancy Services (TCS), and Wipro, are at the forefront of AI adoption. These companies are investing significantly in developing AI-driven platforms that cater to diverse industries such as finance, retail, and manufacturing. By incorporating predictive analytics, automation, and personalized solutions into their services, they enhance operational efficiency and maintain global competitiveness.

Collaborations with international tech giants and academic institutions further bolster India's AI capabilities, ensuring access to cutting-edge technologies and fostering cross-border innovation.

India's startup ecosystem is flourishing, with numerous companies dedicated to AI innovations in natural language processing, robotics, and computer vision. Startups are not only addressing domestic challenges but are also making a mark on the global stage, offering solutions that span healthcare diagnostics, autonomous systems, and education technology.

The government's support, through programs like Startup India, provides these startups with crucial funding, mentorship, and policy incentives. This nurturing environment enables entrepreneurs to experiment, innovate, and scale solutions that have a transformative impact both locally and internationally.

India's commitment to AI extends beyond technological advancements to socio-economic empowerment. By prioritizing AI-driven solutions, India is addressing critical issues such as rural healthcare access, educational equity, and agricultural efficiency. The integration of AI across sectors not only boosts economic growth but also aligns with India's broader vision of inclusive and sustainable development.

In conclusion, India's multi-faceted approach to AI—encompassing robust government strategies, corporate innovation, and entrepreneurial energy—positions it as a rising global leader in this transformative technology. As AI continues to shape the future, India's investments in education, infrastructure, and international collaboration ensure its readiness to capitalize on the opportunities ahead.

Green Technology

India's commitment to sustainable development has positioned it as a leader in green technology, particularly in renewable energy, electric vehicles, and sustainable innovations. With a comprehensive approach that integrates policy support, private sector participation, and international collaboration, India is

THE TRIANGULAR DYNAMICS

advancing its green agenda to align with global climate goals and drive economic growth.

Renewable energy is a cornerstone of India's sustainability strategy. The country is among the global leaders in solar and wind power capacity, with ambitious goals like the National Solar Mission, which targets a solar capacity of 280 GW by 2030. Government incentives, including tax benefits and subsidies, have encouraged significant investment in renewable energy projects, drawing both domestic and international players to accelerate the transition to cleaner energy. These efforts reflect a well-structured approach to reducing carbon emissions and achieving energy security.

Green hydrogen is emerging as another transformative area in India's green technology landscape. Through the Mission Green Hydrogen initiative, India aims to develop green hydrogen as a clean energy alternative produced using renewable sources. This innovation not only reduces carbon emissions but also decreases reliance on fossil fuels. Collaborations with nations like the United States, Japan, and Germany have been instrumental in advancing green hydrogen research, technology transfer, and infrastructure development, ensuring scalability and commercial viability.

Electric vehicles (EVs) form a critical component of India's sustainability roadmap. The Faster Adoption and Manufacturing of Hybrid and Electric Vehicles (FAME) scheme underscores the country's intent to promote EV production and usage. Policies encouraging local manufacturing of essential components like lithium-ion batteries and motors have reduced import dependency while stimulating job creation in the domestic market. Investments in charging infrastructure and supportive government policies are making EVs increasingly accessible to consumers, further reducing pollution and oil imports.

India's focus on sustainable innovations extends to sectors like agriculture, waste management, and urban development. Drip irrigation systems, solar-powered agricultural equipment, and organic farming practices demonstrate India's commitment to eco-friendly farming techniques. In waste management, advancements in waste-to-energy conversion, recycling, and biodegradable materials address pressing environmental concerns while fostering new business opportunities. Smart city initiatives incorporate green technologies in urban planning, improving energy efficiency, reducing emissions, and enhancing the quality of life for residents.

These green technology initiatives are part of India's broader vision for technological self-reliance and economic development. By investing in renewable energy, green hydrogen, and sustainable innovations, India not only enhances its national security by reducing reliance on foreign resources but also drives economic growth through job creation and increased competitiveness. Moreover, these efforts position India as a global leader in sustainability, showcasing its commitment to addressing climate challenges responsibly.

India's inclusive approach ensures that the benefits of green technology reach all sections of society. By democratizing access to sustainable solutions and promoting skill development, India is creating opportunities for equitable growth. This strategic focus on collaboration, innovation, and investment underscores India's determination to play a pivotal role in global technological and environmental progress. As the world looks to sustainable solutions, India stands poised to lead by example, integrating economic advancement with environmental stewardship.

How Tech Disruptions Shape India's Growth Trajectory

Technological disruptions are transforming economies, redefining industries, and reshaping societal norms across the globe. For India, this era of innovation offers both **unprecedented opportunities** and **critical challenges.** The country's ability to harness these disruptions will play a decisive role in determining its **economic growth, job creation,** and **global competitiveness.** India's response to these technological shifts is reflected in its robust **digital infrastructure, vibrant startup ecosystem, workforce transformation initiatives,** and its push toward **global competitiveness.**

Digital Infrastructure

India's robust digital infrastructure lies at the heart of its economic transformation, driving financial inclusion, enhancing connectivity, and

THE TRIANGULAR DYNAMICS

creating new opportunities for growth across sectors. With a comprehensive digital ecosystem, India is reshaping industries and empowering citizens.

Digital payments have revolutionized the way Indians transact, with platforms like Unified Payments Interface (UPI) making financial technology accessible to millions, even in rural areas. UPI's seamless integration into daily life has led to billions of transactions monthly, establishing India as a global leader in digital payments. Initiatives like the Jan Dhan-Aadhaar-Mobile (JAM) trinity have further expanded financial inclusion by bringing millions into the formal banking system. This foundational effort not only promotes cashless economies but also ensures that economic participation becomes more inclusive.

The rise of e-commerce and telemedicine exemplifies the transformative potential of India's digital landscape. Platforms like Flipkart, Amazon, and Reliance JioMart have redefined retail by connecting businesses and consumers nationwide, especially during the pandemic. Simultaneously, telemedicine platforms such as Practo and Apollo 24/7 are bridging healthcare gaps, enabling remote consultations and making medical services accessible to underserved regions. These digital advancements demonstrate how technology is reshaping traditional industries while improving quality of life.

The rollout of 5G networks marks a new era of connectivity in India, promising transformative impacts across sectors. Enhanced bandwidth and low-latency networks are set to boost innovations in manufacturing, agriculture, healthcare, and education. Investments in smart cities further complement this technological leap, as initiatives supported by Internet of Things (IoT) and artificial intelligence (AI) enhance urban infrastructure, optimize energy use, and deliver citizen-centric services.

India's digital infrastructure is more than just a tool for economic growth—it is a driver of societal transformation. By integrating cutting-edge technologies with inclusive policies, India is not only fostering innovation but also ensuring that the benefits of its digital revolution reach every corner of the nation. This comprehensive approach positions India as a global leader in the digital age, capable of leveraging technology to address complex challenges while building a more equitable and connected future.

Startups and Innovation Ecosystem

India's dynamic startup ecosystem, now the third largest globally, stands as a testament to its technology-driven growth and entrepreneurial spirit. By harnessing innovations across fintech, edtech, healthtech, and emerging technologies like artificial intelligence (AI) and blockchain, Indian startups are crafting solutions that address critical challenges both domestically and internationally.

The emergence of unicorns like Paytm, BYJU'S, OYO, and Zomato highlights India's capacity to build globally competitive enterprises. These startups are not merely businesses; they are innovators tackling essential societal needs. For instance, fintech firms are driving financial inclusion with digital payment platforms, while edtech companies are revolutionizing education delivery, making quality learning accessible to millions.

This growth has been bolstered by the active involvement of U.S.-based venture capital firms such as Sequoia Capital, Accel, and Tiger Global, which provide vital funding and mentorship to scale these ventures. Complementing this private sector support is the Indian government's **Startup India** initiative. By offering tax incentives, funding opportunities, and incubation facilities, the initiative has created an enabling environment for entrepreneurship to thrive.

Indian startups are also pioneering advancements in emerging technologies. From blockchain-based digital wallets and cryptocurrency platforms to AI-driven healthcare diagnostics and IoT-powered smart solutions, the innovation coming out of India caters to diverse markets. These technological breakthroughs not only address local needs but also position India as a global hub for cutting-edge products and services.

The country's vibrant startup ecosystem exemplifies its potential as a leader in the global innovation landscape. By fostering creativity, leveraging investments, and embracing transformative technologies, India's startups are shaping the future while cementing the nation's status as a powerhouse of ideas and entrepreneurship.

Workforce Transformation

India's workforce is undergoing a profound transformation as technological advancements reshape the demand for skilled talent. The rapid adoption of artificial intelligence (AI), cybersecurity, quantum computing, and renewable energy technologies across industries has created a pressing need for professionals proficient in these emerging fields.

The IT services sector, led by giants like TCS, Infosys, and Wipro, continues to play a pivotal role in employing tech talent and driving global digital transformation initiatives. These companies have not only maintained India's status as a leading IT hub but also supported global enterprises by offering cutting-edge solutions in areas like data analytics, cloud computing, and automation.

To meet the evolving demands of the industry, initiatives like **Skill India** are equipping millions of Indians with expertise in AI, data science, machine learning, and other high-demand areas. Collaborations with global firms and educational institutions ensure access to top-tier training programs and certifications, empowering India's workforce to remain competitive on the international stage.

India's youth, one of the youngest populations globally, represents a significant demographic advantage. Investments in vocational training, online education platforms, and intensive coding bootcamps are enabling young Indians to acquire the skills needed to thrive in the digital economy. By fostering a culture of continuous learning and innovation, India is positioning its workforce to lead in the technological era.

This transformation underscores India's commitment to not only adapting to but also shaping the future of work. By aligning its education and skill development initiatives with industry needs, the country is paving the way for sustainable economic growth and global leadership in technology-driven sectors.

Global Competitiveness

India's strategic adoption of technological innovations is playing a transformative role in enhancing its global competitiveness. By integrating advanced technologies into key industries, the country is not only driving efficiency and productivity but also positioning itself as a leader in the global economy.

The infusion of **AI, automation, and IoT** into traditional sectors such as manufacturing, agriculture, and logistics has sparked a wave of modernization. From smart farming solutions that optimize crop yields to autonomous manufacturing systems and AI-driven supply chains, these innovations are revolutionizing operations, reducing costs, and increasing output. Such advancements exemplify how India is leveraging technology to reshape its industrial landscape.

This technological momentum is integral to India's ambition of achieving a **$5 trillion economy**. By fostering innovation, improving productivity, and creating a business-friendly environment, the country is laying a robust foundation for sustainable economic growth. Initiatives that support startups, attract foreign investment, and encourage research and development are further accelerating this progress.

A key component of India's strategy is reducing its reliance on imports in critical areas like semiconductors, renewable energy, and pharmaceuticals. Through targeted efforts, the country is developing domestic capabilities to manufacture these essential goods, strengthening its resilience in global markets. Programs like **Atmanirbhar Bharat (Self-Reliant India)** underpin this shift, promoting domestic production and encouraging homegrown innovation.

India's focus on harnessing technology and fostering self-reliance not only enhances its economic sovereignty but also cements its role as a competitive player on the global stage. As the nation continues to integrate advanced technologies across sectors, it is poised to drive sustained growth, create high-value industries, and assert its leadership in the international economic arena.

In summary, technological disruptions are reshaping the trajectory of India's growth, creating opportunities to enhance its **economic resilience, global competitiveness,** and **societal development**. By investing in **digital infrastructure, fostering startups**, and **upskilling its workforce**, India is preparing to lead in a world increasingly driven by innovation.

As India continues to integrate **emerging technologies** into its industries and society, it has the potential to transform itself into a global technology powerhouse. By aligning its domestic priorities with global trends, India can ensure sustained growth, generate millions of jobs, and establish itself as a leader in the **global digital economy**.

Conclusion

The escalating technological rivalry between the United States and China presents India with a transformative opportunity to redefine its role in the global technology ecosystem. As these superpowers vie for dominance in critical fields like semiconductors, artificial intelligence (AI), and green technologies, India stands at a strategic crossroads. By aligning with global powers, fostering self-reliance, and embracing innovation, India has the potential to emerge as a leader in the next era of technological progress.

India's commitment to semiconductors, AI, and green technologies underscores its ambitions to become a global tech powerhouse. Initiatives such as the **India Semiconductor Mission**, the **National AI Strategy**, and advancements in renewable energy reflect a forward-thinking approach. The combination of a vast talent pool, a thriving startup ecosystem, and government-led programs provides a solid foundation for this vision. By investing in fabrication plants, fostering collaborations with partners like the U.S. and Japan, and promoting innovations in areas such as solar energy and green hydrogen, India is addressing global supply chain gaps while creating new economic opportunities.

However, the journey to global leadership is fraught with challenges. India faces significant infrastructure gaps, particularly in areas like semiconductor fabrication, logistics, and energy storage. Addressing these deficiencies will require substantial investment in industrial zones, power grids, and advanced logistics networks. Additionally, while India's workforce is large, there is a shortage of specialized skills in cutting-edge fields like chip design, AI, and green hydrogen technologies. Expanding initiatives like **Skill India** and fostering global educational partnerships will be crucial to bridging this gap.

Navigating geopolitical pressures also remains a delicate task. India must balance its partnerships with the U.S. and China while safeguarding its strategic autonomy. Geopolitical tensions, such as border disputes and the dynamics of alliances like the Quad, could influence India's ability to sustain its tech-driven ambitions. To succeed, India needs a multi-pronged strategy that combines domestic capacity building with robust international collaboration.

Strategic alliances with nations like the U.S., Japan, Taiwan, and the European Union provide India access to cutting-edge technologies and investment opportunities. Strengthening frameworks such as the Quad's supply chain initiative and enhancing partnerships like the **India-U.S. Technology Partnership** will boost India's influence on the global stage. Domestically, clear and consistent policies that encourage R&D, protect intellectual property rights, and ease business operations are essential for fostering innovation and maintaining investor confidence.

Sustained investments in innovation and infrastructure will play a pivotal role in driving growth. Public and private sector collaboration to boost domestic manufacturing, support startups, and enhance access to capital for tech entrepreneurs will accelerate India's progress. Simultaneously, balancing global collaborations with national priorities will ensure that India's autonomy and long-term interests remain intact.

Looking ahead, this technological inflection point offers India a chance to assert its leadership on the global stage. By addressing challenges with foresight and leveraging its strengths, India can position itself as a technology powerhouse capable of meeting domestic needs while influencing global innovation trends. As the nation navigates the complexities of this competitive landscape, its advancements in technology and strategic positioning will shape its emergence as a global leader in the interconnected and rapidly evolving 21st century.

10: The Power of Strategic Autonomy

India's ability to maintain **strategic autonomy** in its foreign policy has been one of its defining strengths. This principle, rooted in the philosophy of **non-alignment**, enables India to navigate complex geopolitical dynamics without being tethered to the ambitions of any single power. In the evolving global order, marked by the intensifying rivalry between the **United States and China**, India's commitment to **independence** while fostering **strategic partnerships** has emerged as a cornerstone of its foreign policy.

This chapter explores how India's modern approach to non-alignment—termed **Non-Alignment 2.0**—equips it to balance relationships with global powers, sustain its independence, and adapt to the demands of a multipolar world.

India's Non-Alignment 2.0: Navigating Between Two Giants

India's foreign policy of **non-alignment**, introduced during the Cold War, was a strategic response to the ideological conflict between the **United States** and the **Soviet Union**. By choosing to avoid alignment with either bloc, India sought to maintain its sovereignty, focus on development, and act as a bridge between the two opposing power centers. In the contemporary geopolitical landscape, where the rivalry between the **U.S. and China** dominates global discourse, India's foreign policy has evolved into a more pragmatic version termed **Non-Alignment 2.0**.

This modern approach enables India to navigate the complexities of a multipolar world, balance competing global interests, and safeguard its

national interests without compromising its autonomy. Non-Alignment 2.0 is characterized by **flexibility, issue-based partnerships**, and a commitment to **strategic autonomy**.

Modern Non-Alignment: The Core Principles

India's updated framework of non-alignment marks a shift from ideological neutrality to a more pragmatic approach, engaging with multiple nations based on specific interests rather than rigid allegiances. This strategy ensures that India remains adaptable and relevant in an increasingly complex global order.

A cornerstone of this modern non-alignment is maintaining equidistance. India avoids exclusive alignment with either the U.S. or China, preserving the flexibility to navigate challenges and opportunities on its own terms. This is evident in India's diverse international engagements. For instance, its active role in the Quad alliance—alongside the U.S., Japan, and Australia—demonstrates its commitment to fostering a rules-based Indo-Pacific and countering China's assertiveness in the region. Simultaneously, India's participation in BRICS and the Shanghai Cooperation Organisation (SCO) underscores its readiness to collaborate with non-Western powers. This dual engagement highlights India's ability to forge partnerships across ideological divides, avoiding entanglement in global rivalries while advancing its own strategic interests.

Unlike the Cold War-era non-alignment, which emphasized ideological neutrality, India's modern approach—sometimes referred to as "Non-Alignment 2.0"—is more issue-driven. Partnerships are forged with nations based on shared goals in specific areas:

> **With the U.S.**: India engages in defense collaborations, technology transfers, and joint counterterrorism efforts. Regular military exercises and deals for advanced weaponry underscore this relationship.

> **With China**: Despite persistent border tensions, India continues robust trade relations, benefiting from China's manufacturing strengths to fuel its own economic growth.

THE TRIANGULAR DYNAMICS

> **With Russia**: Historical ties in defense and energy remain strong, with India sourcing critical supplies such as oil and advanced military systems like the S-400 missile defense system.

This pragmatic, issue-based approach enables India to address its diverse needs while ensuring that it does not become overly reliant on any single power. By balancing its partnerships and strategically managing its global engagements, India continues to assert its autonomy and influence in a multipolar world.

Navigating the U.S.-China Rivalry

The intensifying rivalry between the United States and China has created a complex global landscape, demanding a careful balancing act from nations like India. For India, this dynamic requires preserving its strategic autonomy while fostering constructive relationships with both superpowers.

India's engagement with the U.S. is driven by shared interests in countering China's assertiveness in the Indo-Pacific and advancing its own economic and technological goals. The defense partnership between the two nations has grown significantly, with India participating in joint military exercises such as *Malabar*, bolstering its naval capabilities, and acquiring advanced weaponry to modernize its defense forces. In the technology sector, collaborations in semiconductors, artificial intelligence (AI), and clean energy technologies are helping India strengthen its tech ecosystem and meet its developmental objectives. India's active role in the Quad alliance further highlights its commitment to ensuring maritime security and promoting a rules-based order in the Indo-Pacific, aligning with the U.S. vision for the region.

At the same time, India maintains a pragmatic approach in its engagement with China. Despite ongoing border tensions, trade between the two nations remains robust, with China being one of India's largest trading partners. India's participation in multilateral forums, such as discussions around the Regional Comprehensive Economic Partnership (RCEP), demonstrates its willingness to engage with China on economic matters where mutual benefits exist.

However, India is equally focused on reducing its dependency on Chinese imports in critical sectors like electronics and pharmaceuticals. Through initiatives such as *Make in India*, it is strengthening domestic manufacturing and infrastructure to enhance self-reliance and mitigate vulnerabilities.

By skillfully navigating this rivalry, India aims to balance its relationships with the U.S. and China, ensuring that its engagements serve national interests while maintaining its autonomy in an increasingly polarized world.

Strategic Autonomy in Action

India's steadfast commitment to strategic autonomy underpins its ability to navigate a complex global landscape without compromising its national interests or sovereignty. This principle is evident in its neutral stance on global conflicts and its adept management of competing relationships.

In the context of the Russia-Ukraine conflict, India's refusal to condemn Russia outright or align with Western sanctions exemplifies its independent approach to foreign policy. Despite significant pressure from the United States and its allies, India continues to engage with Russia for energy imports and defense procurement, emphasizing pragmatism in securing its strategic and economic needs. This nuanced stance ensures that India safeguards its interests while avoiding entanglement in geopolitical rivalries.

India's ability to balance strategic priorities is another hallmark of its autonomy. By engaging constructively with both the U.S. and China, India ensures that it does not become overly reliant on either. It addresses security concerns stemming from its border tensions with China while fostering robust economic and technological collaborations with the U.S., particularly in areas such as defense, artificial intelligence, and clean energy.

Multilateral platforms serve as vital arenas for India to exercise its strategic autonomy and amplify its global influence. Active participation in organizations such as the G20, BRICS, and the Quad enables India to shape international agendas, champion the concerns of developing nations, and assert its role as a key player in the evolving global order. This multilateral engagement underscores India's ability to maintain a non-aligned identity while playing a proactive role in addressing global challenges.

Through its commitment to strategic autonomy, India demonstrates the capacity to navigate a polarized world, balancing relationships and advancing its national interests without compromising its sovereignty or independence.

In conclusion, India's **Non-Alignment 2.0** is a testament to its ability to adapt to changing geopolitical realities while staying true to its core principles of **independence** and **sovereignty**. By maintaining equidistance, pursuing issue-based partnerships, and navigating the U.S.-China rivalry with finesse, India has positioned itself as a **balancing force** in an increasingly polarized world.

As global challenges evolve, India's strategic autonomy will remain pivotal to its foreign policy. This approach not only safeguards its national interests but also enhances its role as a stabilizing force in global politics, ensuring that it remains a vital player in shaping the future of international relations.

Balancing Strategic Partnerships While Maintaining Independence

India's foreign policy is a careful exercise in balancing its strategic partnerships with its commitment to **sovereignty and autonomy**. By fostering diverse relationships and pursuing **long-term national goals**, India ensures that its engagements are rooted in its own interests rather than the influence of external powers. This approach enables India to maintain **strategic autonomy** while leveraging its partnerships to bolster its **economic, technological,** and **security capabilities**.

Strategic Partnerships with the U.S. and Other Democracies

India has deepened its relationships with like-minded democracies, including the United States, Japan, Australia, and European nations, by focusing on shared goals such as maritime security, technological innovation, and counterterrorism. These collaborations allow India to pursue its strategic objectives while maintaining its autonomy in decision-making.

The partnership with the United States is central to India's efforts to ensure a rules-based international order and counter China's assertive posture in the Indo-Pacific. In technology, the two nations are advancing cooperation in areas like artificial intelligence, semiconductors, and green technologies through initiatives such as the U.S.-India Strategic Partnership Forum (USISPF). Maritime security is another cornerstone of this relationship, with joint naval exercises like *Malabar* enhancing interoperability and protecting vital trade routes in the Indo-Pacific. In counterterrorism, intelligence-sharing and joint operations have bolstered India's capabilities to address regional and global security threats.

India's active role in the Quad alliance alongside the U.S., Japan, and Australia further underscores its commitment to a free, open, and inclusive Indo-Pacific. Quad initiatives emphasize critical areas such as infrastructure development, offering alternatives to China's Belt and Road Initiative (BRI); supply chain resilience, aimed at diversifying manufacturing and reducing dependency on China; and climate action, fostering collaborations in renewable energy and green technologies.

In parallel, India's engagements with Japan and Australia complement its Indo-Pacific strategy. Japan has been instrumental in supporting infrastructure development within India, while Australia collaborates on critical minerals vital for clean energy and advanced technologies. Additionally, European nations, particularly France and Germany, contribute significantly through defense cooperation and clean energy partnerships, offering advanced technologies and investment opportunities that align with India's development goals.

These strategic partnerships reflect India's pragmatic approach to global alliances, enabling it to address shared challenges while safeguarding its independence and long-term interests.

Engagement with Non-Western Powers

India's pragmatic foreign policy extends beyond Western alliances, encompassing strategic relationships with Russia, China, and Middle Eastern countries. These partnerships are carefully balanced to secure access to vital resources, diversify markets, and address critical strategic needs, while ensuring India's broader national interests remain intact.

India's ties with Russia have remained steadfast, even amid global tensions following the Ukraine conflict. Moscow continues to be a significant supplier of defense equipment, providing advanced systems like the S-400 missile defense system, essential for India's military preparedness. On the energy front, discounted oil imports from Russia have bolstered India's energy security and affordability, offering a vital diversification of supply sources.

The relationship with China presents a more complex dynamic. Despite ongoing border tensions and strategic rivalry, economic engagement between the two nations persists. China remains one of India's largest trading partners, supplying critical components for industries such as electronics and pharmaceuticals. However, India has adopted a dual strategy—while continuing economic ties, it is actively strengthening domestic manufacturing under initiatives like *Make in India* and diversifying trade relationships with other partners to reduce dependency on Chinese imports.

India's connections with Middle Eastern countries, including Saudi Arabia, the UAE, and Iran, play a crucial role in its foreign policy. These relationships are anchored in energy security, with the Middle East being a primary supplier of oil and gas. Collaborative projects in infrastructure development, renewable energy, and trade further underscore the strategic importance of the region. Additionally, India's large diaspora in the Gulf strengthens economic and cultural bonds, reinforcing mutual interests.

Through these engagements, India demonstrates a nuanced approach to diplomacy, leveraging partnerships with non-Western powers to ensure strategic balance, economic stability, and access to critical resources. This pragmatic policy allows India to navigate a complex global environment while safeguarding its autonomy and advancing its long-term objectives.

Economic and Technological Autonomy

India's drive for economic and technological self-reliance forms the backbone of its strategy to maintain independence while fostering strategic partnerships. This vision is embodied in initiatives like *Atmanirbhar Bharat* (Self-Reliant India), which prioritize reducing dependency on imports and building robust domestic capabilities in critical sectors.

The *Atmanirbhar Bharat* initiative focuses on strengthening local industries, particularly in manufacturing, defense production, and technology development. By encouraging innovation and enhancing domestic production, India aims to position itself as a global hub for high-tech manufacturing and exports, reducing vulnerabilities in its supply chains.

In recognition of the critical role of semiconductors in modern technology, India has launched the India Semiconductor Mission (ISM). This ambitious program is designed to attract global leaders like Intel and Taiwan Semiconductor Manufacturing Company (TSMC) to establish fabrication units in the country. By developing a domestic semiconductor manufacturing ecosystem, India seeks to play a pivotal role in the global supply chain while reducing reliance on imports from regions like China and Taiwan.

India's leadership in renewable energy further underscores its commitment to achieving economic and technological autonomy. Programs such as *Mission Green Hydrogen* aim to establish India as a key player in the production and use of clean hydrogen, while initiatives like FAME (Faster Adoption and Manufacturing of Hybrid and Electric Vehicles) are accelerating the country's transition to a low-carbon economy. These efforts not only advance energy independence but also create new opportunities for economic growth and technological innovation.

By focusing on self-reliance and leveraging its strengths, India is laying the groundwork for sustainable economic development. This approach ensures that the nation remains resilient amid global uncertainties while becoming a significant contributor to the world's technological and environmental goals.

Balancing Autonomy and Dependence

India's foreign policy exemplifies a delicate balance between cultivating partnerships and maintaining strategic autonomy. By engaging with a diverse array of nations, India ensures access to critical resources, technologies, and markets while avoiding over-reliance on any single partner or bloc.

India's relationships extend across a broad spectrum of global powers, including the United States, China, Russia, and key Middle Eastern nations. This diversity allows India to draw benefits from multiple sources, be it advanced technology from the U.S., energy security from Russia and the Middle East, or manufacturing inputs from China. Such a wide network not only supports India's economic and strategic objectives but also reinforces its position as a global player capable of navigating complex geopolitical landscapes.

Strategic initiatives like *Atmanirbhar Bharat* and the India Semiconductor Mission strengthen India's domestic capabilities, reducing vulnerabilities to external shocks. These programs aim to build resilience in critical sectors, ensuring that India can achieve its long-term ambitions without compromising its independence in decision-making.

India's diplomatic pragmatism is evident in its ability to engage with both the Quad and BRICS. This duality highlights India's skill in leveraging opportunities from democratic alliances while maintaining constructive relations with non-Western powers. Such an approach enables India to benefit from a broad spectrum of partnerships, from technological and security collaborations with the Quad to economic and trade engagements within BRICS.

This balanced strategy ensures that India remains adaptable and self-reliant while advancing its global ambitions, solidifying its role as a key player in an increasingly multipolar world.

In summary, India's ability to balance **strategic partnerships** with its commitment to **independence** is a testament to its nuanced and pragmatic foreign policy. By engaging constructively with both Western democracies and non-Western powers, India secures its national interests while avoiding entanglement in global rivalries.

Through its focus on **economic and technological autonomy**, India is building a foundation for sustained growth and resilience. As the global order evolves, India's ability to maintain this balance will be critical to its role as a key player in a multipolar world, shaping its path as a **self-reliant and globally respected power**.

Lessons from History and Strategies for the Future

India's foreign policy of **strategic autonomy** is deeply rooted in its historical experiences, offering critical insights into how it has navigated global complexities while preserving its **sovereignty and independence**. These lessons serve as a guide for addressing current and future challenges, helping India adapt to the dynamics of an increasingly **multipolar world**. By learning from its past and implementing forward-looking strategies, India can strengthen its position as a global power capable of balancing diverse interests and partnerships.

Lessons from History

India's foreign policy has consistently demonstrated an ability to adapt to shifting global dynamics, ensuring its national interests remain paramount. This adaptability, rooted in historical experiences, has shaped India's approach to navigating complex geopolitical realities.

During the Cold War era, India adopted a policy of non-alignment under Prime Minister Jawaharlal Nehru, allowing it to avoid ideological entanglements between the U.S.-led capitalist bloc and the Soviet-led communist bloc. This strategy enabled India to secure economic aid, technological support, and investments from both sides without compromising its sovereignty. India's leadership in the Non-Aligned Movement (NAM) further enhanced its diplomatic influence, positioning the nation as an advocate for decolonization and equitable global development.

However, the limitations of this approach were starkly exposed during the Sino-Indian War of 1962. The conflict revealed vulnerabilities in India's non-alignment strategy, particularly its inability to address existential security threats. The lack of strong alliances left India diplomatically isolated during the war, underscoring the need for a more robust and pragmatic approach to national security and defense.

The post-Cold War period marked a significant recalibration of India's foreign policy. The collapse of the Soviet Union in 1991 ushered in a unipolar world dominated by the United States, compelling India to engage more actively with Washington while retaining its strategic ties with Russia. This dual approach ensured continuity in defense and energy partnerships with Russia while fostering new economic and technological collaborations with the U.S.

India's economic liberalization in 1991, led by Prime Minister P.V. Narasimha Rao and Finance Minister Manmohan Singh, further highlighted its adaptability. By opening its economy to global markets, India attracted foreign investments, expanded trade relations with the U.S. and China, and laid the groundwork for its emergence as a global economic power. This period underscored the importance of flexibility in responding to evolving global challenges and opportunities.

India's historical lessons underline the value of pragmatism and foresight in foreign policy. They serve as a blueprint for navigating the complexities of an increasingly interconnected and competitive world, ensuring that India remains both resilient and forward-looking in its global engagements.

Strategies for the Future

As India navigates the complexities of the 21st century, it must craft strategies that bolster resilience, adaptability, and global influence while preserving its strategic autonomy. By focusing on diversified partnerships, domestic resilience, and active engagement in multilateral platforms, India can secure its position as a leading global power.

To reduce dependency on dominant global powers like the U.S. or China, India must deepen its ties with middle powers such as Japan, South Korea, ASEAN nations, and European countries. Collaborations in areas like infrastructure development, technology, defense, and trade will enhance India's global standing and shield it from external shocks. For instance, its partnership with Japan on infrastructure projects and South Korea in electronics manufacturing exemplify the strength of such diversified engagements. Similarly, India's focus on South-South cooperation—fostering relations with Africa, Latin America, and Southeast Asia—can open new avenues for trade and investment. By providing development assistance and sharing technological expertise, India can position itself as a leader among developing nations, as reflected in initiatives like the Asia-Africa Growth Corridor (AAGC).

Strengthening domestic resilience is another cornerstone of India's future strategy. Investments in world-class infrastructure, research and development, and education will enhance global competitiveness. Fostering innovation in critical sectors such as semiconductors, artificial intelligence, and renewable energy will reduce dependency on imports and establish India as a technology leader. Securing energy independence through diversified energy sources—including renewables, nuclear power, and strategic reserves—is crucial, alongside policies promoting sustainable agriculture and efficient supply chain management to ensure food security. Building resilient supply chains by collaborating with trusted partners will mitigate vulnerabilities in key sectors like pharmaceuticals, electronics, and defense equipment.

India's role in multilateral platforms like the G20, BRICS, SCO, and the Quad is pivotal for shaping global norms and addressing shared challenges. Active participation enables India to advocate for equitable policies on climate change, sustainable development, and digital transformation. Its presidency of the G20, for instance, has spotlighted these critical issues on the global stage. Additionally, India's leadership in tackling global challenges such as public health, climate change, and cybersecurity enhances its soft power and solidifies its reputation as a responsible global actor. Initiatives like the International Solar Alliance (ISA) and contributions to global vaccine distribution reflect India's commitment to collective global progress.

By embracing these strategies, India can navigate the shifting global landscape effectively, ensuring its economic, technological, and diplomatic growth while contributing meaningfully to global stability and development.

India's Path Forward

India's foreign policy must remain firmly rooted in the principle of strategic autonomy while evolving to meet the demands of a rapidly changing global landscape. By drawing from historical experiences and adopting forward-looking strategies, India is well-positioned to achieve its aspirations and navigate the challenges of an increasingly multipolar world.

India's rise as a global leader depends on its ability to leverage economic and technological strengths to shape the rules of the emerging international order. Initiatives in advanced technologies, renewable energy, and digital infrastructure will not only enhance its global competitiveness but also establish India as a pivotal player in addressing shared global challenges. By taking a proactive stance in shaping international norms, India can secure a seat at the table where the future of global governance is defined.

Resilience against external shocks is essential for safeguarding national interests. Strengthening domestic capacities in manufacturing, energy, and infrastructure will reduce vulnerabilities to global disruptions. Investments in innovation, supply chain diversification, and sustainable practices will enable

India to remain self-reliant while responding effectively to global uncertainties. This resilience will serve as a foundation for India's long-term growth and stability.

Promoting equitable global development through partnerships with middle powers and fostering South-South cooperation offers India the opportunity to champion inclusive growth. Collaborations with Africa, Southeast Asia, and Latin America can create new avenues for trade, investment, and cultural exchange, positioning India as a leader among developing nations. By supporting sustainable development and providing technological expertise, India reinforces its role as a partner of choice for emerging economies.

In conclusion, India's foreign policy, informed by lessons from history and grounded in strategic autonomy, provides a strong foundation for navigating the complexities of the global future. By diversifying partnerships, bolstering domestic resilience, and actively engaging in multilateral platforms, India can advance its global ambitions without compromising its independence.

As the global order continues to evolve, India's success will depend on its ability to adapt, innovate, and lead. This balanced approach ensures the safeguarding of its sovereignty while enhancing its role as a stabilizing force in international relations. In doing so, India is poised to shape a more equitable, inclusive, and sustainable global future for decades to come.

Conclusion

India's steadfast commitment to strategic autonomy is both a reflection of its historical wisdom and a pragmatic response to the complexities of modern geopolitics. In an era marked by shifting power dynamics, escalating rivalries, and intricate interdependencies, India's ability to balance meaningful engagement with global powers while safeguarding its sovereignty has cemented its position as a pivotal player on the world stage. This nuanced approach blends lessons from history with a forward-looking vision to navigate the challenges of an evolving multipolar world.

Balancing Engagement with Independence

India's strategic autonomy lies in its capacity to collaborate with diverse global actors while avoiding overdependence on any single partner. This balanced approach enables India to pursue multi-alignment—a strategy that bridges divergent and even opposing blocs.

India's participation in the Quad alliance exemplifies its alignment with like-minded democracies to counterbalance China's influence in the Indo-Pacific, while maintaining robust economic ties with Beijing underscores its diplomatic flexibility. Similarly, its enduring defense and energy partnerships with Russia, despite geopolitical tensions and Western pressure, highlight India's unwavering focus on its domestic priorities and sovereignty.

Adapting to a Changing Global Order

As the global landscape evolves, India's success hinges on its ability to embrace change and leverage emerging opportunities. By prioritizing key sectors, India is poised to solidify its position as a global leader.

In technology, India's focus on self-reliance in semiconductors, artificial intelligence, and green technologies reflects its alignment with global trends while addressing national goals. Initiatives like *Atmanirbhar Bharat* position India as a hub for high-tech manufacturing and global trade, reducing dependency on imports. Strengthened defense capabilities, bolstered by partnerships with nations like the U.S., France, and Israel, ensure that India remains prepared to address both regional and global security challenges.

Leveraging Lessons from History

India's approach to strategic autonomy is deeply informed by historical experiences. The non-alignment policy of the Cold War enabled India to navigate ideological divides while securing support from competing blocs. However, events like the Sino-Indian War of 1962 revealed the limitations of non-alignment in addressing existential security threats, underscoring the need for robust defense strategies. The economic liberalization of 1991 demonstrated the importance of reform and global integration in sustaining growth. These pivotal moments have shaped India's capacity to adapt to changing circumstances, equipping it to meet the challenges of the 21st century.

Strengthening Domestic Capacities

India's economic resilience and technological innovation underpin its strategic autonomy. Investments in infrastructure, education, and research and development (R&D) create a foundation for long-term growth and self-reliance. Initiatives in renewable energy, electric vehicles, and digital infrastructure align with India's vision for sustainable and inclusive progress. Programs like *Skill India* and *Startup India* empower the workforce and foster innovation, ensuring India's competitiveness in the global economy.

Asserting Sovereignty and Advancing National Interests

India's approach to strategic autonomy reflects a commitment to asserting its sovereignty while advancing its national interests. By diversifying partnerships and engaging in multilateral platforms, India has positioned itself as a stabilizing force in an increasingly volatile world. Forums like the G20, BRICS, and SCO provide platforms for India to advocate for equitable development, address global challenges, and influence international norms. Leadership in areas such as climate action and public health enhances India's soft power, reinforcing its image as a responsible and forward-thinking global actor.

Looking Ahead

India's ability to innovate, lead, and adapt will define its trajectory in an interconnected and multipolar world. By maintaining its strategic autonomy, India can safeguard its sovereignty while emerging as a guiding force for global stability and progress.

11: Core Sectors for Resilience

Resilience is the foundation of a nation's ability to adapt to global challenges and assert its independence. For India, developing key sectors like **agriculture, energy,** and **manufacturing** is critical to ensuring **food security, energy sufficiency,** and a robust **industrial base**. These sectors not only support domestic needs but also strengthen India's global competitiveness and its position as a self-reliant economic powerhouse.

Agriculture: Food Security and Modernization

Agriculture remains the cornerstone of India's economy, providing livelihoods for nearly half of the population and ensuring food security for over **1.4 billion people**. While it contributes significantly to the nation's economic stability, the sector faces critical challenges such as **climate change, resource constraints,** and **global market dynamics**. To address these challenges, India must focus on enhancing **productivity**, adopting **modern technologies**, and implementing **sustainable practices** to create a resilient and future-ready agricultural ecosystem.

Ensuring Food Security

Food security is a cornerstone of India's economic and social stability, requiring targeted interventions to enhance agricultural productivity and minimize post-harvest losses. A comprehensive approach that combines technological innovation, infrastructure development, and supportive policies is essential to achieve sustainable and equitable food systems.

THE TRIANGULAR DYNAMICS

Enhancing agricultural productivity is critical to meeting the growing food demands of a populous nation. Investments in high-yielding crop varieties, precision farming techniques, and resource-efficient practices such as drip irrigation are transforming traditional farming methods. Precision farming, powered by GPS, IoT devices, and AI, allows farmers to monitor crop health, soil quality, and weather patterns in real time. This data-driven approach optimizes the use of inputs like water, fertilizers, and pesticides, resulting in higher yields while conserving resources.

Government programs like *PM-Kisan*, which provides direct income support to farmers, and the National Food Security Mission, focused on increasing foodgrain production, are instrumental in stabilizing farmer incomes and ensuring the availability of essential staples. These initiatives bridge the gap between technological advancements and grassroots implementation, empowering farmers to adopt modern agricultural practices.

One of the significant challenges to India's food security is the substantial post-harvest losses, with nearly 30% of agricultural produce wasted annually due to inadequate storage, transportation, and processing infrastructure. Developing modern cold storage chains equipped with temperature-controlled environments is crucial for preserving perishable commodities such as fruits, vegetables, and dairy products.

Expanding food processing capabilities adds value to raw produce, converting grains into packaged foods or milk into processed dairy products. This not only increases profitability for farmers but also reduces waste and improves shelf life, benefiting consumers.

Strengthening rural logistics networks, including farm-to-market transportation systems, ensures that agricultural produce reaches consumers quickly and efficiently, minimizing spoilage and enhancing market access for farmers. Integrating these networks with digital platforms for real-time supply chain management can further optimize operations and reduce inefficiencies.

By prioritizing food security through productivity enhancement and reduction of post-harvest losses, India can ensure the availability of nutritious food for its population, stabilize farmer livelihoods, and contribute to global food sustainability. This integrated approach aligns with India's broader goals of inclusive development and resilience in the face of environmental and economic challenges.

Modernizing Agriculture

Modernization is the cornerstone of transforming Indian agriculture into a globally competitive and sustainable sector. By adopting digital technologies, advancing sustainable practices, and integrating with global markets, India can significantly enhance agricultural efficiency, profitability, and resilience.

Technology-driven solutions are empowering Indian farmers, providing them with tools for informed decision-making and efficient operations. AI-based applications analyze satellite imagery and weather data to predict pest attacks, diseases, and water stress, enabling proactive measures to protect crops. Blockchain technology enhances supply chain transparency, especially for exports, bolstering India's reputation in global markets by ensuring traceability and quality.

Mobile applications like *Kisan Suvidha* and *e-NAM* (National Agriculture Market) connect farmers directly with buyers, reducing reliance on intermediaries and ensuring better pricing. These platforms democratize market access, allowing farmers to optimize profits and make informed sales decisions.

Government programs like *AgriStack* are building a unified digital platform to integrate services such as credit access, crop insurance, and advisory support, creating a robust ecosystem for digital agriculture.

Sustainability lies at the heart of agricultural modernization. Organic farming, which eliminates the use of synthetic fertilizers and pesticides, not only improves soil health but also caters to the growing demand for chemical-free produce in both domestic and export markets. Agroforestry, the integration of trees and shrubs into farming systems, enhances biodiversity, sequesters carbon, and provides additional income streams for farmers.

Water-efficient crops like millets, along with techniques such as zero tillage and rainwater harvesting, address the pressing challenge of dwindling water resources. Initiatives under the National Mission for Sustainable Agriculture (NMSA) support the adoption of climate-resilient practices, such as drought-tolerant seeds and adaptive irrigation systems, ensuring the long-term viability of agriculture amid changing climate patterns.

Diversifying agricultural exports beyond traditional staples like rice and wheat opens doors to high-value international markets. Processed foods, organic products, and specialty crops such as basmati rice, millets, and organic spices are gaining popularity due to rising global demand for healthy and sustainable products.

Strengthening relationships with global institutions like the World Trade Organization (WTO) and the Food and Agriculture Organization (FAO) facilitates access to international trade opportunities while ensuring domestic food security. By enhancing export-oriented infrastructure and meeting international quality standards, India can position itself as a leading supplier of premium agricultural products.

Through a combination of digital innovation, sustainable practices, and global integration, Indian agriculture is poised for a transformative journey. These advancements not only promise economic prosperity for farmers but also address environmental challenges, secure food systems, and solidify India's role as a key player in the global agricultural landscape.

Driving Innovation and Sustainability

Innovation and sustainability are shaping the future of Indian agriculture, ensuring resilience and long-term growth. By integrating emerging technologies, climate-smart practices, and community-driven approaches, India is transforming its agricultural sector to meet modern challenges and opportunities.

Agri-tech startups are at the forefront of this transformation, introducing innovative solutions that enhance farm management, streamline supply chains, and improve market access. Companies like *Ninjacart*, *DeHaat*, and *CropIn* are leveraging AI and IoT to make agriculture more data-driven and efficient. These technologies allow farmers to monitor crop health, optimize inputs, and predict market demand, fostering higher productivity and profitability.

India is also scaling up climate-smart practices to promote sustainable agriculture. Solar-powered irrigation systems are replacing traditional diesel pumps, significantly reducing carbon emissions and energy costs for farmers. The adoption of bio-fertilizers and natural pest control methods is being encouraged to minimize the environmental impact of chemical inputs, ensuring healthier soils and eco-friendly farming practices.

Community-based approaches are playing a crucial role in empowering smallholder farmers. Farmer-producer organizations (FPOs) and cooperatives are fostering collaboration by pooling resources, sharing knowledge, and negotiating better prices in the market. These collective farming models enable better utilization of resources, access to advanced machinery, and enhanced bargaining power, ultimately improving the livelihoods of small farmers.

By embracing innovation and sustainability, Indian agriculture is not only addressing immediate challenges but also building a resilient and inclusive future. These efforts ensure that agriculture remains a vital pillar of India's economy while contributing to environmental conservation and social equity.

Future Roadmap

To secure its agricultural future and ensure food security, India must adopt a strategic approach that integrates infrastructure development, education, policy reforms, and global market engagement. The following key strategies will drive modernization and resilience in the sector:

Expanding irrigation infrastructure is critical to reducing dependency on erratic monsoons and ensuring year-round farming. Initiatives like the *Pradhan Mantri Krishi Sinchayee Yojana (PMKSY)* must be scaled up to provide equitable access to water resources. Modern irrigation techniques such as micro-irrigation and rainwater harvesting should be integrated to maximize efficiency and conserve water.

Enhancing agri-education and training will empower farmers with the knowledge and tools to adopt modern practices. Agriculture extension programs, coupled with digital platforms, can bridge the gap between research institutions and grassroots farmers. Collaborations with universities and research bodies will ensure that innovations in fields like precision farming, climate-resilient crops, and bio-technology reach the field level effectively.

Strengthening policy frameworks will support sustainable growth in agriculture. Policies should promote eco-friendly practices while ensuring fair market access for farmers. Comprehensive risk management plans, addressing challenges from climate change, market volatility, and natural disasters, will safeguard farmers' incomes and resilience.

Promoting export-oriented agriculture will unlock high-value markets for Indian produce. Developing specialized infrastructure like export-oriented processing zones and logistics hubs will streamline the supply chain for global trade. Branding Indian agricultural products as sustainable, organic, and premium-quality will enhance their appeal in international markets, attracting higher returns and fostering a reputation for excellence.

By focusing on these priorities, India can transform its agricultural landscape into a modern, competitive, and sustainable sector. These strategies not only aim to ensure food security but also position Indian agriculture as a global leader in innovation, quality, and resilience.

In conclusion, India's agricultural sector is at a critical juncture where modernization, sustainability, and food security must go hand in hand. By integrating **advanced technologies**, adopting **sustainable practices**, and expanding **market opportunities**, Indian agriculture can move beyond subsistence farming to become a globally competitive and resilient sector.

The transformation of agriculture will not only ensure **economic stability** and **livelihood security** for millions of Indians but also position India as a leader in addressing global challenges like **climate change, hunger,** and **sustainable development.**

Energy: Renewable Expansion and Reducing Dependence

Energy is the lifeblood of India's economy, driving **industrial development, infrastructure growth,** and **improved living standards**. As India continues to urbanize and modernize, the demand for energy is surging. To meet this demand sustainably, India has adopted a dual strategy: aggressively expanding its **renewable energy capacity** while reducing its **dependence on fossil fuel imports**. This approach is not only vital for energy security but also aligns with India's global climate commitments.

Expanding Renewable Energy

India stands at the forefront of the global clean energy transition, leveraging its vast natural resources and technological innovation to establish itself as a leader in renewable energy. This shift aligns with its ambitious climate goals and commitment to sustainable development.

India's leadership in solar power showcases its ability to harness abundant sunlight for energy generation. The National Solar Mission aims for 500 GW of non-fossil fuel capacity by 2030, with solar energy playing a pivotal role. Large-scale projects like the *Bhadla Solar Park* in Rajasthan—the largest of its kind globally—underline India's capabilities in utility-scale solar installations. Complementing these efforts are rooftop solar initiatives, empowering households and small businesses to generate their own energy. In rural areas, decentralized solar systems are improving energy access, supporting local industries, and enhancing livelihoods.

In wind and hydro energy, India continues to make strides. As the world's fourth-largest producer of wind energy, states like Tamil Nadu, Gujarat, and Maharashtra lead in onshore wind installations. India is also venturing into offshore wind projects, diversifying its renewable energy portfolio and further expanding capacity. Hydropower remains a cornerstone of India's renewable energy strategy, offering reliable electricity generation while supporting water management and flood control through investments in both large-scale and small hydro systems.

Green hydrogen represents the next frontier in India's renewable energy ambitions. Launched in 2021, the National Hydrogen Mission aims to position India as a global leader in green hydrogen production, targeting heavy industries and transportation as key areas for decarbonization. India's abundant solar and wind resources provide a competitive edge in producing cost-effective green hydrogen, which is set to transform industries like steel manufacturing, ammonia production, and long-haul transportation.

Exporting green hydrogen presents a significant opportunity for India, with countries like Japan, Germany, and South Korea actively seeking sustainable energy solutions. This positions India not only as a leader in renewable energy but also as a key player in the global energy trade.

Through its multifaceted approach to expanding renewable energy, India is setting an example for sustainable development, addressing energy security, and contributing meaningfully to the global fight against climate change.

THE TRIANGULAR DYNAMICS

Reducing Energy Dependence

India's heavy reliance on imported fossil fuels, particularly crude oil and natural gas, remains a significant vulnerability for its economy. Achieving energy independence is essential to enhancing security, mitigating exposure to geopolitical risks, and ensuring economic stability. Efforts to reduce this dependence center on domestic exploration, renewable energy expansion, advanced storage technologies, and energy efficiency improvements.

To enhance domestic energy production, India is advancing initiatives like the *Hydrocarbon Exploration and Licensing Policy (HELP)*, designed to attract investments in oil and gas exploration. By deploying advanced technologies such as enhanced oil recovery (EOR), India is working to maximize output from existing fields. These measures aim to reduce reliance on energy imports while leveraging untapped domestic reserves.

The transition to renewable energy is pivotal in reducing the demand for imported fuels. Scaling up solar, wind, and other renewables is already transforming the power and transportation sectors. Policies promoting electric vehicles (EVs) and biofuels are further reducing dependence on oil, particularly for mobility. This strategic shift supports energy diversification and aligns with India's climate goals.

Energy storage plays a critical role in stabilizing renewable energy supply, given the intermittent nature of solar and wind power. India is focusing on advanced battery technologies, including lithium-ion and solid-state batteries, to ensure consistent energy availability. Partnerships with resource-rich countries like Australia and Chile are being pursued to secure critical minerals such as lithium and cobalt, supporting domestic battery manufacturing. Investments in grid-scale storage solutions, such as pumped hydro storage, compressed air storage, and battery energy storage systems (BESS), are also enhancing grid reliability and enabling greater integration of renewable energy sources.

Improving energy efficiency is another cornerstone of India's strategy. Programs like the *Perform, Achieve, and Trade (PAT)* scheme encourage energy-intensive industries to adopt efficiency measures, achieving substantial reductions in energy consumption and costs. The *Unnat Jyoti by Affordable LEDs for All (Ujala)* program, which has distributed over 360 million LED bulbs nationwide, highlights India's leadership in energy-efficient lighting. This initiative has significantly reduced energy consumption and lowered greenhouse gas emissions while making energy-efficient solutions accessible to millions.

By prioritizing domestic exploration, advancing renewable energy technologies, and promoting efficiency, India is building a more resilient energy landscape. These efforts not only reduce dependency on imports but also position India as a leader in sustainable energy solutions.

Driving Innovation in Energy

India's energy transition is fueled by cutting-edge innovations in technology, financing mechanisms, and policy frameworks, aimed at creating a sustainable and self-reliant energy ecosystem.

Investments in smart grid technologies are transforming energy distribution and management, allowing for better integration of renewable energy sources. These grids optimize energy usage by enabling real-time monitoring, demand response, and efficient load balancing. The use of advanced digital systems ensures minimal energy wastage and enhances grid stability, especially in regions with high renewable penetration.

The rapid growth of electric mobility marks another milestone in India's energy innovation journey. Supported by the *Faster Adoption and Manufacturing of Hybrid and Electric Vehicles (FAME)* scheme, the adoption of electric vehicles (EVs) is reducing reliance on fossil fuels in the transportation sector. Efforts are being intensified to build EV charging infrastructure across urban and rural areas, ensuring accessibility and convenience for EV users. Concurrently, India is promoting domestic production of EV batteries, with a focus on advanced battery technologies, to secure supply chains and drive down costs.

Public-private partnerships (PPPs) have emerged as a cornerstone of India's energy transformation. Collaboration between government agencies and private enterprises is unlocking substantial investments for renewable energy projects, grid infrastructure, and innovative energy solutions. These partnerships not only accelerate project implementation but also foster technological innovation and resource efficiency.

India's leadership on the global stage is exemplified by its role in initiatives like the *International Solar Alliance (ISA)*, co-founded by India to promote solar energy adoption worldwide. The ISA facilitates knowledge sharing, financial collaboration, and policy support, bringing together nations to address common challenges in renewable energy deployment.

By embracing innovation in energy management, electric mobility, and global partnerships, India is accelerating its transition to a cleaner, more resilient energy future. These efforts underscore the nation's commitment to sustainability while positioning it as a global leader in the fight against climate change.

Future Roadmap

India's path toward a sustainable energy future requires a multifaceted strategy that ensures both energy security and environmental responsibility. The following priorities are crucial for achieving these goals:

India must remain steadfast in its pursuit of the ambitious target of 500 GW non-fossil fuel capacity by 2030. Achieving this will require a balanced expansion of solar, wind, and hydropower projects. Large-scale solar parks, offshore wind farms, and small hydro systems will play pivotal roles in diversifying renewable energy sources while meeting growing energy demands.

Diversifying the energy mix is another essential step. India should increase its reliance on biofuels, green hydrogen, and nuclear energy, reducing the risks of over-dependence on a single energy source. Green hydrogen, in particular, offers transformative potential for decarbonizing heavy industries and transportation, positioning India as a leader in clean energy innovation.

Investments in research and development (R&D) will drive the next wave of energy advancements. Focused efforts in developing advanced energy storage technologies, smart grid systems, and efficient renewable energy solutions are critical to maintaining India's competitive edge in the global energy landscape.

Strengthening domestic supply chains for critical minerals such as lithium and cobalt is imperative to support the rapidly growing battery and electric vehicle industries. Building partnerships with mineral-rich nations, alongside establishing robust recycling systems for these resources, will ensure sustainable supply chains.

Empowering rural areas through access to clean, affordable energy is vital for equitable development. Expanding decentralized renewable energy systems, such as solar mini-grids and biogas plants, will not only improve quality of life but also drive rural economic growth and sustainability.

India's energy transition reflects its deep commitment to sustainability, self-reliance, and global climate leadership. By expanding renewable energy capacities, reducing dependence on fossil fuels, and fostering technological innovation, India is paving the way for a resilient energy future.

Through visionary policies, international collaborations, and a focus on inclusivity, India is poised to lead the global energy revolution, securing long-term economic growth while safeguarding environmental sustainability for future generations.

Manufacturing: Building a Self-Reliant Industrial Base

A strong manufacturing sector is the cornerstone of a nation's economic resilience. For India, this sector is vital not only for generating **employment opportunities** but also for reducing **dependence on imports**, enhancing **self-reliance**, and positioning itself as a **global manufacturing hub**. With initiatives like **Make in India**, supported by targeted policies and reforms, India is transforming its industrial base to compete on the world stage.

Strengthening Domestic Manufacturing

India's focus on domestic manufacturing is a strategic move to drive innovation, build industrial capabilities, and attract significant global investments, fostering self-reliance and economic growth.

The **Production-Linked Incentive (PLI) Schemes**, introduced in 2020, are at the heart of this transformation. By offering financial incentives to companies meeting production targets, these schemes have revitalized critical sectors such as electronics, automotive, pharmaceuticals, semiconductors, and renewable energy.

In the electronics sector, global giants like Apple, Samsung, and Xiaomi have significantly expanded their manufacturing operations in India, reducing reliance on imports and establishing India as a hub for consumer electronics production. Similarly, the pharmaceutical industry is leveraging its strength in generic drug production to enhance capabilities in active pharmaceutical ingredients (APIs) and medical devices, reinforcing India's reputation as the "pharmacy of the world."

These initiatives have positioned India as an attractive destination for foreign direct investment (FDI), encouraging multinational corporations to set up production units that cater not only to domestic needs but also to export markets.

India's push toward **defense manufacturing** underscores its ambition for strategic autonomy and reduced dependency on imports. Indigenous projects, such as the Light Combat Aircraft (LCA) Tejas, the Advanced Towed Artillery Gun System (ATAGS), and the Arjun Main Battle Tank, demonstrate India's ability to produce advanced defense equipment domestically.

Collaborations with global defense firms have also played a critical role in enhancing capabilities. Through offset policies, partnerships like those with Lockheed Martin, which manufactures components for the C-130J Super Hercules in India, ensure technology transfer and co-production, boosting local expertise and innovation.

The growth of the defense manufacturing sector not only strengthens India's security but also generates employment and fosters technological advancements. By focusing on domestic manufacturing, India is building a resilient industrial ecosystem that aligns with its vision of self-reliance and global competitiveness.

Integrating Technology in Manufacturing

The modernization of India's manufacturing sector through advanced technologies is pivotal for enhancing efficiency, reducing costs, and ensuring competitiveness in global markets.

Industry 4.0 is at the forefront of this transformation, with technologies such as the Internet of Things (IoT), robotics, artificial intelligence (AI), and 3D printing reshaping the manufacturing landscape. Smart factories are revolutionizing industries like automotive, aerospace, and consumer electronics by automating production lines to enhance productivity and minimize human error. AI-driven quality control systems provide real-time monitoring of manufacturing processes, improving product standards and significantly reducing waste.

Additive manufacturing, particularly 3D printing, is creating new opportunities in sectors like aerospace and healthcare by enabling rapid prototyping and reducing production costs. This innovation allows Indian manufacturers to efficiently produce high-value goods, securing their place in competitive global markets.

India is also prioritizing the **strengthening of supply chains**, especially for critical components like semiconductors and rare earth elements, which are essential for industries such as electronics, renewable energy, and defense. Collaborations with nations like Japan, Taiwan, and South Korea are laying the groundwork for the development of localized supply chains for high-tech industries.

For instance, the **India Semiconductor Mission** aims to establish domestic semiconductor fabrication units, reducing reliance on imports from China and Taiwan. These efforts are not only enhancing India's technological self-reliance but also positioning it as a key player in the global manufacturing ecosystem.

By integrating cutting-edge technologies and securing resilient supply chains, India is building a manufacturing sector capable of meeting the demands of a rapidly evolving global economy. This strategic modernization ensures that India remains competitive while fostering innovation and sustainable growth.

Global Competitiveness

India is pursuing targeted strategies to position itself as a global manufacturing hub, focusing on enhancing export potential and creating a business-friendly environment.

Export Promotion efforts are concentrated on high-value sectors poised for global demand. The textiles industry is leveraging India's traditional strengths while integrating modern techniques to cater to international fashion brands. In engineering goods, India is advancing the production of high-precision components for automotive and aerospace applications, aligning with global standards. Meanwhile, the chemicals and pharmaceuticals sector is expanding its footprint in specialty chemicals and active pharmaceutical ingredients (APIs), capitalizing on the growing demand for reliable and high-quality supplies.

India's trade agreements with regions like ASEAN, the European Union, and Africa are opening new avenues for its manufacturers, reducing trade barriers, and enhancing market access. These partnerships are enabling Indian exporters to diversify and strengthen their global presence.

The **Ease of Doing Business** has seen significant improvements under initiatives like Make in India and Startup India. Simplification of taxation through the Goods and Services Tax (GST) has streamlined compliance, reduced operational costs, and made India an attractive destination for investors. Reforms in labor laws have struck a balance between providing industries with operational flexibility and ensuring worker protections, fostering a more efficient industrial environment.

Additionally, regulatory processes have been streamlined, with faster approvals for infrastructure projects and simplified procedures for business setup. These reforms are encouraging both domestic entrepreneurs and foreign investors to contribute to India's manufacturing growth.

Through strategic export promotion and business-friendly reforms, India is reinforcing its global competitiveness, creating a robust foundation for sustainable industrial growth and global trade leadership.

Driving Innovation in Manufacturing

Innovation forms the backbone of India's manufacturing sector, enhancing competitiveness and enabling the production of advanced, high-value goods tailored to global markets.

Public-Private Partnerships (PPPs) are a cornerstone of this innovation drive, fostering collaboration between the government, private industry, and academic institutions. These partnerships are advancing research and development in critical areas such as aerospace, robotics, and renewable energy technologies. Centers of excellence supported by premier institutions like the

Indian Institutes of Technology (IITs) and National Institutes of Technology (NITs) are acting as hubs for cutting-edge R&D, ensuring that India stays ahead in emerging manufacturing technologies.

Skill Development is another critical enabler, with programs like Skill India and Pradhan Mantri Kaushal Vikas Yojana (PMKVY) equipping the workforce with modern manufacturing competencies. These initiatives ensure industries have access to skilled talent capable of integrating and managing advanced technologies such as robotics, IoT, and AI in their operations.

Sustainability in Manufacturing is becoming a defining feature of the sector as it aligns with global environmental goals. The adoption of energy-efficient processes, waste reduction practices, and renewable energy usage in manufacturing facilities is reducing the sector's carbon footprint. Additionally, programs encouraging the use of recycled materials and sustainable resource management are creating a greener manufacturing ecosystem.

By prioritizing innovation, skill enhancement, and sustainability, India's manufacturing sector is not only meeting domestic needs but also positioning itself as a leader in global markets, capable of delivering advanced, high-quality, and environmentally responsible products.

Future Roadmap

India's aspiration to emerge as a global manufacturing powerhouse hinges on strategic actions that foster innovation, infrastructure development, and global partnerships. To realize this vision, the following priorities must be addressed:

Expanding the **Production-Linked Incentive (PLI) Schemes** to encompass emerging sectors such as electric vehicles (EVs), medical devices, and aerospace will drive comprehensive growth in manufacturing. These sectors hold immense potential to transform India's industrial landscape and position it as a key player in cutting-edge global industries.

Investing in **world-class infrastructure** is critical to supporting large-scale manufacturing and export operations. Developing industrial corridors, logistics hubs, and special economic zones (SEZs) equipped with state-of-the-art facilities will enhance efficiency, reduce costs, and attract foreign direct investment (FDI).

Promoting **innovation and research and development (R&D)** will play a pivotal role in advancing manufacturing technologies. Increased funding and incentives for R&D in areas like AI-driven automation, robotics, and clean technologies will ensure India remains competitive in the global manufacturing ecosystem while addressing sustainability goals.

Fostering **global partnerships** with developed nations and international organizations will provide India access to advanced technologies, investment opportunities, and diversified markets. Strengthened collaborations will enhance India's integration into global value chains and improve its export potential.

Empowering **micro, small, and medium enterprises (MSMEs)** through targeted financial support and capacity-building initiatives will ensure their participation in global supply chains. MSMEs are the backbone of India's economy, and their growth will drive employment generation and innovation at the grassroots level.

By focusing on these strategic priorities, India can transform its manufacturing sector into a globally competitive force, supporting economic growth, job creation, and technological leadership while advancing its vision of becoming a self-reliant and resilient industrial hub.

In summary, India's focus on building a **self-reliant manufacturing base** is central to its economic resilience and global aspirations. By leveraging **PLI schemes**, adopting **Industry 4.0 technologies**, and fostering innovation, India is poised to become a hub for **high-value manufacturing**.

This transformation will not only reduce dependence on imports but also create **millions of jobs**, boost exports, and reinforce India's position as a key player in the global industrial landscape. With strategic planning and sustained efforts, India's manufacturing sector can drive the nation's progress toward becoming a **$5 trillion economy** and beyond.

Conclusion

India's focused efforts to bolster its core sectors agriculture, energy, and manufacturing are crafting the framework for a resilient and self-reliant economy. These foundational sectors are vital not only to addressing the country's domestic needs but also to fulfilling its aspirations of becoming a formidable player in the global arena. By confronting systemic challenges and seizing emerging opportunities, India is positioning itself to thrive in an increasingly interconnected and competitive world.

Modernizing Agriculture for Food Security and Global Competitiveness

India's agriculture sector, historically the backbone of its economy, is undergoing a transformative shift toward modernization, digital integration, and sustainable practices. These advancements address critical concerns such as food security, resource efficiency, and climate resilience while unlocking new opportunities in international markets.

Precision farming, improved post-harvest management, and organic cultivation are driving productivity and creating high-value exports. These initiatives position India to meet the rising global demand for sustainable, premium-quality agricultural products, thereby enhancing its competitiveness in international trade.

Transitioning to Renewable Energy for Sustainable Growth

The move toward renewable energy is a cornerstone of India's strategy for achieving energy security and reducing its reliance on fossil fuel imports. Under ambitious frameworks like the National Solar Mission and the National Hydrogen Mission, India is becoming a global leader in solar power, wind energy, and green hydrogen production.

The adoption of advanced energy storage solutions and smart grid technologies is further improving the reliability and efficiency of India's energy systems, ensuring sustainable economic growth while aligning with global climate goals.

Building a Robust Manufacturing Base for Self-Reliance

India's manufacturing sector, strengthened by initiatives like **Make in India** and **Production-Linked Incentive (PLI)** schemes, is creating the foundation for economic resilience and global competitiveness. The integration of **Industry 4.0 technologies**, localized supply chains, and innovation hubs is reducing dependence on imports and fostering a dynamic industrial ecosystem.

Focused growth in high-tech industries, defense production, and export-driven manufacturing is not only attracting global investments but also solidifying India's reputation as a preferred destination for cutting-edge industries.

Enhancing Economic Stability and Strategic Autonomy

Progress in these core sectors contributes significantly to India's economic stability while reinforcing its strategic autonomy. A self-reliant economy equips India to navigate global challenges effectively, whether they stem from geopolitical tensions, market volatility, or environmental concerns.

By diversifying partnerships, strengthening domestic industries, and promoting sustainable growth, India is safeguarding its economic interests while ensuring resilience against external shocks.

Shaping India's Journey as a Global Leader

Advancements in agriculture, energy, and manufacturing are more than domestic milestones; they represent stepping stones to global influence. India's proactive leadership in addressing critical global challenges—ranging from food security and renewable energy transitions to technological innovation—underscores its emergence as a stabilizing and transformative force on the world stage.

Through the integration of sustainability, cutting-edge technology, and strategic collaboration, India is not only contributing to global progress but also reaffirming its sovereignty and self-reliance.

Looking Ahead

The chapters to come will explore how these advancements in core sectors translate into geopolitical leverage, economic might, and technological leadership. Strengthening these pillars is not just about addressing immediate priorities; it is about positioning India as a leading global power for the 21st century. Through resilience, innovation, and strategic foresight, India is poised to redefine its role in an ever-evolving global order.

12: Diversifying Global Dependencies

As India aspires to assert its autonomy in an increasingly interconnected world, **diversifying global dependencies** is a key strategy. By expanding partnerships beyond traditional power centers like the **United States** and **China**, India can strengthen its economic resilience, enhance security cooperation, and increase its influence on the global stage. Collaborating with regions like **ASEAN, Europe,** and the **Middle East**, while leveraging **regional alliances**, provides India with opportunities to balance its partnerships and reduce vulnerabilities.

Expanding Partnerships with ASEAN, Europe, and the Middle East

India's strategy to diversify its global dependencies hinges on strengthening partnerships with key regions such as **ASEAN**, **Europe**, and the **Middle East**. These regions offer a wealth of opportunities in **trade, technology, security**, and **energy cooperation**, complementing India's ambitions for economic growth and strategic autonomy.

ASEAN: Building Economic and Strategic Ties

The Association of Southeast Asian Nations (ASEAN) plays a pivotal role in India's Act East Policy, fostering deeper economic, cultural, and security ties. With its dynamic economies and geostrategic significance, ASEAN offers India vast opportunities for collaboration and regional integration.

ASEAN has become one of India's most important trading partners, with bilateral trade exceeding $110 billion in 2022. The relationship is driven by robust exchanges in goods, services, and investments, underpinned by frameworks like the India-ASEAN Free Trade Agreement (FTA), which has simplified trade processes and encouraged economic integration.

The growing focus on regional supply chains has opened doors for cooperation in high-potential sectors like electronics, pharmaceuticals, and automotive manufacturing. India's expertise in pharmaceuticals, paired with ASEAN's industrial capabilities, creates mutually beneficial opportunities for scaling production and innovation.

Digital connectivity is another emerging pillar of collaboration. Partnerships with technologically advanced ASEAN nations, such as Singapore and Malaysia, are fueling advancements in fintech, e-commerce, and digital transformation. These initiatives not only enhance economic ties but also position India as a significant player in the region's digital economy.

On the strategic front, ASEAN is crucial for counterbalancing China's growing influence in the Indo-Pacific, particularly in the contested South China Sea. India's defense and security partnerships with ASEAN members like Vietnam, Indonesia, and the Philippines have deepened through joint naval exercises, defense technology transfers, and capacity-building programs.

Initiatives such as the Information Fusion Centre-Indian Ocean Region (IFC-IOR) enhance maritime domain awareness and foster greater cooperation in ensuring freedom of navigation. These collaborations reflect India's commitment to regional stability and its role as a responsible security partner.

By engaging with ASEAN, India underscores its vision for a free, open, and inclusive Indo-Pacific. This partnership not only strengthens India's regional presence but also highlights its proactive approach to fostering shared prosperity and security in Southeast Asia.

Through a combination of economic collaboration, digital innovation, and strategic alignment, India's engagement with ASEAN reinforces its role as a trusted partner in regional development and security. This relationship is integral to India's aspirations for greater influence in the Indo-Pacific and beyond.

Europe: A Trusted Partner in Technology and Sustainability

Europe stands as a critical partner for India in tackling global challenges, including climate change, technological innovation, and geopolitical stability. Anchored by shared democratic values and a commitment to multilateralism, the India-Europe relationship is characterized by collaboration in key areas that align with their mutual aspirations for progress and sustainability.

India's engagement with European nations, including Germany, France, and the UK, centers on research and development in transformative technologies such as artificial intelligence (AI), robotics, quantum computing, and green innovations. These partnerships are driving advancements in critical areas that are shaping the future of global economies and societies.

The India-EU Connectivity Partnership is a cornerstone of this collaboration, aiming to enhance digital infrastructure through initiatives that support smart cities, 5G networks, and cybersecurity. This digital integration not only fosters innovation but also strengthens economic and technological ties between the two regions.

Europe is a major source of foreign direct investment (FDI) for India, contributing significantly to sectors such as renewable energy, pharmaceuticals, and automotive manufacturing. European investments are helping India scale its industrial capabilities and adopt sustainable practices that align with global standards.

Ongoing negotiations for an India-EU Free Trade Agreement (FTA) are poised to reduce trade barriers, expand market access, and unlock opportunities for high-value exports, including textiles, machinery, and chemicals. Partnerships with nations like Sweden and Denmark further emphasize innovation in sustainable solutions, including renewable energy and circular economy initiatives, reflecting a shared commitment to environmental responsibility.

European countries, particularly France, play a pivotal role in enhancing India's defense capabilities. The acquisition of advanced equipment, such as the Rafale fighter jets, and collaborations in naval and aerospace systems underscore the depth of this partnership.

Joint military exercises with European allies foster operational synergy and enhance India's readiness to address regional and global security challenges.

THE TRIANGULAR DYNAMICS

These collaborations highlight Europe's role as a reliable defense partner for India, contributing to regional stability and global peace efforts.

The India-Europe partnership is not merely transactional but deeply strategic, focusing on building sustainable economies, advancing technological innovation, and promoting shared democratic values. As both regions navigate the complexities of a rapidly changing world, their collaboration continues to evolve, addressing pressing global challenges while unlocking new opportunities for growth and progress.

This partnership reinforces India's position as a key player on the global stage, leveraging Europe's technological expertise and sustainable practices to achieve shared goals for a resilient and prosperous future.

Middle East: Strengthening Energy and Cultural Ties

The Middle East remains a cornerstone of India's foreign policy, playing a vital role in ensuring energy security, fostering trade and investment, and deepening cultural and strategic bonds. With a diaspora of over 8 million Indians contributing to the region's economy and bilateral relations, this partnership is both economically significant and culturally enriching.

The Gulf Cooperation Council (GCC) countries, including Saudi Arabia, the UAE, and Qatar, are indispensable to meeting India's energy needs, supplying the majority of its crude oil and natural gas. This energy partnership underpins India's economic stability and industrial growth.

Beyond fossil fuels, India and the Middle East are forging collaborations in renewable energy. Joint initiatives in solar power, green hydrogen, and energy storage technologies signal a shift toward sustainable energy practices, aligning with global climate goals and enhancing energy resilience for both regions.

The Middle East is a crucial trade partner for India, with the UAE alone accounting for bilateral trade exceeding $85 billion annually. The signing of the India-UAE Comprehensive Economic Partnership Agreement (CEPA) in 2022 has streamlined trade in goods and services, boosting sectors such as infrastructure, logistics, and healthcare.

Investment from sovereign wealth funds, such as the Abu Dhabi Investment Authority (ADIA), has been instrumental in financing India's infrastructure projects, startups, and renewable energy ventures. These investments not only strengthen economic ties but also accelerate India's development goals.

The Indian diaspora in the Middle East plays a pivotal role in fostering people-to-people connections and driving economic contributions. Remittances from this diaspora exceed $40 billion annually, supporting millions of families in India and adding to the region's economic vitality.

Strategically, India has bolstered its engagement with the Middle East through agreements in security, counterterrorism, and cybersecurity. These collaborations ensure regional stability while addressing shared concerns such as extremism and cyber threats.

India's relationship with the Middle East is evolving beyond traditional energy dependence to encompass trade diversification, strategic cooperation, and cultural enrichment. This multifaceted partnership reflects India's commitment to a mutually beneficial relationship that supports economic growth, energy transition, and regional security.

As these ties deepen, the Middle East continues to serve as a bridge between India's domestic priorities and its aspirations on the global stage, reinforcing its role as a key partner in India's journey toward sustained growth and international influence.

Driving Innovation and Resilience Through Partnerships

India's diversified partnerships with ASEAN, Europe, and the Middle East reflect its strategic foresight in navigating an evolving global order. These relationships extend beyond economic collaboration, encompassing technology transfer, capacity-building, and contributions to regional stability.

India's partnership with Europe has been pivotal in addressing critical global challenges such as climate change and renewable energy transitions. Investments in carbon-neutral technologies and green infrastructure underscore the shared commitment to sustainability.

With ASEAN and the Middle East, India is tackling pressing issues like food security, maritime stability, and energy transitions. These collaborations ensure mutual growth, create avenues for resource-sharing, and strengthen regional frameworks for addressing shared concerns.

Strategic collaborations with ASEAN, such as the India-Myanmar-Thailand Trilateral Highway, are enhancing regional connectivity and boosting trade. These projects underline India's commitment to fostering regional integration and creating pathways for economic cooperation.

Defense partnerships with Europe and the Middle East are bolstering India's strategic autonomy. Through technology transfer, joint exercises, and co-production agreements, India is enhancing its defense capabilities while contributing to regional security frameworks.

In conclusion, India's partnerships with ASEAN, Europe, and the Middle East demonstrate a multi-faceted approach to global engagement, focusing on economic growth, technological innovation, and strategic security. By diversifying its alliances and reducing over-reliance on traditional power centers like the U.S. and China, India is building a resilient and interconnected network of relationships that supports its long-term autonomy and global aspirations.

As these partnerships evolve, India is cementing its role as a pivotal player in global trade, technology, and geopolitics. This approach not only reinforces India's position as a leading power in the 21st century but also enables it to address complex global challenges with agility, innovation, and a vision for inclusive growth.

Leveraging Regional Alliances for Trade and Security

In an era of geopolitical complexities and shifting alliances, India's strategic engagement with regional groupings such as **BRICS**, the **Shanghai Cooperation Organisation (SCO)**, and the **Quadrilateral Security Dialogue (Quad)** has become vital for enhancing trade, security, and its global standing. These alliances enable India to collaborate on diverse issues, from **economic development** and **infrastructure funding** to **counterterrorism** and **supply chain resilience**, while balancing the influence of major powers like China.

SANDEEP CHAVAN

BRICS and the Shanghai Cooperation Organisation (SCO)

BRICS has emerged as a significant platform for fostering South-South cooperation, uniting Brazil, Russia, India, China, and South Africa—countries that collectively represent around 40% of the global population and over 25% of global GDP. India's active participation in BRICS has unlocked access to development finance, expanded trade opportunities, and facilitated technology transfers among member nations.

The New Development Bank (NDB), established under BRICS, serves as an alternative funding source for large-scale infrastructure projects, reducing dependency on Western-led institutions like the World Bank and IMF. This aligns with India's vision of promoting a multipolar financial order. Additionally, India has championed initiatives within BRICS to encourage trade in local currencies, thereby reducing reliance on the U.S. dollar and strengthening economic sovereignty.

Technological collaboration within BRICS has also proven valuable, providing India with opportunities for joint research and innovation in cutting-edge fields like artificial intelligence, space technology, and renewable energy. These efforts support India's broader goals of technological self-reliance and sustainable growth.

India's engagement with the Shanghai Cooperation Organisation (SCO) underscores its strategic focus on Central Asia, addressing critical issues like counterterrorism, regional stability, and economic connectivity. The SCO serves as a vital platform for India to maintain balanced relationships with major powers like China and Russia while fostering ties with smaller Central Asian states.

Through the SCO Regional Anti-Terrorist Structure (RATS), India has bolstered its efforts to combat cross-border terrorism and extremism, especially in light of the evolving security dynamics in Afghanistan. The SCO's emphasis on fostering regional stability aligns with India's strategic interests in maintaining a secure and cooperative neighborhood.

The SCO's promotion of regional connectivity projects, including international transport corridors, complements India's efforts to improve trade access to landlocked Central Asia and Europe. Initiatives like the development

THE TRIANGULAR DYNAMICS

of the Chabahar Port in Iran align with the SCO's connectivity goals, positioning India as a crucial trade link between South Asia and Central Asia.

By actively participating in both BRICS and the SCO, India is leveraging these platforms to advance its economic, technological, and strategic objectives. These engagements not only enhance India's role in regional development but also underscore its commitment to fostering a balanced and multipolar global order.

Quad and Indo-Pacific Cooperation

The Quadrilateral Security Dialogue (Quad), comprising India, the U.S., Japan, and Australia, has become a cornerstone of India's Indo-Pacific strategy. Initially a loose security arrangement, the Quad has transformed into a comprehensive framework addressing critical areas such as maritime security, infrastructure development, and technological collaboration.

In maritime security, India's participation in joint naval exercises like the Malabar Exercise underscores its commitment to ensuring freedom of navigation and countering China's assertive behavior in strategic waterways, including the South China Sea and the Indian Ocean. India's investments in enhancing its naval capabilities—such as aircraft carriers and advanced submarines—complement the Quad's collective efforts to promote regional stability.

India is also a key partner in the Quad's initiative to develop critical infrastructure across the Indo-Pacific. By focusing on sustainable and inclusive development, the Quad offers alternatives to China's Belt and Road Initiative (BRI). India's expertise in digital connectivity and smart city projects aligns seamlessly with these priorities, reinforcing the Quad's vision of a resilient and equitable regional development framework.

The Supply Chain Resilience Initiative (SCRI), a vital component of the Quad's agenda, seeks to diversify and secure global supply chains by reducing dependence on China for essential goods. India plays a pivotal role in this initiative through its Production-Linked Incentive (PLI) schemes, which target key sectors like electronics, automotive, and solar energy. These efforts position India as a reliable partner in global supply chains, particularly in critical areas like semiconductors, pharmaceuticals, and rare earth elements.

On the technology front, the Quad fosters collaboration in emerging fields such as 5G, artificial intelligence (AI), and quantum computing. India's active engagement in these initiatives strengthens its domestic innovation ecosystem while contributing to the region's technological leadership. This partnership ensures that technological advancements in the Indo-Pacific are shaped by democratic values and transparency.

India's engagement with the Quad, alongside its participation in other alliances like BRICS and the SCO, highlights its adeptness at balancing diverse relationships to address domestic and regional priorities.

Through the Quad, India counterbalances China's assertiveness in the Indo-Pacific while leveraging platforms like BRICS and SCO to collaborate on shared interests. This dual approach allows India to maintain strategic autonomy while addressing critical economic and security concerns.

By participating in regional alliances, India fosters economic resilience through expanded trade, investment, and technology transfer opportunities. This diversification reduces dependency on traditional partners and opens new pathways for growth.

India's multi-alignment approach ensures that it retains the flexibility to pursue its national interests without being constrained by the dynamics of any single bloc or power. In the evolving geopolitical landscape, this strategy strengthens India's position as a stabilizing and influential force, both regionally and globally.

Future Directions

To fully leverage the potential of its regional alliances, India must adopt a strategic and forward-looking approach:

Accelerating infrastructure projects like the India-Myanmar-Thailand Trilateral Highway and the Chabahar Port is crucial for integrating with regional supply chains and trade networks. These initiatives will not only boost economic ties with Southeast and Central Asia but also position India as a critical transit hub in the region.

India should expand its R&D partnerships within frameworks like BRICS and the Quad to advance capabilities in critical areas such as clean energy, digital infrastructure, and defense technologies. Strengthened technological collaboration will bolster innovation and drive economic growth.

By focusing on development initiatives in neighboring regions, including South Asia and Central Asia, India can foster stability and shared prosperity. Investments in these regions will enhance economic integration and reinforce India's leadership as a partner for sustainable development.

Strengthening naval capacities and partnerships under the Quad framework is vital for maintaining a strategic edge in the Indo-Pacific. Enhanced maritime capabilities will ensure the security of critical trade routes and counterbalance regional challenges.

India's active engagement with alliances like BRICS, SCO, and the Quad reflects its ability to collaborate with diverse partners while pursuing its economic and security priorities. These alliances provide India with a robust platform to enhance trade opportunities, deepen technological cooperation, and reinforce its strategic autonomy.

By effectively leveraging these partnerships, India is solidifying its position as a stabilizing force in the global order and an influential player in the multipolar world of the 21st century. This strategic approach ensures that India remains prepared to navigate the challenges of a rapidly evolving geopolitical landscape while contributing to regional and global stability.

Reducing Reliance on Both the U.S. and China

India's engagement with the **United States** and **China** is pivotal to its economic and strategic goals, but overreliance on either nation can expose India to vulnerabilities. A diversified approach to partnerships, combined with a focus on domestic capacity-building, is essential to maintaining **strategic autonomy** in a rapidly evolving global landscape.

Minimizing Economic Dependencies

Economic dependencies, particularly in trade and technology, pose risks to India's resilience. Mitigating these vulnerabilities involves bolstering domestic production and diversifying trade relationships to reduce reliance on a limited number of partners.

India's trade deficit with China remains a significant concern, driven by substantial imports of electronics, machinery, and pharmaceuticals. To address this, India is prioritizing domestic production through initiatives like **Atmanirbhar Bharat** and **Production-Linked Incentive (PLI)** schemes. These programs incentivize manufacturing in critical sectors, including semiconductors, electronics, pharmaceuticals, and automotive components. By fostering local innovation and scaling up domestic capabilities, India is gradually reducing its reliance on Chinese supply chains and enhancing its industrial self-reliance.

In the technology sector, India is focusing on localization by investing in indigenous R&D and forging partnerships with non-Chinese entities. For instance, efforts to develop domestic capabilities in 5G infrastructure, solar panels, and rare earth element processing are creating a more resilient tech ecosystem.

Expanding trade relationships with ASEAN, the European Union (EU), and Africa is a key pillar of India's strategy to minimize economic dependency. By targeting these regions, India is diversifying its export portfolio and reducing overreliance on traditional markets like the U.S. High-value goods such as IT services, textiles, and pharmaceuticals are increasingly finding markets in these regions, supported by trade agreements like the India-EU Free Trade Agreement (FTA) and the Africa-India Framework for Cooperation.

Shifting focus from raw material exports to value-added products, such as processed foods, specialty chemicals, and engineering goods, is further enhancing India's global competitiveness. These efforts not only increase export revenues but also create a more robust manufacturing ecosystem capable of meeting international demand.

In Summary, India's proactive approach to minimizing economic dependencies underscores its commitment to building a resilient economy. By reducing trade deficits, localizing technology, and diversifying export markets, India is laying the groundwork for sustainable growth and greater economic sovereignty. These measures ensure that India can navigate global economic uncertainties while securing its long-term interests.

THE TRIANGULAR DYNAMICS

Balancing Strategic Engagements

India's diplomatic and strategic approach requires a delicate equilibrium between leveraging partnerships and preserving autonomy, especially in its engagements with global powers like the U.S. and China.

India's strategy is rooted in maintaining equidistance between the two superpowers, allowing it to collaborate where interests align while safeguarding its national priorities.

India's partnership with the U.S. spans critical areas such as defense, technology, and counterterrorism. These collaborations address pressing security concerns, particularly in the Indo-Pacific region, where China's growing assertiveness poses challenges to regional stability.

Joint initiatives like the **Quad alliance** and the **Indo-Pacific Economic Framework (IPEF)** highlight India's active role in shaping a free, open, and inclusive Indo-Pacific. These frameworks not only enhance maritime security but also foster economic and technological cooperation, reinforcing India's strategic position in the region.

Despite enduring border tensions and strategic rivalry, India continues to engage with China through multilateral platforms such as **BRICS** and the **Shanghai Cooperation Organisation (SCO)**. These forums provide opportunities to collaborate on shared challenges like climate change, global trade dynamics, and regional connectivity.

By maintaining constructive dialogue through these channels, India ensures it can address broader regional issues without compromising its sovereignty or national interests.

India's neutral stance on contentious global issues, such as the Russia-Ukraine conflict, exemplifies its commitment to strategic autonomy. By avoiding alignment with either bloc in great power rivalries, India retains the flexibility to pursue its economic and security interests on its own terms.

In Summary, India's balanced approach to strategic engagements underscores its ability to navigate complex geopolitical landscapes. Through pragmatic partnerships with the U.S. and constructive engagement with China, India reinforces its position as an independent yet influential global player. This strategy not only enhances India's role in fostering regional stability but also ensures its autonomy in shaping its long-term interests.

Building Alternative Alliances

Expanding relationships with emerging and middle powers is a cornerstone of India's strategy to diversify partnerships, reduce dependency on major powers like the U.S. and China, and strengthen its global presence.

Partnerships with Japan, South Korea, and Australia

Collaborations with key regional players such as Japan, South Korea, and Australia highlight India's commitment to fostering mutually beneficial alliances:

Technology and Infrastructure: Partnerships with Japan, including the Mumbai-Ahmedabad Bullet Train project, reflect a shared vision for advanced infrastructure and economic collaboration. Similarly, South Korea's investments in India's electronics and steel sectors underscore the potential of industrial synergies.

Renewable Energy and Resources: Australia's contributions to India's renewable energy goals, alongside robust trade in natural resources, reinforce India's energy security and economic ties.

Defense Cooperation: Joint efforts within the Quad framework and bilateral agreements with these nations enhance India's defense capabilities and its strategic position in the Indo-Pacific, promoting a secure and stable regional environment.

Strengthening Ties with Africa and Latin America

India's outreach to Africa and Latin America reflects its intention to build meaningful partnerships beyond traditional allies:

Economic Engagement: In Africa, India is focusing on trade and investment in sectors such as agriculture, pharmaceuticals, and infrastructure. These collaborations not only enhance economic ties but also support development in African nations.

In Latin America, growing partnerships in oil, gas, and mining provide India with access to critical resources, strengthening its energy security and diversifying its import sources.

Development Diplomacy: Initiatives such as the **India-Africa Forum Summit (IAFS)** and collaborative efforts in healthcare and capacity-building highlight India's role as a trusted development partner. By sharing expertise and resources, India fosters goodwill and mutual growth in these regions.

THE TRIANGULAR DYNAMICS

In Summary, India's strategy to build alternative alliances with middle powers and emerging economies aligns with its vision of a multipolar world. These partnerships not only reduce reliance on the U.S. and China but also create new avenues for economic growth, energy security, and regional stability. Through a combination of technological collaboration, economic engagement, and development diplomacy, India is forging a resilient network of alliances that bolsters its global influence and strategic autonomy.

Key Strategies for Reducing Reliance

To reduce reliance on dominant powers and achieve greater economic and strategic independence, India is pursuing a multifaceted approach that emphasizes self-reliance, diversified partnerships, and regional integration. Central to this effort is the strengthening of domestic capabilities in critical sectors. By investing in areas such as electronics, semiconductors, pharmaceuticals, and defense manufacturing, India aims to diminish import dependencies and build resilience in its industrial and technological base. Encouraging indigenous research and development while incentivizing private sector participation in high-tech industries is further accelerating this transformation.

Simultaneously, India is expanding its engagement in multilateral platforms to foster diversified alliances. Active participation in trade and security forums not only opens up new avenues for collaboration but also reduces the risks associated with over-reliance on bilateral partnerships. This approach enables India to leverage global networks while maintaining its strategic autonomy.

Regional trade integration is another key strategy. Accelerating initiatives such as the India-Myanmar-Thailand Trilateral Highway and deepening economic ties with ASEAN and African nations are helping India broaden its trade networks. These efforts are creating new market opportunities and enhancing connectivity across regions, strengthening India's role as a hub for trade and investment.

India is also leveraging its soft power to build trust and influence globally. Through cultural diplomacy, a strong diaspora presence, and active leadership in global forums like the G20 and the United Nations, India is positioning itself as a responsible and inclusive global player. These efforts not only enhance its standing but also solidify relationships with a diverse range of partners, ensuring a robust foundation for sustainable growth and resilience in an interconnected world.

In summary, Reducing reliance on both the U.S. and China is a vital component of India's strategy to ensure **economic resilience** and **strategic autonomy**. By diversifying partnerships, building domestic capabilities, and engaging with alternative allies, India is creating a balanced approach to navigating the complexities of a multipolar world.

This strategic rebalancing not only strengthens India's position as an independent global player but also reinforces its ability to chart its course in an increasingly competitive and interconnected world.

Conclusion

India's strategy to diversify global dependencies reflects not only a response to the challenges of an interconnected world but also a proactive commitment to resilience and strategic autonomy. As it positions itself as a key player in the evolving global order, India is leveraging partnerships and alliances to reduce vulnerabilities, foster growth, and enhance its influence on the international stage.

By expanding economic and strategic engagements with regions like ASEAN, Europe, and the Middle East, India is building a broad and resilient network of partnerships. ASEAN offers opportunities for trade, digital connectivity, and security cooperation, aligning seamlessly with India's Act East Policy and strengthening its influence in the Indo-Pacific. Europe serves as a reliable partner in areas such as technology, sustainability, and defense, enabling collaboration on critical issues like climate change and innovation. The Middle East, with its energy resources and strategic significance, not only bolsters India's energy security but also deepens cultural and economic ties through its extensive diaspora. These diverse partnerships collectively enhance India's ability to navigate global uncertainties, reduce reliance on traditional power centers, and improve its competitiveness on the world stage.

India's active involvement in regional alliances such as BRICS, the Shanghai Cooperation Organisation (SCO), and the Quad exemplifies its

THE TRIANGULAR DYNAMICS

diplomatic dexterity in balancing relationships with varied partners. Platforms like BRICS and SCO allow India to maintain constructive engagements with major powers like China and Russia while addressing shared concerns such as economic integration and counterterrorism. Meanwhile, the Quad strengthens India's role in ensuring maritime security and promoting a rules-based order in the Indo-Pacific, countering unilateral assertiveness in the region. These alliances not only bolster regional stability but also amplify India's voice in shaping global governance on issues ranging from security to technology.

In reducing overdependence on the United States and China, India's approach emphasizes strategic autonomy and economic resilience. Initiatives like Atmanirbhar Bharat and the Production-Linked Incentive (PLI) schemes are fostering domestic manufacturing capabilities in critical sectors such as semiconductors, electronics, and pharmaceuticals. Simultaneously, diversifying export markets toward Africa, ASEAN, and Europe mitigates risks associated with concentrated dependencies while unlocking new growth opportunities. This balanced engagement allows India to collaborate with both superpowers on its own terms, steering clear of entanglement in their rivalries and prioritizing its national interests.

India's diversified partnerships and strategic rebalancing are underpinned by a reaffirmation of its sovereignty and global leadership aspirations. Aligning with nations that share common goals and strengthening ties with emerging and middle powers, India is asserting itself as a stabilizing force in a multipolar world. Its leadership in addressing global challenges such as climate change, sustainable development, and digital transformation underscores its commitment to creating an equitable and inclusive world order. By maintaining independence while building coalitions, India is playing the role of a bridge between developed and developing nations, championing democratic and inclusive solutions to global problems.

This strategy of diversification lays the foundation for India's journey toward becoming a leading global power. By investing in strategic autonomy, strengthening domestic capacities, and forging resilient alliances, India is positioning itself to navigate the complexities of the 21st century. Beyond economic and strategic ambitions, this journey is about asserting a vision for a just, sustainable, and equitable future. India's ability to adapt, innovate, and collaborate will be central to its success, cementing its role as a transformative force in a rapidly shifting global order.

As India continues on this path, its ambitious yet achievable goals will redefine its place in the world. By embracing opportunities and responsibilities alike, India is set to emerge as a dominant and stabilizing presence in the new global landscape, exemplifying the values of resilience, innovation, and leadership.

Part VI: India in 2030 and Beyond

13: India's Vision for 2030

India's vision for **2030** is an ambitious yet achievable roadmap aimed at achieving **sustainable and inclusive growth**, positioning itself as a **global leader in technology, trade, and diplomacy**, and ensuring a balance between **external dependencies** and **domestic self-reliance**. This vision aligns with India's aspirations to become a **$10 trillion economy**, while addressing challenges like **climate change**, **geopolitical complexities**, and **rapid technological disruptions**.

The Roadmap for Sustainable and Inclusive Growth

India's vision for sustainable and inclusive growth integrates **economic prosperity**, **social equity**, and **environmental sustainability**. By focusing on empowering marginalized sectors, reducing inequalities, and addressing the challenges of climate change, India is laying the foundation for a **resilient economy** that benefits all sections of society.

Economic Growth with Social Equity

Economic growth is meaningful only when it is inclusive, fostering social progress alongside economic advancement. India's strategy emphasizes empowering the underserved and ensuring equitable access to opportunities, thereby creating a robust and inclusive society.

The role of Micro, Small, and Medium Enterprises (MSMEs) is pivotal in this endeavor. Contributing over 30% to India's GDP and serving as a significant source of employment in rural and semi-urban areas, MSMEs form the backbone of India's economy. Recognizing their importance, the

THE TRIANGULAR DYNAMICS

government has introduced targeted measures to enhance their resilience and growth. Financial assistance programs like the Emergency Credit Line Guarantee Scheme (ECLGS) ensure liquidity during economic disruptions, safeguarding livelihoods dependent on MSMEs. Additionally, efforts to digitize MSME operations through e-commerce integration and digital payment systems are enhancing their operational efficiency and market access. Initiatives like the India Export Facilitation Program are also enabling MSMEs to explore international markets, fostering innovation and competitiveness on a global scale.

Social equity is at the core of India's growth agenda, reflected in a series of inclusive social policies aimed at addressing socio-economic disparities. The Ayushman Bharat universal healthcare scheme stands out, providing coverage to over 500 million individuals and ensuring access to quality healthcare for underserved populations. Similarly, PM-Kisan offers direct income support to farmers, bolstering agricultural resilience and improving rural livelihoods. These programs, coupled with investments in education, healthcare, and rural infrastructure, are bridging the urban-rural divide and creating opportunities for all.

Enhanced rural connectivity under initiatives like the Pradhan Mantri Gram Sadak Yojana has significantly improved access to markets, healthcare, and education, transforming the economic landscape in remote areas. Furthermore, vocational training programs tailored to emerging industries are equipping rural youth with skills necessary to thrive in a dynamic job market, fostering upward mobility and economic participation.

India's approach to economic growth with social equity reflects its commitment to building a society where progress benefits all, ensuring that no one is left behind. By empowering MSMEs, investing in rural development, and implementing inclusive social policies, India is creating a foundation for sustainable growth that aligns economic aspirations with social responsibility. This balanced strategy not only strengthens the economy but also nurtures a more equitable and resilient nation.

Sustainability at the Core

Sustainability is at the heart of India's growth aspirations, emphasizing the importance of addressing global challenges like climate change, resource efficiency, and environmental resilience while pursuing economic development.

India's leadership in renewable energy exemplifies its commitment to a low-carbon future. With a target of achieving 500 GW of renewable energy capacity by 2030, India is positioning itself as a global clean energy leader. Programs like the National Solar Mission have propelled the country to become one of the world's largest producers of solar energy. Landmark projects such as the Bhadla Solar Park, among the largest solar parks globally, highlight India's capability to harness its natural resources for sustainable growth.

The Green Hydrogen Mission represents a transformative step in decarbonizing energy-intensive industries like steel and cement, ensuring their long-term sustainability while driving economic growth. This investment in green hydrogen technology not only contributes to India's climate goals but also opens avenues for technological innovation and global partnerships.

Sustainability is also being embedded in India's urban development through the Smart Cities Mission. By integrating digital technologies with green infrastructure and forward-looking urban planning, the initiative enhances quality of life while reducing environmental impact. Smart traffic management systems, energy-efficient buildings, and waste-to-energy plants are being deployed to create cities that are not only livable but also aligned with environmental goals. Projects like mass rapid transit systems further reduce carbon footprints by promoting sustainable urban mobility, improving connectivity, and enhancing accessibility.

The circular economy is another cornerstone of India's sustainability efforts, focusing on maximizing resource efficiency. Initiatives in waste management, recycling, and the reuse of materials are reducing environmental degradation while fostering job creation in the emerging green sector. These efforts underline a broader vision of aligning economic growth with ecological balance.

India's sustainability-driven approach to development demonstrates a harmonious blend of ambition and responsibility. By prioritizing renewable energy, decarbonizing critical industries, fostering smart urbanization, and promoting a circular economy, India is not only addressing pressing environmental challenges but also setting a precedent for sustainable growth in the global arena. This strategy positions the nation as a leader in crafting a resilient and environmentally conscious future.

Driving Inclusive Growth through Sustainability

India's approach to growth uniquely intertwines economic inclusivity with sustainability, creating a framework that ensures development is both equitable and environmentally conscious. This integrated strategy addresses the nation's immediate socio-economic needs while laying the foundation for long-term resilience and prosperity.

The alignment of social policies with sustainability initiatives embodies a vision of growth that combines equity and opportunity. Programs like PM-Kisan and Ayushman Bharat not only provide a crucial safety net for vulnerable populations but also create an enabling environment where individuals and businesses can flourish. These initiatives reflect a commitment to uplifting underserved communities while fostering conditions for widespread economic participation.

Harnessing renewable energy is central to India's pursuit of a green economy capable of sustaining future generations. By leveraging its abundant solar, wind, and hydro resources, India is reducing its dependence on fossil fuels and building a resilient energy framework. Investments in solar parks, wind farms, and green hydrogen technology not only address climate change but also generate jobs and drive innovation across multiple sectors.

Sustainable urban development is transforming India's cities into hubs of economic activity and innovation without compromising environmental health. Initiatives under the Smart Cities Mission integrate green infrastructure, digital technologies, and efficient urban planning, creating spaces that are both livable and future-ready. From energy-efficient buildings to mass rapid transit systems, India's urbanization efforts prioritize environmental sustainability while enhancing connectivity and quality of life.

India's model of inclusive growth through sustainability exemplifies a balanced approach to development. By aligning social equity with ecological responsibility, the nation is crafting a pathway that not only meets the demands of today but also safeguards the prosperity of tomorrow. This multi-dimensional strategy underscores India's role as a global leader in forging a sustainable and inclusive future.

Future Outlook

India's path to achieving sustainable and inclusive growth by 2030 requires a strategic focus on expanding the reach of transformative policies, fostering green investments, leveraging advanced technologies, and strengthening social equity. This vision reflects a commitment to uplifting all citizens while preserving environmental integrity.

Expanding the reach of flagship programs like Ayushman Bharat and the Emergency Credit Line Guarantee Scheme (ECLGS) will be critical to ensuring their benefits penetrate even the remotest corners of the country. Enhanced awareness campaigns and streamlined accessibility mechanisms can empower marginalized communities, making essential healthcare and financial support universally available.

Promoting green investments through public-private partnerships (PPPs) can accelerate the transition to renewable energy and the development of sustainable infrastructure. Collaborative efforts between the government and private enterprises will drive innovation, mobilize resources, and create employment opportunities in emerging green sectors, solidifying India's leadership in the global push toward sustainability.

Embracing emerging technologies like artificial intelligence (AI), the Internet of Things (IoT), and blockchain will revolutionize public services and industrial operations. These technologies have the potential to enhance transparency, efficiency, and scalability, ensuring that India's growth is both inclusive and future-ready. Digital transformation in governance, healthcare, education, and logistics will further enable equitable access to opportunities across the nation.

Strengthening social equity remains central to India's growth story. Continued investments in education, healthcare, and skill development will empower the most vulnerable sections of society, bridging gaps in opportunity and fostering resilience. Equipping individuals with modern skills and knowledge will ensure their active participation in the rapidly evolving global economy.

India's roadmap to sustainable and inclusive growth reflects a vision of a nation determined to harmonize economic prosperity with social well-being. By fostering innovation, creating equitable opportunities, and championing environmental stewardship, India is setting the stage for a future where progress uplifts every citizen and safeguards the planet. This integrated approach positions India as a beacon of balanced development in an interconnected world.

How India Can Become a Global Leader in Technology, Trade, and Diplomacy

India's path to becoming a global leader in **technology, trade, and diplomacy** is driven by its **innovative talent pool**, strategic geographical location, and **proactive government policies**. By fostering technological advancements, enhancing trade competitiveness, and asserting diplomatic leadership, India is positioning itself as a key player in the evolving global order.

Technology Leadership

India's journey toward technology leadership is underpinned by its thriving startup ecosystem, a skilled workforce, and forward-looking policies that position the nation as a global hub for cutting-edge innovation. With focused efforts in semiconductors, artificial intelligence, digital transformation, and global collaborations, India is transforming its technological landscape to address domestic needs and global challenges.

The India Semiconductor Mission (ISM) is a cornerstone of this strategy, aiming to build a robust domestic semiconductor manufacturing ecosystem. By reducing reliance on imports, ISM addresses critical requirements in sectors like electronics, defense, and automotive. Collaborative efforts with global leaders such as Japan, Taiwan, and the U.S. are enhancing India's capabilities in chip design, wafer fabrication, and advanced testing, positioning the country as a key player in the global semiconductor supply chain.

India's leadership in artificial intelligence (AI) is another critical pillar of its technological advancement. The National AI Strategy focuses on integrating AI into vital sectors like agriculture, healthcare, and education, aiming to foster economic growth while solving societal challenges. Indian IT giants, including TCS, Infosys, and Wipro, are investing heavily in machine learning, data analytics, and AI-driven solutions, ensuring India remains competitive in the global tech arena.

The transformative impact of the Digital India initiative has reshaped the nation's digital landscape. By enabling financial inclusion, advancing e-governance, and fostering smart infrastructure, the initiative has made India a global leader in digital financial solutions. Platforms like UPI (Unified Payments Interface) exemplify this success, offering seamless, real-time digital payment systems. Simultaneously, innovations in blockchain, cloud computing, and IoT are bolstering India's digital capabilities.

India's adoption of Industry 4.0 technologies is revolutionizing its manufacturing and services sectors. By integrating IoT, robotics, automation, and 3D printing, Indian industries are enhancing operational efficiency and reducing costs. Smart factories and advanced supply chain management systems are positioning India as a formidable competitor in global manufacturing, aligning with its broader economic aspirations.

The nation's dynamic startup ecosystem is central to its technology leadership, ranking as the third-largest globally. Innovations in fintech, healthtech, agritech, and cleantech are thriving, with startups like BYJU'S, Ola, Zomato, and PhonePe attracting significant global investments. Strategic collaborations with countries like Germany, France, and South Korea are fostering breakthroughs in quantum computing, renewable energy, and cybersecurity, empowering India to address emerging challenges and solidify its position in future technologies.

India's vision of technology leadership combines domestic innovation with global collaboration, ensuring it not only addresses its own developmental goals but also contributes to global progress. This holistic approach underscores India's growing role as a global innovation hub, capable of shaping the future of technology on the world stage.

Trade Competitiveness

India's trade competitiveness is central to its vision for 2030, with a focus on strengthening global trade networks, advancing value-added exports, and integrating into resilient supply chains. By aligning its policies with emerging global trends and leveraging strategic partnerships, India is poised to solidify its position as a key player in international trade.

The pursuit of Comprehensive Economic Partnership Agreements (CEPAs) with regions such as ASEAN, Europe, Africa, and Latin America is broadening India's export markets and reducing over-reliance on traditional partners like the U.S. and China. Notably, the anticipated India-EU Free Trade Agreement is set to unlock significant opportunities in sectors like pharmaceuticals, textiles, and engineering goods, amplifying India's export potential. Regional integration initiatives, including the India-Myanmar-Thailand Trilateral Highway, are further enhancing connectivity with ASEAN nations, while deepening ties with African countries in infrastructure and natural resource trade is opening new avenues for Indian businesses.

India's emphasis on value-added exports marks a strategic shift toward high-margin sectors with robust global demand. The focus on electronics, precision machinery, specialty chemicals, and pharmaceuticals reflects this intent. Initiatives like the Production-Linked Incentive (PLI) schemes are driving domestic production and innovation in these critical industries, positioning India as a competitive and reliable supplier in global markets.

Supply chain resilience is another cornerstone of India's trade strategy. Collaborative efforts under the Quad's Supply Chain Resilience Initiative (SCRI) are enabling India to diversify its trade dependencies and reduce reliance on China for critical inputs such as semiconductors and rare earth materials. These initiatives not only bolster India's integration into global supply chains but also reinforce its strategic autonomy in navigating an increasingly interconnected world.

Through these concerted efforts, India is building a robust trade ecosystem that aligns with its long-term economic aspirations. By fostering partnerships, advancing domestic capabilities, and focusing on high-value exports, India is charting a course to become a leading force in global trade by 2030.

Diplomatic Leadership

India's diplomatic strategy embodies its commitment to multilateralism, regional stability, and the promotion of a rules-based international order. By leveraging its unique position as a bridge between developed and developing nations, India is crafting a narrative of inclusive leadership and proactive global engagement.

As a leader in multilateral forums, India's active participation in platforms such as the G20, BRICS, Quad, and the Shanghai Cooperation Organisation (SCO) underscores its diplomatic clout. As the current chair of the G20, India is driving discussions on equitable global governance, with a focus on tackling climate change, advancing digital transformation, and improving public health. Through initiatives like the International Solar Alliance, India is showcasing its commitment to collaborative solutions for global challenges, while cultural diplomacy, development partnerships, and strong diaspora engagement enhance its soft power.

In its regional focus, India is playing a pivotal role in ensuring stability across South Asia and the Indo-Pacific. Defense collaborations, maritime security initiatives, and economic connectivity projects are central to this effort. India's active participation in the Quad strengthens its position as a counterbalance to unilateral assertiveness in the Indo-Pacific, safeguarding critical maritime routes and promoting regional security. Collaborative defense and maritime exercises with partners like Japan, the U.S., and Australia further bolster India's strategic presence in the region, enhancing its ability to influence and shape the regional order.

India's journey toward global leadership is driven by a multifaceted approach encompassing technological innovation, strategic trade alliances, and proactive diplomacy. In technology, India is spearheading advancements in semiconductors, artificial intelligence, and digital connectivity, addressing future challenges while capitalizing on global opportunities. On the trade front, its focus on value-added exports, supply chain resilience, and diversified partnerships is driving economic growth while reducing vulnerabilities.

Diplomatically, India's active engagement in multilateral platforms and its dedication to regional stability position it as a key player in shaping the global order. Through sustained investments in innovation, strategic trade policies, and a balanced foreign policy approach, India is steadily asserting its influence on the world stage. This integrated strategy is essential for realizing India's vision of a prosperous, resilient, and globally significant future by 2030. By harmonizing economic growth, technological progress, and diplomatic leadership, India is setting the foundation for its emergence as a central force in the evolving global landscape.

Strategies for Balancing External Dependencies with Internal Growth

To realize its **2030 vision**, India must achieve a delicate balance between **leveraging external partnerships** and **building robust internal capacities**. This dual strategy is essential for fostering **economic resilience**, ensuring **strategic autonomy**, and driving **sustainable growth** in a competitive global landscape.

Reducing Import Reliance

Reducing import reliance has become a cornerstone of India's strategy to strengthen economic resilience and minimize external vulnerabilities. By focusing on self-reliance and domestic innovation, India is addressing critical dependencies across key sectors to foster sustainable growth and strategic autonomy.

The **Atmanirbhar Bharat** initiative exemplifies this vision, prioritizing domestic manufacturing and technological advancement in areas like electronics, pharmaceuticals, defense, and energy. In the electronics sector, India is investing heavily in semiconductor manufacturing and smartphone production, with targeted support through **Production-Linked Incentive (PLI)** schemes. These efforts aim to transform India into a global hub for high-tech manufacturing, reducing reliance on imports and driving innovation.

In the pharmaceutical sector, India is boosting its **Active Pharmaceutical Ingredient (API)** production to diminish dependence on imports, particularly from China, while solidifying its status as a global leader in generics and vaccines. This approach strengthens the supply chain for critical medicines and positions India as a reliable partner in global healthcare.

The defense industry is another area of focus, with projects like the **Tejas Light Combat Aircraft** and the **Advanced Towed Artillery Gun System (ATAGS)** highlighting India's commitment to indigenizing defense production. These initiatives not only enhance national security but also foster technological development and job creation within the country.

Energy independence is central to India's transition to clean and sustainable energy sources. As the country scales up its renewable energy capacity, reducing reliance on imported solar panels and lithium-ion batteries is a top priority. Establishing domestic manufacturing facilities for these components aligns with India's renewable energy goals while creating new economic opportunities. Collaborative ventures with countries like Japan and South Korea in advanced battery technologies and the sourcing of rare earth materials further strengthen India's green energy ecosystem.

By aligning domestic manufacturing capabilities with strategic international partnerships, India is building a resilient and self-sufficient economy. These efforts not only reduce vulnerabilities but also position India as a global leader in critical industries, paving the way for long-term growth and sustainability. This approach reflects India's determination to balance economic independence with global collaboration, ensuring that it remains agile and competitive in an interconnected world.

Strengthening Domestic Capabilities

Strengthening domestic capabilities is pivotal for India's journey toward a self-reliant and resilient economy. By prioritizing innovation, workforce development, and infrastructure, India is laying the foundation for enhanced global competitiveness and robust defenses against external shocks.

Investments in **research and development (R&D)** are central to fostering innovation in high-impact areas such as biotechnology, quantum computing, artificial intelligence (AI), and renewable technologies. Establishing **centers of excellence** through collaborations between academia and industry ensures that India remains at the forefront of cutting-edge advancements. Public-private partnerships (PPPs) are driving breakthroughs in critical sectors like clean energy, healthcare technologies, and cybersecurity, positioning India as a global innovator.

Developing a future-ready workforce is equally important. Initiatives like **Skill India** are equipping the workforce with specialized training in fields such as AI, robotics, and data science, ensuring a steady talent pipeline for high-growth industries. Vocational training programs tailored for the **MSME sector** are enhancing productivity, driving employment, and strengthening small and medium-scale enterprises, which are the backbone of the Indian economy.

Infrastructure development underpins these efforts, supporting domestic manufacturing and enhancing India's integration into global supply chains. Strategic projects like the **Dedicated Freight Corridors (DFCs)** and **Bharatmala Pariyojana** are revolutionizing connectivity, reducing logistics costs, and boosting efficiency for exporters and manufacturers. Investments in digital infrastructure are also expanding access to global markets and fostering innovation across sectors.

This holistic approach to strengthening domestic capabilities is setting the stage for India to thrive in a competitive global landscape. By aligning innovation, skilled workforce development, and world-class infrastructure, India is not only enhancing its economic resilience but also reinforcing its position as a significant player on the global stage.

Strategic Partnerships

India's strategy of cultivating diversified partnerships reflects its commitment to reducing external dependencies while amplifying its influence on the global stage. This approach enhances economic resilience and positions India as a reliable and indispensable global partner.

By fostering **regional collaborations**, India is strengthening trade and investment ties with ASEAN, Africa, and Europe. These efforts open alternative markets and mitigate reliance on traditional partners such as the U.S. and China. Agreements like the **India-EU Free Trade Agreement (FTA)** and partnerships with African nations in infrastructure and technology are expanding India's economic reach, creating opportunities for sustainable growth and innovation.

Strategic alliances with nations like **Japan, South Korea, and Australia** further solidify India's position in the global arena. These partnerships focus on technology transfer, clean energy development, and security cooperation, reducing dependence on China-centric supply chains and boosting India's competitiveness in high-growth sectors.

India is also positioning itself as a vital hub for **global supply chains**, attracting multinational companies that are seeking to diversify operations. Initiatives like the **Quad's Supply Chain Resilience Initiative (SCRI)** highlight India's strategic importance in creating secure and reliable supply chain networks, particularly in critical industries such as semiconductors, pharmaceuticals, and renewable energy.

To support these efforts, India has implemented reforms to enhance the **ease of doing business**, including streamlined tax policies, reduced regulatory barriers, and targeted incentives for foreign investors. These measures not only attract global investments but also ensure that India remains competitive in a rapidly evolving global economic landscape.

By pursuing a balanced and diversified partnership strategy, India is not just reducing its external vulnerabilities but also solidifying its role as a key player in shaping the 21st-century global order. This strategic positioning underscores India's vision of being a resilient, influential, and forward-looking nation on the world stage.

Balancing growth requires a multifaceted approach that integrates innovation, economic diversification, and strategic collaborations. Promoting innovation and the adoption of emerging technologies is a cornerstone of this strategy. By offering targeted incentives and supporting government-backed research programs, India can cultivate breakthroughs in fields like artificial intelligence, renewable energy, and advanced manufacturing, positioning itself as a global leader in high-tech industries.

Shifting the focus to value-added exports is another critical step. Transitioning from raw material exports to high-value goods such as engineering products, specialty chemicals, and renewable energy technologies enhances India's competitiveness in global markets, driving sustainable economic growth while increasing export margins.

Public-private collaborations are pivotal to accelerating progress. Leveraging public-private partnerships (PPPs) can expedite infrastructure development, strengthen the manufacturing base, and scale up research and development initiatives. These partnerships combine government support with private sector efficiency, fostering innovation and delivering impactful results.

Strengthening domestic markets is equally important for achieving balanced growth. By boosting consumption and investment through measures like social welfare programs and employment generation initiatives, disposable incomes can be increased. This approach not only stimulates demand but also builds a resilient domestic economy, creating a robust foundation for sustained progress.

Together, these strategies reflect a comprehensive approach to balancing growth, ensuring that India's economic trajectory is both inclusive and sustainable in a competitive global landscape.

In summary, balancing **external dependencies** with **internal growth** is fundamental to India's strategy for achieving its **2030 vision**. By reducing import reliance, strengthening domestic capabilities, and diversifying global partnerships, India is building a resilient and self-reliant economy that can withstand external shocks and navigate global uncertainties.

This approach not only secures India's economic future but also enhances its ability to assert **strategic autonomy** in a multipolar world. Through sustained investments in **innovation, infrastructure,** and **human capital**, India is laying the groundwork for long-term growth and global leadership in the 21st century.

Conclusion

India's vision for 2030 goes beyond traditional economic expansion, aspiring to build a resilient, inclusive, and globally influential nation. Anchored in sustainability, technological leadership, trade competitiveness, and proactive diplomacy, this vision reflects a comprehensive approach to addressing domestic priorities while contributing meaningfully to global challenges.

India's focus on resilience underscores its ability to navigate economic disruptions, geopolitical shifts, and environmental challenges. Initiatives like **Atmanirbhar Bharat** and investments in renewable energy and infrastructure highlight its emphasis on strengthening domestic capacities. Programs like **Ayushman Bharat** and **PM-Kisan** ensure that the benefits of growth are equitably distributed, bridging socio-economic divides and fostering inclusive development. Sustainability remains central, with leadership in solar energy, green hydrogen, and other clean technologies positioning India as a global advocate for climate resilience.

Technological innovation, robust trade policies, and strategic diplomacy are the pillars supporting India's emergence as a global power. Investments in semiconductors, artificial intelligence, and Industry 4.0 technologies are driving innovation, with initiatives like **Digital India** transforming the nation into a global tech hub. Through value-added exports, trade diversification, and supply chain resilience, India is enhancing its competitiveness and reducing dependency on traditional partners. Diplomatically, India's active role in platforms like **G20**, **Quad**, and **BRICS** demonstrates its commitment to equitable and inclusive global governance, bridging the interests of developed and developing nations.

Achieving these goals requires a delicate balance between strengthening internal growth and leveraging external partnerships. Domestic investments in R&D, workforce upskilling, and infrastructure modernization ensure economic resilience and competitiveness. Focused efforts to reduce import dependence in critical sectors such as electronics, pharmaceuticals, and energy are pivotal for self-reliance. On the global front, partnerships with regions like ASEAN, Europe, and Africa diversify economic relationships, while strategic frameworks like the **Quad** and **Supply Chain Resilience Initiative** (SCRI) reinforce India's role in regional security and global supply chains.

India's vision extends beyond addressing national challenges; it aims to contribute to the broader global community. Leadership in renewable energy and green technologies serves as a model for sustainable development in emerging economies. Efforts to promote peace and cooperation in regions like South Asia and the Indo-Pacific reinforce India's position as a stabilizing force in global geopolitics. By addressing global challenges such as climate change, digital transformation, and public health, India demonstrates its commitment to creating an equitable international order.

To realize its 2030 vision, India must continue fostering innovation, promoting inclusivity, strengthening resilience, and engaging strategically. Enhancing investments in cutting-edge technologies, ensuring social equity through education and healthcare, building renewable energy and manufacturing capacities, and balancing global partnerships with domestic priorities are crucial for maintaining strategic autonomy while fostering interdependence.

India's roadmap envisions a nation that is economically robust, socially equitable, and environmentally sustainable. By leveraging its unique strengths and embracing diverse collaborations, India is well-positioned to assert its influence on the global stage. As it navigates the complexities of a multipolar world, its ability to balance domestic aspirations with international responsibilities will shape its trajectory toward becoming a leading global power. With visionary leadership and sustained efforts, India's vision for 2030 is not just an aspiration—it is a path toward creating a future of shared prosperity and global significance.

14: The Triangular Dynamics Redefined

As the world transitions into a **multipolar order**, India finds itself at a pivotal juncture where it can play a defining role in shaping the future of global geopolitics and economics. The **triangular dynamic** between **India, the United States, and China** is not just a framework of competition and collaboration but also a platform for India to assert its identity as a **balancer and a leader**. This chapter explores India's emerging role, offers lessons for key stakeholders, and concludes with a vision for India's future in this critical triangle.

India's Role in Shaping a New World Order

India stands at a crossroads in the shifting dynamics of the global order, leveraging its **strategic location**, **economic potential**, and **diplomatic engagement** to emerge as a **stabilizing force**. As geopolitical rivalries intensify, India's unique position enables it to play a pivotal role in fostering **regional stability**, **economic resilience**, and **global cooperation**.

A Mediator in a Fragmented World

In a world increasingly divided by geopolitical tensions, India's balanced and pragmatic approach positions it as a natural mediator capable of fostering dialogue and cooperation among rival powers.

India's engagement with both the U.S. and China exemplifies its strategic autonomy and nuanced diplomacy. Through its participation in the **Quad**, India collaborates with democratic nations to uphold a rules-based international order, safeguard maritime security, and counter unilateral actions in the Indo-Pacific. Simultaneously, India's active involvement in **BRICS** and the **Shanghai Cooperation Organisation (SCO)** underscores its ability to work with China and Russia on shared goals such as development financing, counterterrorism, and regional stability. This dual engagement highlights India's unique capacity to navigate complex global dynamics without aligning exclusively with any single bloc.

As a staunch advocate for multilateralism, India emphasizes inclusive global governance that addresses the concerns of both developed and developing nations. Initiatives like **Vaccine Maitri**, which supplied COVID-19 vaccines to over 70 countries, reflect India's commitment to equitable global progress and solidarity with the Global South. By championing initiatives that prioritize collective well-being, India is fostering trust and reinforcing its role as a responsible global actor.

In bridging divides and promoting cooperation, India not only enhances its diplomatic clout but also contributes to a more stable and equitable international order. Its ability to mediate and align diverse interests places it at the forefront of efforts to address global challenges in an increasingly fragmented world.

Leading the Global South

India's leadership on the global stage is increasingly defined by its role as a representative and advocate for developing nations. Through its active participation in platforms like the **G20** and the **United Nations Framework Convention on Climate Change (UNFCCC)**, India is addressing critical issues such as climate change, debt relief, and sustainable development. By amplifying the concerns of the Global South, India ensures that the voices of emerging economies are heard in shaping global policies and priorities.

Initiatives like the **International Solar Alliance (ISA)** demonstrate India's commitment to sustainable growth and climate action. By championing renewable energy, India is not only addressing its own energy transition but also providing a model for other developing nations to achieve low-carbon, sustainable development.

India's deepening ties with **Africa** and **Latin America** highlight its dedication to fostering global cooperation. Investments in infrastructure, agriculture, and digital connectivity in these regions showcase India's expanding global footprint and its focus on creating mutually beneficial partnerships. These efforts not only strengthen economic and cultural ties but also underscore India's commitment to equitable growth and shared prosperity across the Global South.

In championing these initiatives, India is asserting itself as a leader of developing nations, bridging the gap between emerging economies and the global order, and driving an agenda of inclusive and sustainable progress.

Economic Resilience and Global Influence

India's expanding economic strength, underpinned by its focus on self-reliance and innovation, is reshaping global supply chains and positioning the country as a hub for technological progress and sustainable growth.

As the world seeks alternatives to China-centric supply chains, India emerges as a compelling and reliable partner. The Production-Linked Incentive (PLI) schemes are transforming key sectors like electronics, pharmaceuticals, and automobiles, fostering domestic manufacturing and reducing dependency on imports.

Infrastructure modernization efforts, such as Dedicated Freight Corridors (DFCs) and advanced logistics systems, are enhancing India's connectivity and efficiency, making it an integral part of global trade networks. Strategic collaborations, such as those within the Quad's Supply Chain Resilience Initiative (SCRI), are attracting multinational companies looking for secure and stable production bases.

India's proactive approach to emerging technologies underscores its ambition to lead the next wave of global innovation. Initiatives like the India Semiconductor Mission (ISM) and investments in green hydrogen and artificial intelligence (AI) reflect a strategic focus on industries of the future. These investments are setting the stage for India to play a pivotal role in high-tech global markets.

The Digital India program and advancements in e-governance have demonstrated India's ability to scale technology-driven solutions, significantly improving access to services for millions of citizens. These efforts showcase India's capacity to blend technological innovation with societal benefits.

THE TRIANGULAR DYNAMICS

India's thriving startup ecosystem, the third-largest in the world, is driving transformative breakthroughs in sectors like fintech, healthtech, and agritech. Startups are not only addressing domestic challenges but also creating solutions that resonate globally, attracting substantial investment from international venture capital. This dynamic ecosystem is cementing India's reputation as a global hub for cutting-edge innovation and entrepreneurship.

In combining supply chain diversification, technological leadership, and a vibrant innovation ecosystem, India is building economic resilience and asserting its influence on the global stage. These strategic moves not only enhance its competitiveness but also solidify its role as a key player in shaping the future of global trade and technology.

Strengthening Regional Stability

India's geographical position and strategic alliances position it as a pivotal player in fostering peace and stability across South Asia and the Indo-Pacific. Through a combination of maritime security initiatives, connectivity projects, and regional partnerships, India is asserting its influence and counterbalancing growing geopolitical challenges.

India's Indo-Pacific strategy is focused on maintaining a free and open maritime domain. As a key member of the Quad, India actively participates in joint naval exercises such as Malabar, enhancing coordination and preparedness to safeguard critical sea lanes. Investments in maritime infrastructure, including the development of strategic ports and the modernization of naval capabilities, strengthen India's ability to counterbalance assertive actions in the region. These efforts are essential for securing the Indo-Pacific as a stable and inclusive region.

Connectivity initiatives are equally critical in enhancing India's regional influence. Projects like the India-Myanmar-Thailand Trilateral Highway and the development of the Chabahar Port serve dual purposes: boosting trade links with ASEAN and Central Asia while amplifying India's strategic reach. These ventures underscore India's commitment to fostering economic integration and regional stability.

In South Asia, India is reinforcing its leadership by addressing the region's developmental and security needs. Development aid, energy partnerships, and targeted collaborations with neighboring countries such as Nepal, Sri Lanka, and Bangladesh demonstrate India's proactive approach to counterbalancing external influences. For instance, India's cross-border energy projects, including electricity trade with Bhutan, Nepal, and Bangladesh, highlight its dedication to promoting sustainable development and mutual growth within the region.

By leveraging its strategic location and fostering collaborative initiatives, India is not only ensuring regional stability but also solidifying its role as a responsible and influential leader in South Asia and the Indo-Pacific. These efforts reflect a comprehensive approach to addressing both immediate challenges and long-term strategic goals.

A Vision for Leadership

India's vision for leadership in a new world order reflects its unique ability to balance diverse relationships, build economic resilience, and champion regional stability. Guided by strategic autonomy and a steadfast commitment to inclusive growth, India is transitioning from being a participant in global dynamics to a key architect of their evolution.

With its strategic geopolitical location, vast economic potential, and skilled diplomatic acumen, India is poised to address pressing global challenges, mediate escalating geopolitical rivalries, and drive initiatives for a more equitable and sustainable future. This pragmatic and forward-looking approach ensures that India's influence resonates not just across its region but on the global stage, shaping a world order that aligns with the principles of cooperation, stability, and shared progress.

Lessons for Policymakers, Businesses, and Citizens

India's journey toward becoming a **global power** is a collective endeavor that requires the involvement of all stakeholders—**policymakers, businesses,** and **citizens**. Each group plays a pivotal role in shaping India's ability to navigate the **triangular dynamics** involving the U.S. and China, while simultaneously strengthening its global position. Here are the key lessons and strategies for each stakeholder:

THE TRIANGULAR DYNAMICS

For Policymakers: A Strategic Path Forward

Policymakers must adopt a balanced and forward-thinking approach to ensure India's strategic autonomy while leveraging global partnerships to advance national interests. Maintaining flexibility, investing in domestic capacities, and engaging proactively in multilateral platforms are key to achieving this vision.

Balancing Engagement with Autonomy requires a pragmatic foreign policy that safeguards India's independence in global affairs. Managing the U.S.-China rivalry demands avoiding over-reliance on either power while fostering balanced relationships that serve India's economic and security objectives. India's neutral stance on complex issues like the Russia-Ukraine conflict underscores its ability to uphold autonomy while navigating the intricacies of global geopolitics.

Investing in Domestic Strengths is critical to enhancing global competitiveness and reducing external vulnerabilities. Modernizing infrastructure through initiatives like the Bharatmala Pariyojana and Dedicated Freight Corridors strengthens connectivity and reduces logistics costs, fostering seamless integration into global supply chains. Manufacturing growth, driven by Production-Linked Incentive (PLI) schemes, attracts investments in key sectors such as electronics, pharmaceuticals, and automotive, positioning India as a reliable player in global markets. Parallelly, education reforms must focus on expanding access to quality learning and aligning curricula with evolving industry needs, equipping the workforce for emerging opportunities in the knowledge-driven economy.

Proactive Multilateralism will enable India to influence global norms and build alliances aligned with its vision for sustainable and inclusive development. Engaging actively in platforms like the G20, BRICS, and the Quad reinforces India's role in shaping global conversations on climate action, digital governance, and public health. At the same time, strengthening South-South cooperation through partnerships with African and Latin American nations expands India's influence in emerging markets, fostering equitable development and mutual growth.

By aligning these priorities, India can position itself as a resilient, self-reliant, and influential force in the global arena while advancing its long-term vision for sustainable and inclusive progress.

For Businesses: A Blueprint for Growth and Resilience

Indian businesses must adopt a forward-looking approach to remain competitive and sustainable in an evolving global landscape. Embracing innovation, diversifying markets, and prioritizing sustainability are key strategies for long-term success.

To **embrace innovation**, businesses need to leverage emerging technologies like artificial intelligence (AI), IoT, robotics, and blockchain. These technologies drive efficiency, reduce costs, and enhance productivity. Digital transformation, including the automation of processes and the adoption of Industry 4.0 solutions, is essential for maintaining competitiveness in global markets. Startups in fintech, healthtech, and agritech are leading this wave of innovation, attracting global venture capital and creating solutions for both domestic and international challenges. Established businesses can collaborate with these startups to integrate cutting-edge ideas into their operations.

Diversifying markets is vital for mitigating risks associated with over-reliance on traditional trade partners like the U.S. and China. Businesses should actively explore opportunities in emerging markets such as ASEAN, Africa, and Latin America. Expanding exports to these regions not only reduces geopolitical risks but also unlocks new avenues for growth. Trade agreements like the India-EU Free Trade Agreement and partnerships in the Indo-Pacific region provide access to high-value markets, offering opportunities to expand market share and drive profitability.

Focusing on **sustainability** ensures long-term viability and aligns businesses with global trends toward a low-carbon economy. Adopting renewable energy sources like solar, wind, and green hydrogen can significantly reduce energy costs while minimizing environmental impact. Integrating circular economy practices, including recycling, waste reduction, and resource efficiency, positions businesses as leaders in sustainability and attracts environmentally conscious consumers and investors.

By integrating these strategies, Indian businesses can not only thrive in an increasingly interconnected world but also contribute to India's broader vision of becoming a global economic and technological powerhouse.

THE TRIANGULAR DYNAMICS

For Citizens: A Roadmap to Empowerment and Contribution

Citizens are central to India's progress, and their active engagement in adapting to economic changes, contributing to nation-building, and representing India on the global stage is crucial for achieving national aspirations.

To **adapt to a changing economy**, embracing lifelong learning and upskilling is essential in a technology-driven world. Programs like Skill India and initiatives focusing on AI, data analytics, and cybersecurity equip individuals with the tools to thrive in future job markets. Citizens should cultivate an entrepreneurial mindset, embracing innovation and creating new opportunities that drive economic growth and foster self-reliance.

Engaging in **nation-building** strengthens India's social fabric and aligns with its growth vision. Active participation in civic initiatives, environmental conservation, and community development enhances societal well-being. Volunteering for local projects or supporting government schemes contributes to inclusive growth. Citizens can further advance sustainability by adopting energy-efficient practices, reducing waste, and championing renewable energy solutions, creating a greener and more resilient India.

As **global ambassadors**, citizens and the Indian diaspora play a pivotal role in enhancing India's global image. Sharing Indian culture, traditions, and achievements fosters international goodwill and strengthens cultural ties. Whether through arts, cuisine, or festivals, showcasing India's heritage promotes mutual understanding and appreciation. The diaspora, in particular, contributes significantly through remittances, investments, and by fostering bilateral trade and collaborations, reinforcing India's global influence.

By adapting to economic changes, actively participating in nation-building, and representing India's values on the world stage, citizens can play a transformative role in shaping India's future as a vibrant, inclusive, and globally respected nation.

Key Takeaways

India's vision of becoming a global leader requires cohesive action from its stakeholders—policymakers, businesses, and citizens. By fostering innovation, prioritizing sustainability, and maintaining strategic autonomy, each group plays a vital role in propelling the nation forward on the global stage.

This united effort will strengthen economic resilience, enhance global competitiveness, and position India to effectively navigate the challenges of an evolving world order. As India charts its course, these guiding principles will pave the way for a future marked by prosperity, inclusivity, and leadership.

Closing Thoughts on India's Future Between Two Giants

The triangular dynamics between **India, the United States, and China** are reshaping the global geopolitical landscape. While the U.S. and China continue to dominate in terms of economic and military might, **India's rise as a stabilizing force** rooted in **strategic autonomy**, **economic resilience**, and **diplomatic finesse** underscores its growing significance. This unique positioning enables India to influence global norms, mediate tensions, and emerge as a key player in addressing pressing international challenges.

The Path Forward

India's future lies in its ability to navigate a complex global landscape while leveraging its strengths to drive domestic and international progress. This vision combines pragmatic diplomacy, strategic innovation, and inclusive development.

India's relationships with global powers demand a nuanced approach. Constructive engagement with the U.S. on defense, technology, and shared democratic values must be balanced with pragmatic collaborations with China on trade and multilateral platforms like BRICS and the Shanghai Cooperation Organisation (SCO). India's neutral stance on geopolitical conflicts, such as its approach to the Russia-Ukraine war, underscores its strategic autonomy, avoiding entanglement in power rivalries. By fostering ties with middle powers like Japan, South Korea, and Australia and expanding collaborations with regions like Africa and Latin America, India diversifies its engagements, minimizing vulnerabilities and reinforcing its sovereignty.

India's influence extends beyond its borders, with leadership in addressing critical global challenges. Initiatives like the International Solar Alliance (ISA) and the National Green Hydrogen Mission position India as a leader in renewable energy transitions, setting sustainability benchmarks for emerging economies. With its expertise in digital governance through programs like Digital India, India can shape global norms for financial inclusion and e-governance, ensuring technological advancements benefit developing nations. The Vaccine Maitri initiative, which showcased India's pharmaceutical prowess during the COVID-19 pandemic, highlights its role as a global health leader. Continued investments in healthtech and biotechnology will further solidify this position. India's focus on equitable development, particularly through partnerships with African and Latin American nations, reinforces its leadership as a voice for the Global South, advocating for economic parity and resource accessibility.

India's demographic advantage and innovation ecosystem are pivotal to its ascent. With over half of its population under the age of 30, empowering youth through education and skill development is critical. Initiatives like Skill India and STEM education programs are preparing the workforce for high-growth industries such as AI, robotics, and biotechnology. India's vibrant startup ecosystem, ranked third globally, is a driving force behind innovation and economic growth. Policies like Startup India and enhanced access to venture capital will continue to nurture this ecosystem.

Strategic investments in infrastructure are transforming India's economic landscape. Projects like the Bharatmala Pariyojana and Dedicated Freight Corridors are enhancing logistics, reducing costs, and boosting trade competitiveness. Smart city initiatives and expanded digital connectivity ensure that India remains resilient and competitive in a rapidly evolving global economy. Expanding research and development funding in renewable energy, semiconductors, and advanced manufacturing is vital for cementing India's position as a global innovation hub.

India's path forward is defined by its ability to balance power dynamics, lead on global challenges, and harness its internal strengths. Through a combination of pragmatic diplomacy, sustainable development, and strategic investments in people and innovation, India is poised to shape the 21st century as a leader in an interconnected and equitable world.

SANDEEP CHAVAN

India's Vision for the Future

India stands at a pivotal juncture, poised to influence the global order while preserving its sovereignty and the diversity of its partnerships. As the nation pursues its vision for 2030, its trajectory will be guided by principles of inclusivity, sustainability, and global responsibility. This vision reflects a deeper ambition: to be a bridge between developed and developing nations, offering solutions to shared challenges while asserting its leadership in an interconnected and competitive world.

India's role is not confined to balancing the influences of global powers; it is about creating an independent and influential space where India leads by example. By leveraging its strengths in diplomacy, economics, and innovation, India is positioned to redefine its global standing. Its actions today will leave a lasting legacy, establishing its identity as a leader in a multipolar world.

Balancing Partnerships

India's nuanced approach to diplomacy allows it to maintain strategic autonomy while fostering partnerships that advance its national interests. This balance ensures that India remains an influential voice without being drawn into the rivalries of superpowers.

India's collaboration with the United States enables advancements in technology, defense, and geopolitical stability, especially in the Indo-Pacific region. Simultaneously, its pragmatic engagement with China through trade and multilateral platforms like BRICS and the Shanghai Cooperation Organisation (SCO) underscores its ability to navigate complex relationships. Its enduring ties with Russia further demonstrate a commitment to maintaining diverse and stable partnerships. Platforms like the Quad and BRICS exemplify India's capacity to bridge ideological divides, fostering cooperation on global challenges such as climate change, public health, and digital governance.

Building Resilience

Resilience is the cornerstone of India's ability to withstand global uncertainties and emerge stronger. By focusing on self-reliance and innovation, India is preparing for a future that balances growth with sustainability.

Economic self-reliance is being driven by initiatives like Atmanirbhar Bharat, which bolster manufacturing and reduce import dependencies in critical sectors such as semiconductors, green energy, and pharmaceuticals. Technological advancements in AI, renewable energy, and quantum computing are positioning India as a leader in future industries. Its leadership in climate resilience, particularly through the International Solar Alliance and investments in green hydrogen, underscores India's commitment to environmental sustainability and long-term economic stability.

Fostering Inclusive Growth

India's vision for the future is rooted in inclusivity, ensuring that progress uplifts all segments of society. Empowering communities through initiatives like Skill India and Digital India equips youth and marginalized populations with the tools needed to thrive in a technology-driven economy. Investments in rural development, healthcare, and education aim to bridge the urban-rural divide, fostering equity and cohesion.

India's leadership extends to advocating for the Global South, championing issues like climate justice and debt relief. By aligning its domestic goals with its global responsibilities, India is redefining what it means to be a developing nation with global influence.

A Bridge, a Balancer, and a Beacon

India's approach to triangular dynamics between itself, the United States, and China is not about choosing sides. Instead, it is about creating a space where India thrives on its own terms. India is emerging as:

> - **A Bridge**: Facilitating dialogue and cooperation between developed and developing nations, India addresses shared challenges with inclusivity.

> **A Balancer**: Navigating global rivalries with pragmatism, India ensures its engagements align with its strategic goals.

> **A Beacon of Hope**: Demonstrating that sustainable development, inclusive growth, and strategic autonomy can coexist to inspire a more equitable and harmonious world.

A New Era of Global Harmony

India's commitment to innovation, diplomacy, and collaboration positions it to lead the world into a new era of progress. Its leadership model—centered on inclusivity, sustainability, and shared prosperity—offers a pathway for global governance that prioritizes humanity over hegemony.

The journey toward global leadership will not be without challenges, but India's ability to adapt, innovate, and persevere ensures its continued rise as a force for stability, equity, and peace. By fostering partnerships, harnessing its unique strengths, and staying true to its vision, India is shaping a new world order defined by cooperation and shared success.

India's moment to lead is here, and its actions will not only redefine its own future but also usher in an era of harmony and progress for all.

References

The following references have been used to provide credibility, support factual accuracy, and enhance the insights presented in this book. This comprehensive list serves as a resource for further exploration of the topics discussed.

Government and Policy Documents

1. **Ministry of External Affairs, Government of India** – Policy briefs, reports, and statements on India's foreign policy and strategic alliances.
2. **Ministry of Commerce and Industry, Government of India** – Updates on trade agreements, economic initiatives, and the Production-Linked Incentive (PLI) schemes.
3. **Ministry of Power, Government of India** – Reports on renewable energy progress and the National Green Hydrogen Mission.
4. **Digital India Program** – Official updates and publications on India's digital transformation initiatives.
5. **NITI Aayog** – Policy papers and frameworks for AI adoption, renewable energy, and sustainability goals.

International Organizations and Platforms

1. **United Nations Development Programme (UNDP)** – Data and reports on sustainable development and India's contributions.
2. **World Bank and International Monetary Fund (IMF)** – Insights

on India's economic trajectory, trade balances, and global competitiveness.
3. **International Solar Alliance (ISA)** – Publications on renewable energy initiatives and global partnerships.
4. **Quad Reports** – Joint statements and updates on Indo-Pacific strategies and supply chain resilience.

Research Papers and Journals

1. Academic journals such as *Economic and Political Weekly* and *International Studies Quarterly* for analysis on India's diplomatic strategies and economic policies.
2. Studies published in *Journal of Renewable and Sustainable Energy* for technical insights into India's clean energy transition.
3. Research on AI and digital governance from *Indian Journal of Information Technology*.

Books and Thought Leadership

1. **Kishore Mahbubani**, *The Asian 21st Century* – Contextual perspectives on Asia's role in the global order.
2. **Shashi Tharoor**, *The New World Disorder and the Indian Imperative* – Analysis of India's role in a multipolar world.
3. **Raghuram Rajan**, *The Third Pillar* – Insights into balancing state, market, and community for sustainable growth.

Industry Reports

1. **McKinsey & Company** – Reports on India's manufacturing capabilities, startup ecosystem, and global trade potential.
2. **Boston Consulting Group (BCG)** – Studies on AI, digital transformation, and renewable energy innovations in India.
3. **KPMG India** – Analysis of infrastructure modernization and industry 4.0 adoption in Indian industries.

Media Sources

1. **The Hindu** and **The Indian Express** – Coverage of India's foreign policy, trade negotiations, and economic developments.
2. **Business Standard** and **Economic Times** – Industry-specific insights on startups, manufacturing, and technology trends.
3. **Reuters** and **BBC News** – International perspectives on India's geopolitical and economic strategies.

Websites and Digital Platforms

1. **PRS Legislative Research** – Updates on Indian legislative measures and their implications.
2. **India Brand Equity Foundation (IBEF)** – Comprehensive data on India's industrial performance and trade outlook.
3. **Invest India** – Resources on investment opportunities, policies, and sector-specific growth.
4. **World Economic Forum (WEF)** – Publications on India's role in global initiatives and sustainability leadership.

Acknowledgment of Primary Sources

Efforts have been made to incorporate insights from a wide array of credible sources, ensuring that the narrative reflects both the depth and breadth of India's vision and initiatives. For direct quotes, data points, and historical references, the above sources have been invaluable.

This reference section is designed to not only support the book's arguments but also to provide readers with a roadmap for their own exploration of the themes discussed.

Acknowledgments

This book is the culmination of countless hours of research, reflection, and collaborative effort. It represents not only my vision but also the contributions, encouragement, and support of many individuals and organizations. I would like to take this opportunity to express my deepest gratitude to those who have made this work possible.

To my **family**, thank you for your unwavering love, patience, and belief in my endeavors. Your support has been my anchor, and your understanding has allowed me the freedom to dedicate myself fully to this project.

To my **friends and colleagues**, your insights, constructive feedback, and honest discussions have enriched this book. Your encouragement has been a source of inspiration during moments of doubt.

To the **students and readers** who have been my silent motivators, your curiosity and thirst for knowledge have driven me to present ideas with clarity and purpose. You are the reason I strive to make complex concepts accessible and engaging.

I am deeply indebted to the **academics, researchers, and professionals** whose work has provided the foundation for the ideas presented in this book. Your contributions to the fields of economics, technology, geopolitics, and sustainability have been instrumental in shaping my understanding.

To the **policy experts, diplomats, and thought leaders**, thank you for your guidance and for offering nuanced perspectives that have added depth to my writing. Your ability to connect global realities with India's aspirations has inspired me to think beyond the obvious.

To the **publishing team**, thank you for believing in this project and for your meticulous attention to detail. Your expertise has transformed my manuscript into a polished and meaningful work.

To the **unsung heroes of research and data analysis**, whose studies, reports, and insights have formed the backbone of this book, your efforts are greatly appreciated.

Lastly, I am grateful to the **spirit of India**—a nation of boundless possibilities, resilience, and innovation. The journey of this book is, in many ways, a reflection of India's journey, and I am honored to contribute to the narrative of its bright future.

This book is dedicated to all those who believe in the transformative power of ideas and actions. It is my hope that it will inspire and empower readers to dream big, act boldly, and contribute meaningfully to the ever-evolving global story.

With heartfelt gratitude,
Sandeep Chavan

About the Author

Sandeep Chavan is a seasoned educator, counselor, and industrial engineer with over two decades of experience in both the industry and academia. A graduate in mechanical engineering, the author has dedicated their career to bridging the gap between theoretical knowledge and practical applications, empowering individuals to navigate the complexities of the modern world.

As a prolific writer and thought leader, Sandeep Chavan has delved deeply into subjects spanning economics, technology, geopolitics, and sustainable development. Their unique ability to simplify complex concepts and present them with clarity and depth has made them a trusted voice among professionals, students, and policymakers alike.

In addition to their contributions to teaching and industrial management, the author has been actively involved in mentoring aspiring leaders, encouraging them to think critically and embrace innovative solutions for real-world challenges. Their passion for fostering a global perspective is reflected in their writing, which emphasizes the importance of collaboration, inclusivity, and resilience in shaping a better future.

This book represents the author's commitment to exploring India's role in a rapidly evolving global order. By combining rigorous research with visionary insights, Sandeep offers readers a comprehensive guide to understanding the opportunities and challenges that lie ahead.

When not writing or teaching, the author is deeply engaged in inspiring the next generation, working tirelessly to instill the values of curiosity, adaptability, and purpose in all their endeavors. Sandeep's work is a testament to their belief in the transformative power of knowledge and action to create a more equitable and harmonious world.

Don't miss out!

Visit the website below and you can sign up to receive emails whenever SANDEEP CHAVAN publishes a new book. There's no charge and no obligation.

https://books2read.com/r/B-A-EPGPC-FVXIF

BOOKS 2 READ

Connecting independent readers to independent writers.

Did you love *The Triangular Dynamics*? Then you should read *Culture, Identity & Change: The Evolution of Indian Society*[1] by SANDEEP CHAVAN!

[2]

"Culture, Identity & Change: The Evolution of Indian Society" by Sandeep Chavan, is an insightful journey through the rich history, dynamic present, and promising future of India, aimed at inspiring young Indians and global Indians alike. The book explores the profound transformations in Indian society, shaped by a unique interplay of tradition and modernity, regional diversity, and global influences. Its purpose is to deepen readers' understanding of India's social fabric, which blends ancient customs with contemporary challenges and innovations, positioning youth as the driving force for meaningful change.

The book begins by tracing India's origins, from the early civilizations that shaped social norms to the impacts of colonial rule, which redefined the country's cultural and economic landscape. By examining the social structures, family roles, and caste dynamics that continue to influence Indian society,

---

1. https://books2read.com/u/4Eva7A

2. https://books2read.com/u/4Eva7A

readers gain a comprehensive view of the factors that have historically shaped identity and relationships in India.

With a focus on current and emerging issues, the book addresses challenges like urbanization, poverty, and economic inequality, which create disparities but also provide opportunities for progress. It highlights the pivotal role of education, not just as a foundation for individual growth, but as a powerful tool for collective social transformation. The book underscores that education, coupled with critical skills, is key to empowering young Indians to bridge gaps and foster a more equitable society.

Central to this narrative is the role of youth in driving social movements, from grassroots activism to digital engagement. It delves into the rise of technology as a medium for civic participation, enabling young Indians to champion causes, express their identity, and interact with a global audience, thus building a sense of both national and global citizenship.

Looking forward, the book discusses future trends and pathways, including sustainable development, digital transformation, and social inclusivity. It emphasizes the potential of innovation to address pressing issues and to harness India's demographic dividend.

"Culture, Identity & Change: The Evolution of Indian Society" invites young Indians to reflect on their heritage, envision their role in society, and engage actively in shaping an inclusive and progressive India. The book serves as both a tribute to India's resilience and a roadmap for the future, encouraging readers to contribute to a balanced and inclusive evolution of Indian identity in a globalized world.

Read more at www.gyrusvision.com.

Also by SANDEEP CHAVAN

It's Not AI, It's AHI - Amplified Human Intelligence
The Decision Paradox
The Four Sapiens
Malicious Script of Indian Polity
The IIT Legacy & Global Impact
The IIT Legacy & Global Impact
You are just a Version of Your Original
Win the Game You Didn't Choose
Always Keep Your Bags Packed
Reveal to Shield - Learn the Game of Facades
Engage Beyond Elections
Culture, Identity & Change: The Evolution of Indian Society
The Triangular Dynamics

Watch for more at www.gyrusvision.com.

Milton Keynes UK
Ingram Content Group UK Ltd.
UKHW021121031224
452078UK00011B/981